CW01091391

PILOTING THE
PANAMA CANAL

PILOTING THE PANAMA CANAL

EXPERIENCES OF A PANAMA CANAL PILOT

Charles Gaines and Esther E. Miles

Writers Club Press

San Jose New York Lincoln Shanghai

Piloting the Panama Canal
Experiences of a Panama Canal Pilot

All Rights Reserved © 2001 by Charles Gaines & Esther Miles

No part of this book may be reproduced or transmitted in any form or by any means, graphic, electronic, or mechanical, including photocopying, recording, taping, or by any information storage retrieval system, without the permission in writing from the publisher.

Writers Club Press
an imprint of iUniverse.com, Inc.

For information address:
iUniverse.com, Inc.
5220 S 16th, Ste. 200
Lincoln, NE 68512
www.iuniverse.com

ISBN: 0-595-18107-4

Printed in the United States of America

Dedicated to Leydiana,

whose beauty and vivacity bring joy to my life

Acknowledgements

The author acknowledge the support of Leydiana, who listens with patience as these stories are repeated. Her Spanish translations have been very helpful. Thanks is due to the chief pilot of the Panama Canal, Captain Chet Lavalos, who arranged a transit on the Nordmax for the authors and to pilot Captain Julio Candanedo who graciously shared the wheelhouse with us.

In addition, Martha Shephard's time and effort in reading the manuscript, correcting errors, and offering recommendations are very much appreciated.

Contents

1

GETTING TO PANAMA

March, 1978

Carl Turner went to sea for six months, followed by six months off with pay. He had been ashore for nearly 6 months. For several years he had been going to sea as first mate on a coastwise chemical tanker. Although he had an Unlimited Masters License and had served as a ship's captain, he chose to serve as first mate, since he could draw overtime pay as first mate, an option not available to him as captain. The net result was a fatter paycheck with less responsibility and less paperwork. He thought this was a pretty good contract.

Back in 1974 Carl had hired a private detective to catch his wife, Edna on drugs. He suspected she had been doing drugs for years. What the detective found was that Edna and Jude, Carl's younger brother, were living together. Carl wondered how many men she had been with. He tried to get a divorce, but Jude told the judge that Edna was a good wife and there was no reason to grant a divorce. Jude wanted that fat paycheck to continue to come to him and Edna. So the divorce proceedings dragged out for three years until Carl was successful in getting an attorney who was able to secure the final decree in 1977. Carl had agreed to child support for his three children. During the time he was ashore he technically didn't have a job, so the court awarded Edna a child support payment of only $200 per month, but Carl increased it voluntarily to $400 per month. He told the court that he would go back to sea—he would get another job. He bought a car for himself and a new Pontiac Firebird for his daughter, Maureen, and paid her way to college at the University of Texas. He went back to sea and paid off both cars.

During his time ashore Carl attended the Maritime Institute of Technology and Graduate Studies in Baltimore, taking courses in Automated Bridge, Cargo Storage, and Radar Upgrade to update his skills in light of new technology. While there, he met a friend of his, Jack Lyons, who was passing out applications for Panama Canal Pilot. Jack was serving as a recruiter of pilots for the Panama Canal Company. Carl had been through the Panama Canal many times, and he knew what the job entailed. He listened to Jack run off his spin about Panama. Carl told Jack, as Jack handed him the application, "I'm almost 55 so I know they're not going to give me a job. Most of the fellows who went down there were young, less than 35 with at least a year's master's time."

"Well, Carl, things have changed," Jack replied. "With all the riots and other problems we have in Panama, we can't get young captains with sea time to go there, so we're taking people like you. We can't discriminate because of age anymore, anyway, in government employment. I think you've got an above average chance."

Carl filled out the application. Then he went back to sea as first mate.

Six months later Carl was in the Master Mates and Pilots Union Hall in Houston. He asked the dispatcher and patrolman if they had correspondence for him concerning his Panama Canal Pilot application. Carl told them about a conversation with Jack Lyons who told Carl that Carl had the appointment. There was supposed to be a telegram for Carl in the union hall. Carl asked Alice, the dispatcher, "It's been over a month since the telegram should have arrived here. Where is it?"

Alice took care of the paperwork for the port of Houston. She looked all around. In a few minutes she called Carl in the office and told him, "Here it is, Carl. Here's your telegram."

Carl opened it up. He read:

CONGRATULATIONS STOP YOU HAVE BEEN ACCEPTED AS A PILOT IN TRAINING IN PANAMA STOP CALL THE FOLLOWING NUMBERS FOR INSTRUCTIONS FOR TRAVEL TO PANAMA.

All the numbers Carl was to call were listed. He made the calls and asked the person on the other end of the line to give him six weeks to two months in order to make one more trip to sea. Then he would be able to pay up his child support in advance and come to Panama with a little money in his pocket.

Mr. Peterson, personnel manager, agreed, "Sure, that's all right. Go ahead. Give us a call when you are ready to come down."

Carl shipped out on a container ship for Rotterdam and then returned to Houston. Jude was still living with Carl's ex-wife, Edna. He told Edna and Jude that he was going to Panama. Edna told Carl, "You can stay here when you come to Houston and stay upstairs with the children in the spare room."

Carl saw red. He angrily declared, "Look, with you and Jude, my brother, sleeping down below in the master bedroom? You want me to stay upstairs with the children on my time off—on my vacation—you must think I'm CRAZY!".

"That's the American way, isn't it?"

"It may be for some, but it's damn well not my way. As much as I love my children, I won't do it!"

The conversation got hot and heavy. As Carl walked away, Edna got in back of him and held Carl's arms down at his side so he couldn't move. He started to turn around to shake her off, but Jude got in Carl's face and started pounding him in the face and stomach. Carl raised his hands in a sheer rage and broke Edna loose. He whirled around and smacked her. She hit the wall and slid down the wall to the carpet. Jude cursed Carl calling him every ugly name he could think of. The three children were sobbing. Jude went to see how badly Edna was hurt. Carl walked through the living room and kitchen to get away from them. He held the door closed. Jude charged at the door and tried to get through, but Carl held the knob tight. Jude cursed Carl through the door, calling him a bastard and son-of-a-bitch.

"Well, sonny boy, If you want this door opened so badly, here it is." Carl let go of the knob. The door flew open. Jude stood there, completely surprised. Carl smashed him one. He started backward through the kitchen, the living room, and was heading for the dining room when Carl slammed the door and left, shouting, "*GOOD-BYE!*"

Carl got in his car and drove to Interstate 10. Seeing that his car needed gas, he pulled into a gas station and filled his tank. When he went inside to pay for the gas, the cashier blurted out, "Good God, man, do you need an ambulance or a doctor? You are bloody all over. What's happened to you?"

"Gee, I didn't even know it. I guess my feeling hasn't come back yet."

Carl rubbed his hand around his neck. It was all covered with blood. His shirt was all bloody.

"I could use a little clean up. I had a fight with my brother and my ex-wife who are living together, and it turned into a brawl. No need to call an ambulance or police or anything. I'll just clean up a bit and go on home."

Carl cleaned up in the bathroom. One of the station attendants gave him a clean T-shirt. Carl got in his car, drove to his apartment, and telephoned Mr. Peterson, personnel manager in Panama. He was to drive his car to New Orleans and turn it in at the New Orleans Army Port of Debarkation where it would be shipped to Panama. He was asked when he wanted to go. He replied, "Today".

"There's a flight out on Braniff tonight. I can get you on it," Mr. Peterson informed Carl.

Carl was provided a ticket and transportation to the airport. Arrangements had been made for Carl's use of a car and driver upon his arrival in Panama.

He enjoyed the two and a half hour flight. As he flew over the warm waters of the Gulf of Mexico, he remembered the winters he had spent aboard chemical tankers on coastwise trips to New Jersey, Staten Island, New York, Boston, and Maine. Work on a chemical tanker for the Keystone Tanker Company was not the most comfortable or physically safe job Carl ever held in his 30 years sailing experience. When he loaded chemical products, he had to contend with toxic chemical fumes, the heat and humidity of Texas and Louisiana summers, and the bone-chilling cold of New England winters. A tanker would discharge cargo at Bayonne, New Jersey and proceed up Kill Van Kull waterway, stopping at five to seven different docks. Unlike dry cargo vessels, in which shore side longshoremen load and unload cargo, chemical tankers charged the ship's crew with that responsibility. The five officers consisted of the captain and four mates. While loading and discharging cargo the officers were constantly on overtime, even while they were sleeping. Carl's overtime rate was $19 per hour. At least two officers and three crewmen had to be in attendance at all times. One mate could sleep while the other three discharged cargo on deck. Crewmen couldn't go ashore while cargo was being discharged. They were lucky to get ashore for a few beers, a haircut, some magazines and newspapers before they headed south.

Several types of chemicals, including styrene, from which plastic is made, and methanol-cunene, would be discharged at one time. As many as 17 grades of chemicals might be shipped on one vessel. These were very valuable cargoes. For example, one spoonful of a certain chemical could make one gallon of vinegar. One of the chemicals transported on these tankers was the very dangerous carbolic acid. Anyone who inhaled these fumes would be lucky to be alive even if hospitalized, so ships transporting carbolic acid were enclosed. The fumes just went up the mast and killed the birds. When the cargo was low in the tanks, they had to be stripped by regulating the valves. The main pumps shut down and a small air driven pump, called a blotter pump, was used to remove every quart of chemical.

On north bound voyages the crew kept a close ear to the radio for the weather. The weather from Texas to Louisiana, across the Gulf of Mexico and from the Dry Tortugas to Florida and on to Cape Hattaras was generally good to tolerable. Further north, someone would frequently come into the officers' salon and give the sad news; "New York has sleet and ice. The temperature is 20°. New Jersey is the same."

New England winters were bitter cold with ice and snow. Carl started to feel the cold even before he arrived. "It must be the power of suggestion or maybe just the fact that I'm a Florida cracker," he thought. The off duty mate could sleep not more than four hours at a time, since the mates on deck in the ice, snow, sleet, biting wind and freezing rain had to be relieved every hour. Even though Carl had bought the very best of heavy weather clothing, he felt the bitter cold after only 30 minutes on deck.

After pumping at each dock for a few hours the ship went on to another dock, with the crew handling tugboat lines and half-frozen dock lines. After shifting the ship to the next dock the crew went back to work discharging cargo.

As Carl's plane neared Panama City, he could see the Bridge of the Americas spanning the Pacific Ocean's entrance to the Panama Canal. To his right he saw many ships at anchor waiting their turn to transit the Canal, and the Balboa Yacht Club with private boats at anchor. To his left was Balboa Harbor with which he would soon become very familiar.

When Carl arrived in Panama, he spotted a government car and driver holding up a sign that read "Captain Turner". At this time the Panama airport was not modern, just a tarmac. Carl never thought he would make as much money in Panama as he did going to sea, but he didn't care. When his plane arrived in Panama, he went down the ladder and walked toward the terminal. He stepped aside, knelt down and kissed the ground, and said to himself, "Thank God I'm in Panama. I'll never be cold again."

2

PILOT IN TRAINING

The Beginning

Well, that put Carl in Panama City. This is a city of contrasts, with beautiful 2 story Spanish style homes as well as numerous dwellings that could only be characterized as shacks. The old school buses were painted with garish colors with pictures of all sorts of things on them, including naked women. Carl's driver took him through Paitillia, a section of lush, high rise apartment houses, along Panama Bay where raw sewage is discharged. Carl was soon to learn that the locals referred to this part of the bay as "Rio Caca". They continued past Chorillo, a slum with washing hanging from every conceivable spot and garbage everywhere, into the downtown area, and then along the highway that parallels the Panama Canal, past dense jungle on both sides of the road. They traveled the 50 miles across the isthmus to Cristobal on the Atlantic side. They went to Coco Solo, a community near Cristobal, to Carl's apartment on Severn Street. The driver showed Carl his apartment, one of four in a two-story building. The apartment house was painted white, and the yard was neatly kept. Carl's apartment had been partially furnished with rental furniture and a nice refrigerator. Everything looked just fine. Carl was physically and emotionally exhausted, so he hit the sack.

The next morning when Carl awakened, a car and a passenger awaited him. Carl guessed the passenger was a pilot. Captain Paul Simon introduced himself. Paul said, "I'm supposed to be your sponsor."

"Aren't you supposed to be working?" Carl inquired.

"I'm off on sick duty. I've been injured, so I have some time off. I'm ambulatory, so I can show you around."

"Well, that's fine. Things in this icebox are all rotten. Somebody stocked it with food." Carl remarked.

"Yes, the pilots' wives did that. They thought you were going to be here two months ago. What happened to you?"

"I had to make another trip to sea to get some pocket money and pay off all my child support in advance. It's not long since I've been divorced."

"Oh, I see. All right."

Paul accepted Carl's story and asked for no further explanation. He showed Carl where the post office was and got Carl assigned a post office box. Paul showed him the location of the Cristobol hospital and then took him to the Processing Center in Cristobal. Here Carl was given identification cards. Then they went to the boathouse in Cristobal where the clerk checked Carl out a 14-channel radio for lock channels, towboats and Marine Transit Control. The tour ended at Gatun locks. During his years as a merchant seaman, Carl had seen Gatun locks at least ten times, he guessed. After that they returned to Carl's apartment in Coco Solo.

Sand Fleas and the Inner Tube Boat

The sand fleas in Coco Solo were horrible. They were biting Carl all over.

He told Paul, "I've got to get an air conditioner in here to get rid of these damn sand fleas."

"Nobody's going to do it today, not this late."

It wasn't really late, about 3:00 P.M., so Carl offered, "Why don't you run on home? I'll take care of this myself. The government is not going to put an air conditioner in here for me; I know that."

"If you're trying to get rid of me, I'll just go," retorted Paul who had become somewhat irritated by this time. Carl was getting irritated at Paul's telling him common sense things that he already knew.

"Well, go."

Paul left. Carl went to the commissary, which was close to his back yard. He stocked up on food and toiletries—whatever he needed. The commissary housed a super market downstairs and household goods, including hardware, upstairs. The household goods section included beds, air conditioners, and furniture, an entire line of home furnishings. Carl chose the best, most powerful air conditioner he could find. He gave the clerk $10 to deliver it to his house. He walked to the window and pointed to his apartment on the 2nd floor on Severn Street. It was just behind the commissary.

The clerk said, "Sure, Captain. Okay."

Carl paid cash for the air conditioner. He tipped one of the boys in the super market $5 to take his groceries up to his apartment. Carl had his arms full of groceries also. He had no sooner put the groceries on the counter than he heard a knock on the door. His air conditioner had been delivered.

He thought, "That didn't take long. This is sure contrary to what Captain Simon said."

Carl put his groceries away. He had cleaned out the refrigerator the night before. Then he went back downstairs and found a carpenter shop close by. He knew it must be a government facility since it was in the Panama Canal Zone. In 1987 everything in the Zone was owned by the U.S. Government.

Carl spoke to the first man he saw, a Panamanian U.S. Government employee, "I need an air conditioner installed in my apartment. Is there anyone here who can do anything like that?"

"Yeah, Captain. We could do that work for you when we get off duty. We have some other work to do here and all…"

"These sand fleas are biting me pretty bad. Could one of you come up and take a look at it and see if you could get it in a little sooner than that?" Carl asked as he gave him a $20 bill.

"That'll hurry things along pretty good, Captain."

"Well here's another twenty," Carl added for insurance, since he already knew something about Panamanians.

"Captain, I do believe we can put off what we have to do here. We'll have that air conditioner installed for you in two hours."

"Thank you very much."

Carl's air conditioner was running in a little less than two hours. The sand fleas were gone. Carl went to a package store and stocked up his kitchen with beer and other booze. Back at the apartment he called for a car and driver. When it arrived he told the driver, "I don't have any official business on this trip, but I'd like to go over to Gatun Lake near the dam. I believe there will be some damn good fishing where they used to have that atomic ship on the bank of the lake. It was a liberty ship whose engine was taken out and atomic generators installed to supply Gatun Locks with electric power."

"Sure, Captain, I know where it is."

They drove over to the lake by the dam and looked all around. It looked like a great fishing spot. Carl's favorite pastime was fishing. Whenever he arrived at a new location, he made it his business to scope out the promising fishing places. This looked like a good one, rife with aquatic weeds. When Carl was at Gatun boathouse, he could see large bass swimming in the clear water. "What do they call this place?" Carl asked.

"A lot of the people from Colon come over here to swim. It's a pretty popular swimming hole. They call it Colon Beach."

"That's just fine." Carl had learned from Paul that he would have plenty of time to swim at the beach, since pilots are called for a transit only between 0600 and 0900. If a pilot isn't called during these hours, he will not have a transit until the next day.

Carl got the driver to take him to a big Texaco station in town. Carl went in and bought the biggest inner tube he could find and another scrap one that he could cut up. Then he had the driver take him home. Carl went back to the commissary and bought a lot of contact cement and fishing equipment. He cut up the scrap inner tube and made strips out of it, cemented the strips across the top of the other inner tube to make a seat. The next day Carl tied an ice chest alongside his rubber "boat", got some live minnows and flippers for his feet like the ones scuba divers use, and went fishing. He loved to fish. Gatun Lake is full of *sargentos*. They are similar to bass, but they have stripes, so they call them *sargentos*, sergeant fish. They are beautiful, colorful fish, bright red, orange, and blue. Somebody imported them from Argentina. They are very aggressive and have eaten nearly all other species of fish in the lake. They are cannibalistic as most fish are, but here they seem even more so. The largest one Carl ever caught was about seven pounds. Some days he could catch as many as a hundred fish in a day if he fished from sunup to sundown. He caught 40 or 50 *sargentos*, or sergeant fish, similar to bass, and gave his neighbors all they could eat. He was extremely happy. This experience, along with the warm weather, put a good taste in his mouth for Panama, especially in contrast to the last year he had spent in the U.S.

Tugboat Rides

Carl began his stint as a pilot in training, a PIT, by riding on tugboats. For his first two months, Carl was the lowest rated P.I.T. in the Panama Canal. In the morning his car and driver took him to the Cristobal boathouse. He was assigned to ride on the "Harry Burgess", a new tractor tugboat, the first one of its kind to be put into use in Panama. He went to the wheelhouse of the tug and introduced himself as PIT Carl Turner. The tugboat captain said he had Carl's name on the list for PIT.

The tugboat captain, Bill, was a very nice guy. He introduced Carl around. Bill was a stocky man with a jovial, round face, brown hair, and strong hands. He was very helpful. He told Carl, "Whenever they run out of captains like you to come here, they will take tug boat captains like me for PITs."

"That's great. I am sure all you tugboat captains will make it," Carl assured Bill. "They are hiring old men like me now. I understand that in the past they only hired PIT's 25 to 40 years old with at least one year's sea time as a master. When I left Houston no captains were applying for this job. They have families that don't want to leave the states and they are familiar with the riots here in Panama."

The Harry Burgess was made fast to the ship S-8. The ship had the designation of S-8 on the list of transits for the day since it was the eighth southbound ship to transit the canal. Ships that require four pilots are assigned two tugs. At times the tugs must assist the stern around the curves, bends in the channel, particularly in the Gaillard Cut and approaching the locks, if the pilot tells the tug, "Stern to port" or "Stern to starboard".

After assisting at Gatun Locks they returned to Cristobol Harbor. Bill took Carl all around the harbor, calling out the numbers of all the docks and piers. Later Carl got off the tug and got on the pilot boat, which took him to the pilot station at pier 8 where he called for a jitney to take him to lunch. Jitneys are cars used to take pilots to and from work. They are often top of the line Chevrolets or similar models, quite new, plush, and comfortable. Since Carl didn't yet have his car, he had a jitney at his disposal. The Panama Canal Commission had given Carl a number of chits, or meal tickets. His jitney driver took Carl to the Cristobal Yacht Club. Carl invited him to come in and have lunch with him, since he had extra tickets and would enjoy the company of another person. The jitney driver, who was black, looked shocked. He had never before had a pilot invite him to lunch. Soon Carl and the jitney driver became good friends. Carl told the driver that everyone called him "captain", but he was just a PIT, and the senior pilots let him know it. Later, Carl made friends with a lot of drivers and dispatchers. He was to discover that their friendship would come in very handy.

The Zonie Engineer

One day while Carl was riding on Bill's tugboat, an engineer walked up and accosted him with, "Are you one of these new PITs? You bastard; don't you know this place is going to hell? You are crazy to come down here and go to work. Don't you know about all the riots and killing here in Panama? When this new treaty begins to be implemented in October 28, 1979, Panama will begin to take over everything there is. You must be crazy. Why don't you pack up and get the hell out of here? What are you doing down here anyway? You are real stupid!"

He kept on and on.

Finally Carl told him, "Don't curse at me any more."

He turned his back to the engineer. Bill was about twice Carl's size. He stepped in.

"Look, you're the chief engineer of all the tugboats on the Atlantic side, and you are here to take care of the engineering problems on this boat, but you can't come in this wheelhouse on this tugboat telling the people who are training to be pilots-cursing them and pushing them around. Carl wants to be here. He went to sea for thirty-two years. This is his chance to stay ashore for the remainder of his maritime career. I don't blame him. So why don't you shut your damn mouth and go down in the engine room and do what it is you do and then get off the damn tugboat? That's what you get paid for. Get your ass out of here. Go down in the engine room where you belong. Stay down there until you're ready to go ashore. Then I'll put your crummy ass ashore."

The engineer turned to Carl one more time, "What are you here for? You look like you're a hundred years old. I don't know how old you are, but whatever it is, most everybody your age had worked and retired. You're coming out here as an apprentice. You ought to be ashamed of yourself."

By this time, Carl's anger was rising. He could feel the heat boiling up from within. "Aw, get the hell out of here. Kiss my ass."

The engineer turned to Bill one last time as he moved toward the engine room, "I know all you big shot tugboat captains are soon going to be pilots. Go to hell."

Bill took a swing; the engineer ducked; so the blow missed him. But the engineer got the message and went below. Carl never saw him anymore during the time he was on Bill's tug.

"What's wrong with the people here?" Carl asked Bill.

"Look, Carl. The engineer is a Zonie and his father was a Zonie. They are American citizens who have lived and worked in the Canal Zone for three generations or more. They get paid U. S. civil service wages and pensions, use of the commissary and lots of other privileges. The treaty the senate recently ratified will give Panama the Canal Zone in another year and the entire canal, lock, stock, and barrel after a 22-year transition period. He is bitter toward anyone who comes to Panama to do any job that will keep the canal operating. Many of the Zonies in Panama hate the United States government with a passion for signing the treaty to give the canal to Panama. They are in fear of losing their jobs and don't know what is going to happen to them. Even if they can keep their jobs, they are afraid they will have to accept much lower Panamanian wages and small pensions. They are ready to curse out any new hires who come here. They don't want the canal to operate any more. They are bitter and will do anything to disrupt unity. They are doing everything they can to disrupt work here, hoping the treaty won't go through. But you know it's going to be implemented. We're not stupid. They're the guys who are stupid. The President, the Secretary of State,

Congress, and all these people signed this treaty. On October 28,1979 it's going to be implemented. The Panama Canal Zone will be under Panamanian control. I'm afraid you're going to meet a lot of people like that engineer. I'm going to be assigned as a PIT soon because people like you are running out. Most younger or middle-aged people like you are not going to come here. They're going to start taking us off the tug-boats. I know that. It's just a matter of time before I get an appointment as a PIT."

Bill went on to explain more about the attitude of the Zonies. "There is a class difference between the Zonies and the Panamanians. The Zonies' are U.S. citizens whose children are educated at the expense of the U.S. government. With this good education they can secure the best jobs in the Panama Canal Zone. They use their positions as U.S. civil service employees to secure part time work for their teen-age children ushering and selling concessions in movie theaters and working in the commissaries. The teenagers get full U.S. civil service pay and benefits for all the hours they work. This establishes the teenagers' seniority in civil service positions, since even these part time jobs come under civil service. With the implementation of the treaty these good jobs will go to Panamanians. From 1979 until noon on December 31, 1999, the Zonies can keep their jobs, but all the new hires have to be Panamanian citizens. If higher positions open up, and a qualified Panamanian is available, that position will go to a Panamanian regardless of more senior, qualified American citizens or third nationals. After noon on December 31, 1999 all former U. S. civil service positions are to go to Panamanians. People who occupy these positions will be employed by the Panamanian government. Panama, not the U.S, will set wages and benefits. Zonies know this and resent it. Zonies do not want a successful Panama Canal operation after 1979. Most people know, however, that the operation will be a success because of the civil service pensions, even if other factors are not favorable. U. S. civil service pensions are paid at the rate of 2-½% of a person's average pay for the last three years times years of service, beginning in October 1979. That is higher than a Social Security percentage. That engineer must be getting $65,000 a year, as long as he's been on the job here. At this rate, if he works at his job for twenty-five years, his retirement pay will probably be about $4,000 per month. The rest of the Zonies will bellyache and bitch, but they'll stay on the job until 1999, if they don't retire before then, and train the Panamanians to run the canal. They won't take a chance on being fired because they want their pensions. They are not going to let go of their security. They may not like the canal being turned over to the Panamanians, but it's like one Zonie said, 'After 1985 everything we need, except liquor in a bottle store, will have to be bought in Panama. Brother, those prices in Panama are absolutely ridiculous. They won't give me anywhere near the service that they will give to their own. But I've got a pension, and I guess I'm going to be like the rest of the Zonies. I'm going to let the U. S. Government roll me over a barrel, strip my shirt down to my bare back, turn me over to Panama and let the Panamanians all take a whack at cutting me up.' Zonies and Americans are going to suffer plenty. They will be discriminated against and they will have to grin and bear it. Panamanians justify discrimination by say-ing that the Americans discriminated against Panamanians by not hir-ing them to build the canal and hiring black Caribbean's at 10 cents an hour instead."

"Yeah, okay, Bill" Carl said, "I guess you're right. But I've been going to sea all my life except for a couple of years when I was in the army. My family is all broken up. We had a big pow-wow in Houston. I hired a private detective to find out if my wife was on drugs. He found out she was in bed with my brother. They had been robbing me blind for the 15 years I had been married to that bitch. I'm down here trying to make a new life. I enjoy the weather, fishing, tropical fruit, the beauty of the lawns, trees, and flowers. You know? I especially appreciate running into guys like you. I'll probably see you in the canal again, Bill. Maybe I'll be riding with you again tomorrow. They say I'm to ride these tugboats for 4 weeks. Is that right?"

"Yes, that's right, 2 weeks on the Atlantic side and 2 weeks on the Pacific side. Look here, we don't have an assignment right now. Let me show you around. Let me wheel you over to the Cristobal Yacht Club. That's the 'watering hole'. The pilots will get you to stop off there, buy cups with ice, soda and Scotch whiskey. Whether you want it or not, they're going to be shoving it to you. You're going to be drinking in that jitney all the way home. They're always like that. If you don't want it, tell them, 'Hell, no.' But you've got to be forceful. Just about all these pilots are half drunks."

"Yeah, well, I believe that. Seamen drink a lot, but they don't do drugs."

"That's right, Carl. I don't know of any pilots who have ever been on drugs, but they sure do booze it up."

"You sure got that right." Carl agreed.

"I'll take you over to piers six, seven, eight and nine. You can see all the slips and the ships docked there. The boathouse is at the end of the slip at dock eight. I'll show you dock 16, the fuel oil pier where ships take on bunker fuel. You'll be taking a lot of ships in there to take on bunker fuel."

Bill took Carl to the places he had mentioned as well as around the harbor where it is somewhat shallow and around the buoys marking the various anchorages. Then they went to where the small boats anchored, the yacht club anchorage as Bill called it. They crossed the harbor to the anchorages on both sides of Limon Bay. In short, Bill took Carl all over the port. Carl didn't need any more rides because he already had the harbor well fixed in his mind. Because of his many years of professional seagoing experience, it didn't take Carl long to size up the harbor, but he had six more days to go. He was hoping he would be with Bill every day, but Bill told Carl he had only four more days of day work. This would take Carl through Friday. Carl's next workday would be on Monday.

"Bill, I sure do appreciate your showing me around. I look forward to piloting with you someday."

"Yeah, okay, Carl. Take it easy. If you need any help just let me know. I have a car you can borrow,"

"Thanks, Bill, but I have a car the Commission assigned me until my car gets shipped here. About how long do you think it will take for my car to arrive? I'm having one shipped from New Orleans."

"You should have your car in about seven to ten days."

"I sure hope so, because I don't like to depend on the Commission and tie up a car and driver."

"Don't worry about it. They have about a hundred. If they said you'd have a car and a driver, you'll get one. Take it."

"Okay, Bill, see you tomorrow."

Bill was right. In another year he was a PIT, and he rode with Carl on an observation ride through the Canal. Carl was glad to see him again. Bill was a nice fellow. Later on Carl made transits with him.

The Broken Down Jitney

On the Monday after Carl's first week was up, he was assigned a car to go to Balboa and ride the tugs on the Pacific side for 2 weeks. He was in the boathouse on the Atlantic side waiting for a jitney to take him to Balboa. Just as his car arrived, in walked a pilot with three other pilots. One of them asked, "Is that your car out there, Captain?"

"Yes, that's my car," Carl answered.

"Well, we're taking it."

"Who are you?"

"I'm the president of the pilots association. It's in the contract that the men getting off work have priority on these cars. You're a PIT, aren't you?"

"Yeah, so what?" Carl retorted.

"We're taking your car! You get on that phone and call you another one."

Not to be intimidated, Carl told him, "You get on the phone and call one for me."

"NO! YOU get on the phone and call!"

The three pilots went outside and got in Carl's car. Carl thought, "Hell, I'll just sit here all day. If he wants to take my car and driver I won't do anything. I'll just collect my pay and call Marine Transit Control later on and go on back where I came from."

In a few minutes the pilot who commandeered Carl's car turned around and stormed through the door.

"Have you called yourself another car?" he yelled.

"Hell, no. You're taking my car so it's up to you to get me another one."

"**Well get out of my way.**"

"Don't you shove me around."

Carl had determined that this must be the nature of senior pilots to push new hires around. Perhaps he was a Zonie, too. Carl's age, fifty-five, apparently irritated them even more. This was the second time in his first week in Panama that he had run into such a belligerent attitude. He remembered that one of them had told him, "Most of the men your age are retiring."

Senior pilots did not like older men to begin piloting in the Panama Canal. As the demand for pilots increased and the supply decreased, the age requirement was lifted to 45 and then was eliminated entirely. Senior pilots hired before 35 years of age felt that Carl's presence in Panama lowered their standards. They discouraged older pilots who came to the canal. Some left, but the more they harassed Carl, the more determined to stay he became. He wasn't going to let these surly, uncouth bastards beat him. He enjoyed the warm climate, the fishing, and, most of all, transiting the canal.

The angry pilot walked around the other side of the table, reached over, grabbed the telephone, and called Marine Transit Control (MTC). He raised all kind of hell screaming that pilots getting off transits are entitled to the first car home. He told MTC he was taking Carl's car and for them to send another car for Captain Turner to take him to Balboa. He quoted his contract stipulations, which called for the preferential treatment he sought. He slammed down the phone and stormed out of the door, got in the jitney, and drove off.

Carl waited for a while. Sure enough another car and driver pulled up. Carl went outside.

"Are you Captain Turner?" the driver asked.

"Yes, I'm Turner."

"This car is going to Balboa."

"That's for me."

Carl got in the car, and they started out. They drove until they got two or three miles from Balboa at the transfer point, a crossroads. Trans-isthmus jitneys go only from Balboa to Cristobal and back. Local jitneys pick up pilots from the two transfer points, called crossroads, one on the Pacific side and one on the Atlantic side, to their homes or to a boathouse. Carl and his driver saw a car alongside the road. It looked like another jitney. A pilot was sticking half his body out of the window, all red-faced, waving his arms.

Carl exclaimed in surprise, "Well, I'll be damned if it isn't old Captain Asshole. Driver, that's the same pilot who commandeered my car at Cristobal and called for another car for me. What's wrong with that car?"

His driver told Carl, "The hood's open, Captain. The car is broken down."

Then the occupants of the disabled car got out. They started waving their arms and calling, "Stop, Stop!"

Carl said to his driver, "What do you suppose they want? This car?"

"Well, it looks like it."

"Keep going. Crank her up, put the pedal to the metal, and let's go."

As they drove off, Carl stuck his head out the window and laughed, "Ha, ha, ha, ha."

"I didn't make any friends this day," he thought.

Tugboat Captain Johnson

When they got to the boathouse at Balboa, Carl telephoned Marine Transit Control, told them of the car trouble, and received his tug assignment. Carl took a pilot boat to his tug. The tug was working on the sterns of ships heading up toward Miraflores Locks. The young fellow who worked as captain of this tug told Carl he was expecting to get on the pilot force pretty soon.

"How long have you been here?" Carl asked him.

"About nine years. I've been a captain on a tug for about four of those. If they run short of PITs, I'm pretty sure I'm going to make it."

"Well, Johnson, I guess you will. I hope you do."

Johnson was an amiable fellow. He showed Carl all around. When they finished putting all the north bound supers in the Miraflores Lock, everything was dead until that afternoon when the really big supers, also called Panamax ships, started coming south. Johnson took Carl all over Balboa Harbor and then over to Rodman Navy Base and ran around all the buoys in the harbor so that Carl would be familiar with them. The tugboat then docked at the pier not far from the pilots' station. Carl called a car, and he and the jitney driver went to the Balboa Yacht Club for lunch. The Yacht Club was a two story building with a restaurant upstairs and a bar and pier downstairs where 30 to 150 feet transiting yachts and those belonging to local Panamanians and Americans were anchored. The restaurant had large curved glass windows on the second story overlooking a golf course. On the opposite side of the large dining room, windows overlooked the Bridge of the Americas and entire entrance to the canal on the Pacific side where one could see ships passing, going both north and south. The scenery was beautiful. The tables had linen tablecloths, good china and silver, and excellent food. It was an elegant place to relax, enjoy the view, and dine. Later on, when the U. S. turned the Yacht Club over to the Panamanians, it fell into disrepair and was torn down in January of 1999. The nearby golf course was done away with to make way for a new hotel and convention center being built by an Asian firm.

During the rest of his training period Carl worked with a few nice fellows and met some more nasty pilots. He soon discovered that nobody liked to work with a PIT. Pilots expressed it this way, "I do not let PITs work. When you have pilots to train, it's a pain in the ass."

Carl's answer was, "I don't want to work; I don't need to."

Early Repeats

When Carl had finished his 4 weeks of riding on the tugboats, he had a three-day holiday. He was still living at Coco Solo on the Atlantic side of the isthmus. He went to Fort Davis, a few miles north of Gatun, to fish. Instead of using his inner tube "boat" he rented a fishing boat and motor from the army and went out onto Gatun Lake. He was successful catching the *sargentos* with just a hand line and live minnows. He had bought two dozen minnows for a dollar from Panamanian children who sold them by the side of the road on weekends and holidays. He caught enough fish to feed everyone in his apartment house. He took his transit radio with him to listen to conversations of transiting ships on Gatun Lake and between ships passing through Gatun Locks. He thought this would be good training for him. He'd hear Marine Transit Control (MTC) calling the ships. He heard on the radio, "Captain Thomas, would you and Captain Brown be available for an early repeat tomorrow?"

"No, thank you. No, thank you." This went on from ship to ship.

"Is Captain Emmett there?"

"No, Captain Emmett is indisposed—in the head. He says 'no'".

This went on and on. Carl laughed and laughed. He thought it was the funniest thing he had ever heard. An early repeat means that a pilot would work out of rotation. He would finish up late in the afternoon and then go out again early the next morning instead of being called to work according to the rotation list. If pilots could work overtime on Saturday and have an early repeat for Sunday, they'd voluntarily take it. There was no overtime pay for a repeat if the total hours worked for the week was forty or fewer. If forty hours had already been worked that week, a repeat on the weekend meant overtime pay for the pilot. If the early repeat were during the week, pilots would refuse because they were trying to negotiate for higher pay. At this time pilots' pay was substandard. They did not have a union; instead they had an organization called the Panama Canal Pilots Association. Since pilots were employed by the government, they could not strike, so they found other ways to apply pressure. The Association was affiliated with the Masters, Mates, and Pilots Union, which gave the association a little clout. In the National Maritime Union, the union Carl had belonged to as an unlicensed person, and then the Masters, Mates and Pilots Union, the MMP, as a licensed person, if ships' crews didn't get the kind of contract they wanted, they would vote to strike and start to walk the picket line. Pilots were not required to belong to the association, but, if a pilot went to Panama as a PIT and didn't belong to it, he would not get any assistance learning the job. Learning piloting requires hands on training and experience. If a person can't take control and handle that ship himself, with some supervision, he will not learn essential piloting skills. This is a unique piloting situation, requiring more skill than most places in the world. Maneuvering a ship into a cement box like a lock, transiting a large lake prone to violent thunderstorms, negotiating the sharp turns and narrowness of the channel through the Gaillard cut, coping with locks spilling water while entering them, both fresh and salt water, and harbor piloting are all required.

Later on, after this business with pilots refusing to take early repeats during the week and ships stacked up on each side of the canal, the Pilots Association and the Panama Canal Commission got together and put early repeats on a bonus system. Under the bonus system the first transit a pilot makes in his two week pay period entitles the pilot to just a pittance of a bonus. On the next transit the bonus was a little more. The third transit netted a bonus of $300-$400. For each additional transit, up to seven transits, the bonuses increased. The eighth transit's bonus was $1,000. This system seemed to satisfy everybody. Also in this contract pilots were paid $50 an hour for travel in the jitneys to and from their assigned duties on the opposite side of the isthmus from where they lived. Many times the ride would take an hour and a half, depending on traffic. Pilots were issued a flashlight, a pair of gloves, and a pair of non-slip shoes. When the contract with the Panama Canal Commission expired, the flashlight, gloves, and shoes expired with it.

Test for 225' Solo Pilot

Carl got a call telling him that his car had arrived. After he picked it up, he came back to his apartment, answered the phone, and found that he was to go for a week of seminars in Balboa to become familiar with the nautical charts of the isthmus. A senior pilot, an official in the transit office, would conduct the seminars. They included describing all the buoys and ranges, and becoming familiar with the signal arrows at the lock entrances. The latter are large arrows indicating which lock side to enter and when the lock is ready to be entered. Complete mastery of the canal was mandatory for pilots, since the shipmaster has to relinquish full control of the navigation and movement of his ship to the Panama Canal pilot while in Canal Zone waters, according to the Federal Code of Regulations. The propeller does not turn over one time unless the pilot says so. The anchor comes up and goes down when the pilot orders it to. All orders around the locks come strictly from the pilot. The captain relays the pilot's orders to the quartermaster and officer on duty. No one does anything until the pilot orders it done.

After the week of seminars was over, Carl began to ride as a PIT. After twenty training rides, working at times taking control of the bridge, called "taking the con", he was called to Balboa to take his pilot's examination. He was to stay at a hotel in Balboa for a week, or as long as was necessary, for that examination. He laid out the courses and charts and marked all 101 navigational aids, buoys and ranges, from the Cristobal breakwater to the sea buoy on the Pacific side. The last buoy was 1A. Carl marked all 101 buoys, answered all the questions, and did all the math in a day and a half. He was sitting over in the corner with color crayons starting to color the charts, coloring brown for land, blue for water, color coding buoys and ranges, and the like when the test examiner came over and told him, "Look, that's not necessary. You just turn in what you have. No need to color all that stuff up. You have been assigned here for the entire week. Be our guest. If you have any family members with you, they can stay at the hotel also as our guests."

Carl's daughter, Elaine, was with him. She was having a good time touring Panama City. Carl played at various casinos to keep his mind off the family situation he had left in Houston and studied his *Pilot Handbook*, the federal code of regulations for the Panama Canal. He was enthusiastic about his new job. At the end of the week Carl went back to Cristobal and began piloting ships of 225' or less. If there were no small ships that he could take through the Canal as control pilot, Carl had to ride as a PIT with senior pilots assigned to larger ships.

Special Korean Fishing Day

When he was still a 225' pilot, there was a fleet of 25 or more Korean fishing boats who needed to transit through Gatun locks and on through to the Pacific side. They must have been 60 or fewer feet long. Marine Transit Control had ordered all the fishing boats to lock up in the same lock chamber at the same time. One boat tied up to each of the two tugs and nested alongside. A string of 4 or 5 boats nested alongside the first fishing boat tied to the tugs. One boat had to tie up to the lock wall with the rest of the boats nesting alongside her. Contrary to regulations, the boats were not equipped with horns that could be heard at least one nautical mile. Instead, each boat had small, hand held, compressed air horns which are commonly used on small yachts and sailboats. As each boat tried to maneuver and make fast to the next, they turned every which way, all sounding their horns at once, and bumping into each other. All a person could hear was, "Beep, beep, honk, honk, get away from here. You're hitting my boat. I'm going to call for an investigation."

It was a comical sight! The lockmaster, the pilots, and finally the crews all started laughing. Pilots could talk to the lockmaster and to each other on their transit radios. One of the pilots called to Carl, "This is the biggest circus I ever saw! It reminds me of being in a carnival with bumper cars. Look out! Here comes one at you. He'll crash you for sure. He's going around in circles."

The lockmaster was going half-crazy. He had to bring the water in the lock.

The crews on the fishing boats started screaming, "Stop the water. We're all banging into each other."

Finally all the fishing boats were tied up and the lockmaster was notified that all was in readiness to let the water in *very slowly*. The lock was finally filled and the gates opened. Then another mad scramble ensued as all the boats, like a flock of baby chicks without a mother hen, made their way through the channel to the next lock. Confusion reigned supreme yet another time as the boats tied up in preparation for going through the second lock. The performance was repeated at the third lock. At long last the boats were crossing Gatun Lake. Some of the boats took the "Banana Channel", although they weren't supposed to. This is a shortcut which cut off a dogleg across one part of Gatun Lake. At one time it had been used for small ships, but was later closed to canal traffic.

Just as the boats finished crossing Gatun Lake and reached Gamboa in preparation for entrance into the Gaillard Cut, the pilots radioed, "Transit, transit, this is S10-echo. Where is my relief?"

Each of the boats was assigned a letter in addition to their South 10 transit number. E was identified as "echo", h was "hornet" and so on. The reply came, "This has been declared a special fishing boat day. All of you will make the entire transit all the way to the Pacific Ocean sea buoy. You will not get the usual relief pilots at Gamboa."

Some of the pilots did not hear the message given to the other pilots, so the message had to be repeated many times. Some of the pilots quoted from the Pilots Association contract with the Panama Canal Commission, "Marine Transit Control, slow vessels and fishing boats are to have pilot relief at Gamboa. Where is my relief?"

The answer was, "I repeat, this has been declared a special fishing boat day. All of you will make the entire transit all the way to the Pacific Ocean sea buoy."

In due time the boats began to gather near the Miraflores Locks. Since they had orders to go into the lock chamber as a total group, and all of them traveled at somewhat different speeds, some of the boats milled around waiting for the slower boats or for those who had gone the long way through the regulation channel instead of the "banana channel". Carl had gone through the regular channel. Horns began blaring again. Boats bumped into one another as they sought a nesting place. This 'malfunction junction' was reenacted at Pedro Miguel Lock and at both Miraflores Locks. Finally the brood of fishing boats made their way under the Bridge of the Americas and into the Pacific Ocean. At the sea buoy the pilot boat arrived to take the pilots to the boathouse on Naos Island. It circled around trying to get all the pilots off the fishing boats and on to the pilot boat. The fishing boats were in a hurry, heading for Korea. Pilots were calling to Marine Traffic Control, "This is south 10-echo. Come, get me. I don't want to go to Korea."

The pilot boat finally rounded up all the pilots and made its way to the boathouse. The jitneys on the way home rocked with laughter as the pilots recalled this unique, rollicking transit experience.

3

PILOT IN TRAINING

Ships to 526'

Pilots were promoted by the number of transits they had made. After 20 transits a PIT takes the test for 225'; 40 more transits are required to qualify for the check ride to be promoted to 440'; 40 more transits for 526'; 40 more for Step One. When a pilot reaches Step One, he is no longer a PIT; he is a pilot in the Panama Canal. Beginning with Step One tonnage is figured in. Pilots become qualified to take ships through the canal that are of thirty, forty, sixty, eighty tons depending on their examinations and experience. From the beginning pilots attend seminars conducted by senior pilots in charge of transit control. Beginning with Step Two, pilots could do bow jobs on ships with a beam of from 90 to 106'. Bow pilots work on the bow of the ship to assist the control pilot with managing the locomotives on the center lock wall as ships approach and proceed through the locks. In about eight years a pilot can become a senior pilot. At this level he can pilot any size ship.

After 40 transits, a checkride, and six months time Carl was promoted to a "440'". With each promotion he was given a $3,000 increase in salary. On October 8, 1978 Carl was sent a copy of a memorandum from the pilot training officer notifying him of his promotion to 526', allowing him to pilot ships up to 526' solo. A PIT gets a "checkride" for 225', and for promotions to pilot ships up to 440', and 526'. A checkride is a transit with a more senior pilot who then fills out an evaluation sheet. Until Carl got his promotion to 526' pilot he was considered a PIT serving under the supervision of a senior pilot. This only happened when there were no ships available on which he was qualified to solo. It was his prerogative to simply observe during the transit. However, when the senior pilot asked him what his qualification was and he replied, "I'm a 526' the senior pilot would often say, "You can just run this ship, then. I'll have the night off and spend my time in the bar."

If Carl liked the senior pilot and they had gotten along well together, he would agree to this arrangement. He had been to sea all his adult life. He knew he could handle the ship through the canal with no problem. However, if the senior pilot had been unkind or arrogant, Carl would refuse to transit the ship alone and would simply observe.

After Carl received his promotion to 526', no more evaluation sheets were filled out by a senior pilot. Now all Carl had to do after a transit was to turn in his time card and keep a record of the transits he made as either solo or bow pilot. A lock chamber is 1,000' long by 110' wide. The maximum length of a ship that can transit the canal is 950', maximum width is 106' and maximum depth is 60'. Ships near maximum dimensions are called Panamax ships and are assigned two bow pilots to help guide the ship through the locks.

Geoff Jones and the Pioneer Reef

One day Carl got a transit, riding as PIT with a senior pilot, Captain Geoff Jones. He'd heard that Jones was a nice guy, but at first Carl didn't think so. This was to be an all night transit on a small ship, only 350 feet long. As they started their southbound transit toward the Gatun Locks, Captain Jones said little. They were the last southbound ship that transited that day. After the anchor was up, they were under way, and had cleared Gatun Locks, Jones turned to Carl, and asked, "Aren't you going to do anything?"

"Sure," Carl answered," I'm going to do something."

"Well, go ahead and do it. I guess I'll let you work a little as we cross Gatun Lake. It's 22 miles long and the channel is so wide, I don't think you'll get in any trouble."

"Okay, Captain."

Carl gave the order to heave up the anchor, gave the engine orders, then the courses to the helmsman and brought the ship in to the Cristobal channel and toward the locks. Carl had the computer print out for the transit, so he knew pretty well what was going on. Captain Jones didn't say anything at first. Then he jumped Carl's ass; "You better get on your own side of the channel. There is a ship that has just cleared the west side of the lock. Get over a little more."

Carl said, "Okay."

So he got over, but he knew he had been far enough over. Hell, he'd been going to sea all his life.

"Watch it. Watch what you're doing," Jones hollered.

It seemed Carl couldn't do anything right, at least in Jones 's eyes. When they got close to the locks, Carl slowed the ship and got into position. The nose eased into the lock.

"You don't use tugs on this size ship. It's only 350 feet long. Let's see you put it in there."

Carl answered, "Okay, all right. Here goes."

Carl gave the various orders to the mate on watch and the helmsman, doing good work in his own mind. "You're coming in too wide. Don't you see that knuckle over there? That's what opens up ships, stupid people getting too far away from the center wall. Get her back over close to the wall. Call in on center one."

"Okay. Center one call in." Carl obeyed.

This went on and on until Carl got the ship in the lock and four locomotives made fast. They started through the locks. When they had cleared the third lock, Jones said, "I'm going to go down and take a little rest. By the way, what step are you?"

"I'm 526," Carl answered.

"Take the con for a little while," Jones ordered.

They proceeded across Gatun lake. Carl didn't know what Jones went down for, but he found out later. He needed his insulin shot. He had a severe case of diabetes. Carl found out that he followed the shot with glasses full of whiskey. Carl didn't know at the time that Captain Jones was an alcoholic. When he returned to the bridge, he said, "Let me take over."

When this transit began Geoff had called the ship's captain and asked him for some whiskey. The old man had brought a bottle to him. He had a glassful of it. The old man started to take the bottle back.

"Just leave that bottle right there." Geoff told the captain.

The captain left the bottle.

Carl said to himself, "How can a man take insulin shots and drink all this bloody whiskey? My God, I don't see how the man can stay alive."

Geoff was in his fifties but looked at least 65.

Finally, in a somewhat belligerent tone he asked, "What license you got? What packet are you from?"

"What license do you have, Captain?" Carl asked in return

"I have an unlimited Master's License. I've been a sea captain. Did you come off the tugs?"

"No, I didn't come off the tugs. I have a license just like you do, Unlimited Ship Master, Oceans."

"I thought you were off the tugboats. That makes a difference. I'm glad to see that. They've been taking so many guys off the tugboats here lately that I thought you must be one too." He went on and on.

Finally Carl said, "I've heard about you, Captain. Many people have told me that you were a commander in the navy. I also heard that your wife is from Australia."

"How did you find this out?"

"I was talking to Paul Simon. He comes over, and we have coffee together a lot."

"That's right. Did you ever sail to Australia?"

"I sure did."

"What ship were you on?"

"I was on the Pioneer Reef."

"Well, I'll be damned! I was on the Pioneer Reef. That's where I met my wife, Tess."

"That's funny. I met a passenger on that ship, too. I married her. Her name is Edna."

"I'll be damned! You can take the con. I'm going to call for some sandwiches."

If the food aboard ship were not acceptable or the galley was closed for the night, the pilot could call for sandwiches. There were usually a variety of sandwiches, about six kinds. Also, if the water were questionable, the captain would send out a cooler of water.

After this Jones got real friendly with Carl. Finally he said, "What's the matter with your glasses?"

"They're fogging up on me."

"Hell, throw them away. You don't need them, do you?"

"You know, I believe I can see better without them."

Carl threw the glasses over the side. He had gotten the glasses in Coco Solo. They were poorly made and of little help.

The two men kept on talking about the Pioneer Reef. "Do you remember anybody calling that ship the Pioneer Grief?" Jones inquired.

"I heard the story about a bunch of people drowning for some crazy reason."

"Let me tell you the story. We were docked at Willamaloo Docks. The quay is made of concrete. They use big bundles of sticks like this to keep the ships from scraping on the cement. You know what they are?"

"Sure, fenders about six feet in diameter, right?"

Through the bundles ran an iron shaft attached to chains on both sides which reached up to the quay and was secured to the dock. There were spaces between the fenders.

"The gangway was out. The chief engineer was going ashore. When he was at the top of the turntable and started down the gangway, he had a heart attack. He fell over between the fenders and the side of the ship. He was struggling in the water, pinned in the small space. The captain saw him and jumped over to save the engineer, and they both drowned. You're not going to believe this! It was either the purser or one of the other mates who jumped over. They all drowned. I'm pretty sure it was four officers who drowned; the engineer, the captain, and two other officers. Carl, can you imagine? I wasn't there. I was ashore dating my wife. Can you believe it? These four men jumped over without a life jacket. No one even threw a ladder over the side. No one even put a line down that they could hold on to. They all drowned. When the story came out in the Sydney newspaper, with pictures of the ship and the ambulances taking the drowned men away, along with the quay where it happened, they renamed the ship the Pioneer Grief, G-R-I-E-F, instead of R-E-E-F. When were you on that ship, Carl?"

"I don't remember just when it was. It was in the fifties. I stayed on that ship for one trip. I met my ex-wife, Edna, while I was on that ship. She was a passenger going from Sidney, Australia to New York. She already had her entry into the United States, her green card, and her resident alien status. She had a job in New York waiting for her. She was engaged to marry some fellow in New York and was planning to marry him until she met me. That marriage turned out to be a big mistake, but that is another story. You know somebody burned the boilers on that ship. We had all kinds of trouble. It took us 50 days to go from Brisbane, Australia to the Panama Canal. From there we struggled up to Trinidad. That captain really knew his business. Water was rationed. We got a bucket of water a day to bathe. He had everybody working in shifts, killing one boiler at a time, and rolling in new tubes. This whole thing was a nightmare. The captain and the chief engineer were very good friends, but when the engineer on watch burned the boilers and the chief engineer turned to the bottle, that was the end of that friendship."

"Who was the captain on there when you were on?"

"Captain Pierce."

"I know Pierce, but they flew a captain over there to take over the ship when the skipper was drowned. His name wasn't Pierce, so Pierce must have come on the next trip as permanent master. Did you know the chief mate?"

"Yeah, I know the chief mate."

"What was his name?"

"We called him Useless."

"Oh, yes, Ussery."

"That's right. We called him "useless" because we all hated him for his constant criticism. Useless had his wife aboard while in Australian waters which was against regulations. However, if anyone else brought a guest or anyone aboard, even to tour the ship, Useless would run them off. He was thoroughly disliked. We figured the captain was single because he frequently brought showgirls aboard."

The two men chatted all the way through the canal. Just before they cleared Miraflores Lock, the last lock before going to sea, Jones got out Carl's performance sheet. Each time he worked as a PIT, the control pilot was required to fill out a performance record on him. Jones gave Carl an excellent rating, filled out his slip, brought it into the wheel-house, and handed it to him. He invited Carl to come over and visit him and Tess, his wife.

Carl asked him, "How does your wife like it here? A lot of the women don't like their husbands coming here. They don't like Panama. It isn't very comfortable during the long rainy season, putting up with arrogant Panamanians, and all the TV programs in Spanish. The U.S. Forces Channel #8 is not much better."

"My wife is no different," replied Jones.

"How is your marriage coming along?" Carl asked Jones.

"Carl, my furniture has gone back and forth to Australia so many times that it has more sea time than I do. She has left me many times."

"I divorced my wife. I couldn't take it any more. That's a long story. I kind of wish I were married to somebody down here. It gets awfully lonely by myself, but I'm afraid of marriage."

"Well, Carl, you were on the Pioneer Reef. You got on when I got off. Well, I'll just be damned."

When they got through with this conversation, Geoff told Carl, "You're doing real good, Carl. Ease up on the wheel. Give me a little port helm as we begin our entrance into Miraflores."

Simon had let Carl take the ship through the Gaillard Cut, and now he let Carl lock down at both Pedro Miguel and Miraflores locks. He had no complaints.

"Okay, Captain Carl. You are doing just fine. You can see that old Carl is now a captain and doing good work. I wonder why," Carl thought as he recalled his many years of experience on the high seas.

As they prepared to climb down the Jacob's ladder to the pilot boat, Geoff turned to Carl and said, "Give me your phone number, Carl. I'll give you a call. When you are in Balboa and you have some spare time, maybe when you get off early in the afternoon, you can come over to my house. We'll have coffee and cake. I'd like you to meet my wife."

"Okay, George. I'll do that."

Carl had been on the transit all night, starting at 5:00 p.m. He got off the ship at 3:30 a.m. The pilot boat took then to the "mine dock" where a jitney was waiting. The boathouse on Naos Island was called the mine dock, since trains used to run there to refuel coal-burning ships. The jitney drove them along Amador Road. Geoff got out at Williamson Place, an apartment complex on the Pacific side. From there Carl went to the pilot station at Pier 18 where he got a trans-isthmus jitney for the 50 mile ride to the Atlantic cross roads where he transferred to another local jitney to take him to his home in Coco Solo. Carl's neck was cramped from the trans-isthmus part of the ride, since he was very tired and had slept in a cramped position in the jitney. It took him only about 60 seconds to go to sleep. At the crossroads on the transisthmian highway, 2 ½ miles out of

Colon, he transferred to another local jitney. The last lap of his journey took him to Coco Solo to his apartment on Severn Road. He arrived home at 7:00 a.m.

Geoff and Carl became very good friends. Geoff had a Commander's Comission in the Naval Reserve. At the time of this writing, in late 1999, Captain Geoff Jones lives somewhere in the panhandle of Florida. He is dying. He was an excellent captain, but alcohol, coupled with his diabetic condition, broke his health.

Satin Shirt Gunderson

At 0700 one morning Carl received his call from MTC. "Good morning, Captain Turner. You are assigned to ride with Captain Gunderson on North 21. The vessel is the Herr Vostog, 85' beam, 700' long, docked at Pier 15."

"Okay, transit. I have the trip information. Thank you," Carl replied. He thought, "Man, oh, man, I've heard this pilot on my radio many times. He is tough on PITs."

Pilots didn't like the way he would egg on PITs and junior pilots—steps 1-5. "Satin Shirt" Gunderson, as he was called because he liked to wear satin shirts both when he was piloting and when off duty, was one of the best pilots in the canal. He was known for his fast transits. Often he would call on his radio to the vessel ahead of him, "Is that you, N-19 just calling in at Gamboa?"

"Yes, this is N-19 at the Gamboa check point," would come the reply.

"Well N-19, I am about 500 yards astern of you. Can't you move along faster? Don't you want to go home before sunup? The locks are waiting for you. If you don't step on it I'm going to pass you in Gamboa Reach and take your lockage. I have piloted that ship you're on and there is nothing wrong with that ship. Speed up!"

At other times around the locks, he would call on his radio to another ship, "South 8, what's the matter? Why are you stopped? The locks are not going to come to you. You are holding up the parade. Can't you see your locomotives are back and you have the arrow? We will be here all day. Earn your pay. Move, just move! Do something."

Since Carl was living at Coco Solo, the trans-isthmian jitney would take him the fifty miles to Pier 18 in Balboa. Carl met Gunderson at the Pier 18 reporting office. He called Marine Transit Control (called ACDC 1 and ACDC 2 before 1979). As Carl and "Satin Shirt" were walking down to dock #16, "Satin Shirt" asked, "What license do you hold? What companies did you work for in the U.S.? What step are you? How many transits have you made?"

The only answers he liked was that Carl had been a ship master with an unlimited U.S. Coast Guard license and that he had been a tanker mate and master. On the bridge of the Herr Vostog Gunderson asked, "What time are you going to get under way?"

Carl answered, "In 20 minutes. N-19 is passing dock #6 now." Dock #6 is a check point. Carl did not have the transit card and was reluctant to ask Gunderson for it. As soon as the 20 minutes were up and N-19 cleared dock#6, Carl gave the order, "Let go all lines. Let me know when we are clear."

"Lines clear, sir," the quartermaster informed Carl at the proper time.

"Midship, half astern." The ship's engine started with a whirl of revolutions, then settled down to half speed, about 60 rpm. The ship was backing very fast astern. Satin Shirt screamed, "Thrust bow to port. Stop engines! Then port 20°, half ahead and stop." The ship stopped dead in the water. By this time they were in the middle of Balboa Harbor. Satin Shirt's face was ashen with rage. He bellowed, "What's the matter with you? Don't you know that this ship is a 21 knot vessel? Are you crazy?"

"I do not want to work with you. I will just observe," answered Carl.

"Observe, my ass! You are going to work and learn to be a pilot. I may meet you sometime and I want to know what kind of a pilot you are!

Here, look at this transit card. I will straighten this bucket out; then you can take over and put her in the lock."

The German officers and crew members winced at the term "bucket". Actually the ship was no bucket; she was a beautiful ship. The German officers and crew were cool and calm. They knew that if the ship were damaged, the U.S. Federal code of Regulations stipulates that the Panama Canal Commission would have to pay. The captain knew not to interfere. It was a wonder there was no damage as the docks were in deplorable condition with twisted iron beams jutting out all along them. When docking, the ship must be placed parallel to the dock, keeping her about 2 or 3 feet off the dock and breasting her in gradually. Gunderson saved the day by thrusting the bow out. He talked Carl through the lock approaches. Finally he said, "I will say one thing, Carl. You have a big pair of balls. I am going to help you. I can't stand these slow pokes and scaredy cats. You were a chief mate on a chemical ship. You have the nerve and intelligence to be a good pilot. Pay attention. You have to visualize every move you make in this canal. You get me? Visualize before you make your move. Then when things are not going as planned, make corrections fast. In time all this will come to you automatically."

After clearing Gamboa "Satin Shirt" was on the radio again. "All right, you guys; you can do better. Step on it or I will take the first lockage available at Gatun."

The ship had a lot of speed and after Satin overtook N-17 and had N-19 in his sights, he said on the radio, "Okay, N-17, when we get to Buena Vista I am going to pass you on two whistles."

"ACDC 2 Transit; this is N-17. N-21 is going to pass me. I have told him no, it's too dangerous, but he said that he will pass me anyway. Isn't this against regulations?" the pilot of N-17 radioed transit.

"No, it isn't against regulations in the part of the lake you are in. He only accepts responsibility for any accidents until he is clear of your vessel. Good luck." Came the reply.

Carl could hear the powerful diesel engine digging in. N-17 was passed with ease. Now N-15 was ahead. "Silk Shirt" would have to pass this vessel in the Gatun reaches. He could not do it at his present speed. He would have to slow down from Pinua Blanco to the Gatun Reach. N-15 had the arrow on the west side of the Gatun Locks. The arrow was down on the east side. "Silk Shirt" went for the east side. Screams and loud protests could be heard everywhere including threats that all the transits Silk Shirt's ship had passed would write letters. N-15 was in the middle of the approach blocking Silk Shirt, or he thought he was. But Satin Shirt came close around his stern. Carl thought he was going to hit N-15, but he passed safely close to the stern of N-15, swung the bow to port, and put a violent back in her. The bow swung back to starboard and just sat there. Silk Shirt's ship got its locomotives, and Satin Shirt gave the con to Carl. Satin Shirt said, "Do not try this until you have been here for awhile. Okay?"

Carl said, "Okay". The stern was closing in on the center wall. "What are you going to do?" asked Satin Shirt. Carl put the rudder to port 5° and ordered a tap ahead. Satin Shirt called this a "kick". He was right. "I jacked her over a bit," Carl said.

"Jack, my ass! You gave her a kick ahead. You are no farm boy from Minnesota. You are a rebel just like me," Satin Shirt screamed. Carl knew Satin Shirt was right.

Satin Shirt had been a captain with Texaco Company. He had carried two pistols in his belt when he was a captain, so Carl had been told. It was rumored by pilots that didn't like Satin Shirt that he shot a seaman on one of his ships and Texaco fired him. Satin Shirt was a 32nd degree Mason, a Shriner. Later, Carl saw him in Shriners' parades. He wore a fez, a white robe, and banged big brass cymbals. "Clang! Bang! Clang! Hi, Carl," he would call.

Much later Satin Shirt shot a Guardia officer in a bar in Panama City. He was hauled before the chief pilot who threatened to fire him. Satin Shirt exploded and told the chief pilot what he could do with the job; he quit. Since his buddies were Shriners, he thought he could get his job back any time, but he was mistaken. He thought that the Shriners would stick together, no matter what, but not this time. Satin Shirt took his pension. All this was speculation, of course, but Satin Shirt did leave his job as pilot prematurely. Carl liked Satin Shirt; he was an able pilot. Carl was sorry to see him go, and hoped that he would get his job back.

No Whistle or Telegraph

Carl made some more crazy trips. One time when he was a 440-foot pilot, he was assigned to a Korean fishing boat about 90 feet in length. Since there was no ship of a length to fit his grade, Carl was assigned any smaller ship coming through to give him his required number of transits for promotion. At this time pilots worked according to starts. The more starts a pilot made, the more money he made. Pilots also were paid overtime. However, as a 225,440 or 526 pilot Carl did not make any starts, nor did he get a single hour of overtime. His starting salary was $32,000 per year. Needless to say, he got in lots of fishing.

This Korean fishing boat was a real nightmare. Later Carl thought he really shouldn't have taken him through the Canal. He really didn't have to according to the Federal code of Regulations. The ship didn't have a whistle. The telegraph to the engine room was broken. There was no telephone or voice tube for communication. The captain was using a sledgehammer to beat on the wheelhouse deck to signal his orders to the engine room. Carl told the captain, "Look. Whew! This is really something terrible here. I really don't know that I can take this ship through."

The captain had a good command of English but spoke with a clipped Korean accent. The crew had been at sea for a long time. Carl guessed they were going to unload and then scrap this boat when they got home, but he didn't know for sure. If the captain wanted the ship to go ahead, he just picked up the sledgehammer and bang the wheelhouse deck one time. If he wanted to go ahead at half speed, he'd bang it two times. For "Go ahead full", he'd bang it three times. He had bang, bang orders for going astern. One bang, stop, another bang meant astern. One bang, stop, two bangs meant half astern. These signals were driving Carl crazy. However, the ship steered and handled very well.

Carl told the captain, "I'm going to have to call transit. I don't think you will get a pilot to take this ship through in the condition it is in."

"Captain, if you will get us through and forget the regulations, I sure will appreciate it. We're going to have to get it through if we have to hire a tug to pull us through. If we have to do that it's going to cost this company an awfully lot of money."

"It will take 15 hours for a tug to take you through, and we can't spare the tug to do it, since they are all tied up moving ships through the locks. You are right; that would be a terribly big bill," Carl agreed.

"Would you please take us through and make the best of it? If anything happens and we have an accident, we won't hold you accountable."

"Okay, here we go," Carl assented.

Carl bang, banged along. He was going slow ahead approaching Gatun Locks.

He ordered, "Captain, stop the engine."

It took a long time to stop. Carl's heart was in his throat, as it seemed the ship would not stop before it hit the lock gate. The captain finally picked up the hammer and beat on the deck until the engine stopped. He gave the order to go astern, but instead we went ahead. Carl thought he was going to smash right into the soft nose, but he didn't. They finally got these signals straightened out. The captain knew the signals really well, but Carl didn't. He didn't know how the engine room got them all confused, either. The chocks were rotten, so he talked to the locomotives and asked them to be real careful. The ship didn't need much help to steer it through the locks. Carl asked the locomotives, "Just give us a little tap when we need it, but don't pull the bits through the chocks, because she's a rusty bucket."

Carl went on through the night with this "rusty bucket". He went below to go to the toilet and found that the toilet had been broken off even with the deck. There was just a hole. He had to fill a bucket with water and pour it down the hole to wash it out. Carl looked down in the engine room. He saw a big guy, half asleep, with a big rag in his hand leaning on something. He wondered if this was the engineer he had to depend on. The captain assured him that he was an oiler.

This is the type of transit that is real, real tough. Pilots could get a passenger ship through the canal and they'd think they were on the bridge of the Waldorf Astoria. But this is one of the worst transits Carl ever made. Anyway, he cleared the Gatun locks and asked if the captain had a cold beer and kimchee on board. Carl liked beer and kimchee. Sure enough he brought a lot of Korean beer and a big bowl of kimchee. Some kimchee is mild, and some of it is hot. This was real hot stuff. Carl understood that putting cut cabbage in the ground with condiments such as hot sauce made kimchee. It's real tasty. Carl must have drunk a six pack or more of beer to cool off the kimchee, but he got the ship through to the other side. When he got ready to get off, the captain brought him a half gallon bottle of Korean rice wine in a velvet bag. He told Carl it was the best rice wine ever made in Korea. In addition he gave Carl a bottle of Johnny Walker Black Label.

"Well, Captain, I sure do appreciate this," Carl told the captain.

He replied, in his clipped Korean accent, "Captain, you took this ship through the Canal. If you hadn't done it, it would have cost us an awful lot of money. We divide up the expenses. The boat gets so much; the owner gets so much, and the crew gets so much. If we had to take a tugboat through here, it would come out of the owner's share. Then the owner will take it out of our share. You saved us thousands of dollars and a lot of time. If you hadn't helped us, I don't know when we would ever have gotten through. Thank you, Captain. Thank you. I hope I see you again. I'll never forget you."

"Okay, Captain, good-by." Carl felt sorry for the captain and the crew. He knew the captain was right about the price of the tug and the distribution of the costs.

Carl put both bottles in his transit bag, boarded the pilot boat, and headed ashore.

He said aloud, "Whew! With the condition of this ship, it will be one of my worst transits, but a very rewarding one, I am sure."

Aggressive Latino Captain

One day in 1989 Carl piloted a Panamanian dry cargo ship, about 450 to 500 feet in length, considered a comparatively small ship. A Latino captain was on the bridge. An American tanker transporting volatile chemical cargo had been placed in transit ahead of the Panamanian ship, since the dangerous nature of the cargo mandated the American ship's exclusive use of the lock chamber. Two small ships, like the dry cargo ship Carl was piloting, could occupy a lock chamber at the same time; this is called a tandem lockage. The Latino captain was apparently unaware of the volatile cargo regulation and seemingly had a great deal of hatred for Americans. He started his tirade as soon as the transit started, saying, "Look at that! I've been waiting to take my turn at the lock. That American ship was put in the chamber in front of me. That's discrimination if I ever saw it. This is Panama's canal. Panama owns this canal. That tanker was put in ahead of me for political reasons. This is all political."

Carl told the captain, "Look, Captain. I'm going to tell you something right now. According to the treaty Panama will not control the canal until noon on December 31, 1999. That's ten years from now. Until then the United States has strict control of this canal. The Americans will be running things lock, stock, and barrel."

The captain went on and on telling Carl how imperialistic the U.S. was, grabbing the Philippines, Guam, Puerto Rico, and now Panama for its own selfish profit. Carl got sick and tired of this constant harangue. He needed to concentrate on the ship's operation. The captain's vitriolic diatribe was interfering.

When Carl arrived at the anchorage at Gatun he put the ship at anchor. When the captain asked why he had anchored the ship, Carl replied that he didn't have to take his verbal abuse. The captain called the ship's agent and told him that the pilot had put the ship at anchor. The agent wanted to know why. The captain handed Carl the radio, saying, "The agent wants to talk to you."

Carl told the agent he had taken all the harassment he could stand, and related what the captain had been saying to him.

The agent tried to soothe Carl's feathers, saying, "Captain Turner, you have helped us get difficult transits through in the past. We really need to get that ship out of here. I've been in touch with the owners earlier today, and they are anxious to get this ship through the canal. I sure would appreciate it if you would help us out now. What can I do to help you complete this transit?"

"Get this captain off the bridge. Put the first officer in the wheelhouse," Carl said.

"Okay, pilot. I'll see that the captain will put the first mate on the bridge. The second mate can go forward on the bow. If you will accept these terms, please lock down."

"Okay, Mr. Agent. When it is our turn to lock down, we'll heave up and continue through the canal. When we get to Cristobal, the captain can have his bridge back. I don't care what he does with it then."

"Thank you very much, Captain Turner. I've dealt with you on a similar occasion with a tugboat if you remember."

"Yes, I remember. On that occasion the agent and company official took the captain off and sent him to Cristobal on the train as requested."

"You took care of that situation for us when all the other pilots had turned it down. I really appreciate your cooperation. Let me talk to the captain," the agent answered.

"Okay, Mr. Agent. Thank you very much."

Carl gave the radio telephone to the captain who listened to the agent. All Carl heard the captain say was, "Oh, I see. All right. I'll do as you say."

His face had turned white. When he got off the phone, he turned to Carl and said, "I'm going to my office. I'll send my first mate up here. You won't see me for the rest of the trip."

When a ship approaches and transits a lock, the federal code of regulations states that the captain must be on the bridge. Both the agent and Carl were willing to violate this regulation in order to complete the transit. The rest of the transit was made in peace. Carl wondered why the captain hated Americans so much. He was to encounter this attitude many times as an intense spirit of nationalism grew in Panama.

English Speaking Ship Personnel

The captains and most of the officers on all the ships that go through the Panama Canal speak English. They go to school to learn to speak English no matter what country they come from. These men are cadet trained from the lowest rank on the bridge up to captains. The reason the Panama Canal Commission prefers to hire ex-shipmasters of ocean going vessels as Panama Canal pilots is that the U. S. government insures vessels that transit the canal. Also, ex-shipmasters command the respect of captains whose ships' movements and navigation the pilots command during the canal transit. Ex-shipmasters know the workings of all facets of a ship's operation from the engine room to the wheelhouse. Such a person can, therefore, deviate from the printed word for piloting when the situation warrants. Ship captains expressed to Carl and to other pilots who hold Masters Ship Licenses that they resent the

Panamanian pilots whom they call "coconut busters" or "towboat appointees" taking over ships other than small boats or tugs because they have no maritime background whatsoever. They resent such people taking over control of their ships. However, the shipowners sent them there. They have to get the ships through the canal. Many different people, if they have the talent, regardless of maritime background, can be trained as pilots. What rankles is the idea of someone of less maritime stature taking over their ships.

4

THREE STORIES

A Special ID Card

In July of 1978 the Panama Canal Commission sent a letter telling Carl to go to the office at Pier 16 in Balboa. Although he already had a U.S. Government ID Card, he was to get a Panamanian Identification Card, with his picture glued on it, which would authorize him to enter and board ships on official business. He lived just a few blocks from Pier 18 and was one of the few pilots to get such a card. Dr. Hugo Torrijos, Minister of Property and Treasury and Director General of the Navy, signed Carl's card. This is the same man who was defeated in his run for president in the May 1999 elections. Carl's card expired on April 2, 1988. Such cards were sealed in plastic. When the Panama Canal Zone was turned over to Panama on October 28, 1979, the Panamanian Government wanted to charge $10 to issue the new cards. Since the U.S. had paid for the machine to make the cards, the Panama Canal Comission refused to pay. From that time on, only the U.S. Government ID card was required for pilots. The Panamanian government continued to issue such cards to Panamanian longshoremen and to other Panamanian personnel who worked on the docks.

The Cattle Boat

At 0630 Carl got his call from MTC. "Good morning, Captain Turner," was the greeting.

"Good morning," Carl answered.

"Captain, you have 1300 today. Your transit, the m/v cattleman carrier IV, S14x is at anchor at Gatun anchorage. Your Gamboa time is 1800 hours".

"What time is the transit scheduled to clear?"

"Clearing time at Miraflores is 2200; and, by the way, you should take a clothes pin with you, as many pilots complain about the smell."

"Oh, I don't care," Carl nonchalantly replied, "As long as I get to transit by myself. Thank you."

At 1030 Carl looked out the window and noted that a jitney was parked in the driveway. Carl took the local jitney to the pilot station at pier 18 where his trans-isthmian jitney was waiting. Since two other pilots were already seated in the back seat, Carl took a seat in the front. All the way from Balboa to the crossroads on the Atlantic side the back seat pilots passed a bottle of whiskey back and forth. Neither one spoke to Carl. Instead, they talked about a merchant officer they both knew at one time. Carl felt as though he had lice or leprosy; he was so completely ignored. Since he hadn't had the opportunity to make many friends among the pilots yet, his feelings of dislike toward some of the senior pilots intensified.

At the Atlantic crossroads Carl transferred to a local jitney which took him to the Gatun boathouse where he called MTC for transit information for ship S14x. The x after the ship number denotes that the ship has been delayed for a day. Transit told him, "Captain Turner, your S14x and your Gamboa time is 1800 hours. You will take the west side of Pedro Miguel lock following S10x and the west side at Miraflores following S12x."

Southbound transits are given even numbers; northbound transits are assigned odd numbers. "Thank you, transit," Carl answered as he turned to the dispatcher, "I am ready for a launch to go to S14x."

"Okay, Captain Turner. We will not have to look for your transit. It is a cattle boat. The launch captain can just follow the smell," the dispatcher chuckled Carl.

As the pilot boat approached the vessel, Carl saw that her draft was up 14' 9". He noted from the transit card that the ship was 350' long with a 40' beam. Carl climbed up the pilot ladder and proceeded to the bridge.

"Good evening, Mr. Pilot. My name is John Thompson. Welcome aboard," greeted the captain.

"Thank you. My name is Carl Turner. Howdy, Mr. Mate."

"Good evening. I'm Jerry Smith."

"Pilot, what time do we get underway? We have been at anchor in Cristobal for two days and now an additional day at anchor in Gatun Lake," Thompson inquired.

"Let me call transit and verify my schedule, Captain Thompson," said Carl as he turned to his radio, "Transit, transit, this is S14x for a radio check."

"S14x you have a good radio. No change in schedule, 1800 at Gamboa," verified MTC.

"Okay, thank you, transit," turning to Captain Thompson, "Captain, here is a print out for all the south bound vessels. Your vessel is marked in yellow highlighter. You can see that we will clear Miraflores at approximately 2100. Okay? If you don't mind I'd like to go aft and look at some of the Holstein calves you have on board. I once took a course in animal husbandry from the University of Florida and am interested in the livestock." Carl knew he had plenty of time before the vessel needed to get underway. He had 5 hours to get to Gamboa. They were already through Gatun Locks; it would only take about 3 hours to get across Gatun Lake to Gamboa.

"It's okay by me," said Thompson, "Mr. Wyatt will show you around. He is in charge of the cargo and his gang works only for him. The owner of the cattle makes all the arrangements for his livestock. The ship's crew has nothing to do with them."

Wyatt introduced himself and admonished Carl, "I'll be happy to show you around, but I warn you that the smell is worse below than it is here. Better put these rubber boots on. You know there is always some "brown mud" about. Ha-ha!"

Carl and Wyatt toured the three decks; Carl noted that all the cattle looked to be very expensive calves about six months old. Just as they were passing the last pen on the way back to the bridge, the calves backed excitedly into a tight corner. One of them apparently had diarrhea and sprayed Carl from the waist down. He was glad he had left his shoes and socks in Wyatt's locker. Wyatt's face was ashen. "I warned you, Captain Turner. Now I suppose you will go ashore and leave us here another day."

"Not at all, Wyatt. Just have someone fetch me a bucket of water and a bar of soap on the boat deck. I feel like a swim today, anyhow," Carl good-naturedly assured Wyatt.

On the boat deck Carl stripped to his birthday suit. By this time Captain Thompson appeared. "Pilot, what happened?"

Carl related the episode and asked if he would have a sailor wash his clothes and then take them to the bridge. Thompson complied with, "Sure, Pilot. We'll have a pair of clogs and a robe for you, as well."

Carl soaped up with the bar of soap and the bucket. Then, without further adieu he jumped off the boat deck and swam around the ship even though the ship was at anchor close to a buoy and within sight of the Gatun Yacht Club. Given the circumstances Carl didn't give a damn; the water was clean and cool, about 80' deep at this spot. He returned to the bridge in the captain's robe and clogs. About twenty minutes later a sailor brought his clean clothes and asked Carl where he wanted them hung.

"Son, get me about 30' of 9 or 12 thread and meet me on the flying bridge."

The sailor promptly came to the flying bridge with Carl's laundry and the manila rope. "Put a bowline on one end, snap it to the halyard, open up the lay of the line and attach a pinch of the sleeve on the line, so on and so on, until you have all my laundry flying in the breeze", Carl instructed. "Okay?"

"Mr. Pilot, your clothes won't come off, will they?"

"Not if you do as I have shown you!"

Carl returned to the bridge where Captain Thompson had a fine meal waiting for him. It was a big, thick steak, French fries, a green salad, and an ice cold Budweiser. Carl had become used to the smell by this time. He loved animals. Because of the small size of the ship he was the only pilot; this was just the way he liked it. After the meal Captain Thompson and Wyatt asked Carl about his animal husbandry course. He began, "I was in the airborne army during World War II. After the war, in 1945, I had a few years of college tuition paid for through the GI Bill, so I took a correspondence course from the University of Florida. I completed all the assignments for a six-month period; then heard nothing. At the time I was a bo's'n on the S/T "Antelope Hills" and away from the states for a year shuttling oil from a pipeline in Lebanon to Genoa, Italy. Things went fine until the ship's Captain French was taken off and a new skipper came aboard. We were on articles for a year, since we had signed a contract with the captain to sail foreign for a year unless the ship went back to the U.S. before the year was up. We had only been out for six months when Captain French got off. He wanted to be relieved; he was not on articles like the crew was. He was a U.S. citizen from the Cayman Islands. The new skipper was an American who had emigrated from Norway. He was about 75 years old. I received no more course material. Everything just stopped. I couldn't understand it, since my previous assignments had been returned and been marked "A" or "B". When the vessel returned to the states, I went to the crew's mess room to get my mail and there, scattered all over the place, were dozens of large manila envelopes all opened. There was all my missing course material. A sign on the blackboard read, 'Anyone who wants this material can have it. The ship has no use for it.' I was furious. I went to the captain's office. All the shore officials were there. I shouted, 'You stupid old son of a bitch, don't you see that all these envelopes were addressed to me. Look—Bo's'n Carl P. Turner. I ought to kick your ass, you old bastard!'

'All mail coming to this ship in manila envelopes belongs to the ship. Ship's business comes in brown envelopes,' was all the excuse he would give.

I went for him with fists balled up ready to hit him; but the officers held me back. 'I have lost my GI Bill because of you! You stupid ass hole!'

'Bo's'n, if you hit this old man the Coast Guard Commander will have your papers pulled and you will have to stand trial. Why don't you go get your pay? You were grossly wronged, but you should let the captain go home in peace.' the port captain told me. The captain planned to go to Norway to retire.

I had calmed down a little by this time and answered, 'Oh, let him go, but you know that he ran the ship aground in the sandy bottom of the Persian Gulf. I heard that his ship ran aground more than once. Give him to the Coast Guard.'

Now you see, Captain Thompson, what happened to my animal husbandry career. Okay, Captain; let's heave up. It looks like we're ready to go."

"Okay, Mr. Mate. You can call for water on deck to wash off the anchor. This is a muddy bottom."

"Right, Captain," obeyed the mate.

Captain Thompson turned to Carl and remarked, "Mr. Pilot, I sure am sorry you lost your GI Bill, but I am glad you have a pilot job now."

After the ship was under way, Carl stepped out on the flying bridge. He passed very close to about ten ships at anchor. He knew there would be a lot of calls about his "flag halyard", so he had his radio turned off. Pilots would come out on the flying bridge of their transits and shout all kinds of crazy remarks. One that Carl remembered in particular was: "Hey, Carl, you look like the raft that Robinson Crusoe was on."

He meant that the "flag halyard" looked like Robinson Crusoe's sail.

Halfway down Pena Blanca Reach Carl had the clothes hauled down. They had dried without a wrinkle. He dressed in the wheelhouse and continued on with the transit.

When the vessel locked down in Pedro Miguel and Miraflores, all the lock personnel shouted, "Phew, phew! Get that thing out of here. Give them the fast water, Mr. Lockmaster. Give them a double culvert. Give them the spill. Spill that water through all those holes!"

Everyone in the wheelhouse laughed. They were grateful for a fast transit. When the ship arrived at buoys #2 and #1 in the Pacific Ocean, Carl's pilot boat came alongside. Before departing Captain Thompson and Wyatt each gave Carl a bottle of Johnny Walker Black Label. "Thank you very much. I'll take this as a compliment," Carl told then.

"Captain Turner, you do smooth work, never touching the wall anywhere. We hope to see you again."

Carl bade them good-bye and shook hands all around. The pilot boat captain told him when he had descended the pilot ladder, "Man, you must have suffered today."

"On the contrary, I had a wonderful day. It's not the ship you get; it's the people aboard and the pilots you ride with that make a good transit."

Carl's car was waiting for him at the mine dock, Naos Island. He was driven home and was soon ready for bed.

Captain Wig-Wag

Carl's next transit was with a step five or six pilot. He wasn't a senior pilot, but he acted like he had been in the canal all his life. He was called "Wigwag" because he always had a tug on the stern everywhere he went except across Gatun Lake. He was a Dutchman whose real name was G. Wiggars. He came from Indonesia. His father was a Dutchman who had a huge plantation in Indonesia. His father remained in Indonesia and later married an Indonesian. When World War II broke out Wiggars, who was a five-year-old child at that time, and his mother escaped to Singapore. The rumor was that Wiggars and his mother were hiding under a garbage can in Singapore when the Americans found them. They made their way to the Philippines. When the Philippines were evacuated, they were taken to Guam and then to Pearl Harbor. They finally got to the United States where they became United States citizens. In this way Wiggars had grown up and gone to school in the United States, gotten his citizenship when he was twenty one years of age, and eventually got his Masters License. He had worked for the United Food Company. This company doesn't have any more ships under the American flag since the competition of foreign flagships put them out of business a long time ago.

Carl was told that Wiggars was going to be a real smart-ass. Since Carl was a 526' pilot, he really didn't need any more help from another pilot. He thought he was ready to move up to 20,000 or 30,000 ton ships, whichever was assigned by MTC. They didn't have a transit for Carl that day in his classification, so MTC assigned him to ride with Wiggars. At the Atlantic side boathouse there is a room with telephones for pilots to call in for transit instructions as well as a number of lounge chairs. About ten girls were working in the main office out front. The dispatcher had an office too. He assigned pilot boats. Carl was standing just inside the doorway

"You're Captain Turner, aren't you?" Captain Wiggars greeted Carl.

"That's right."

"You're a PIT?"

"Yeah, I'm still a PIT on ships over 526.'"

"You stay here in this pilot's waiting room. When I want you I'll call for you," he said as he left the room.

Carl sat down in an easy chair near the doorway. He listened to a lot of commotion and laughter. Then he noticed one person crawling on the floor on his hands and knees and under the desks.

The person on the floor said, "Has anybody seen this little old gray headed PIT running around here anywhere? I'm looking for him. I gotta take him out on the Canal today and teach him a few tricks in the canal. Ha, ha, ha, ha. He should be retired, but here he is, an old man just learning all the tricks."

Carl said to myself, "Just listen to this asshole."

The heckler kept making smart remarks. Everybody except Carl was laughing. Finally Wiggars stood in the door and said, "I got a pilot boat coming for us. We're going out to the ship. Are you ready to go out?"

"I'm ready to go out. I figure I'll go out and have just a nice tourist's ride in the Canal." Carl answered Wiggars. He knew that, as a PIT, he was not required to work, but merely observe.

"No, no. You're going to do some work on this ship."

So Carl made the trip with Wiggars. However, Carl never was given the con (control of the ship) throughout the transit.

Wiggars made disparaging remarks about Carl to the captain, "Look here," he'd say, "Look at this trashy old man they're bringing down, right in front of me."

The Old Man looked at him and he looked at Carl and thought, "Where did I get this crazy pilot?"

The seamen standing by and the officers in the wheelhouse just looked at the deck.

Wiggars went on, "Now that the treaty has been implemented they're going to start bringing Panamanians in from the tugboats and God knows where they're going to get them. I understand they have a maritime academy in Panama where they graduate pilots and send them out on Texaco ships that carry oil products from a refinery in Colon Province. The Texaco ships' officers have the Panamanian cadets to make coffee on the bridge for a year or two and then they come back as PITs."

Texaco operates Panama's only refinery. The Panamanian government put pressure on Texaco to allow cadets attending the Nautical Escuela, located in Panama City, to ride on their tankers. Before they begin their final year in the nautical school, they go out on Texaco tankers. They don't yet know how to navigate. They just make coffee for the officers and observe. After two years they come to the canal as PITs. The men who begin their piloting experience in this way have "palanca", or political pull. They come from influential families. Panamanian PITs who graduate from Central or South American academies go directly to the canal as PITs without riding on Texaco's tankers.

Wiggars went on, "They're going to flood the place with tugboat captains too. Can you imagine? These guys are coming on as PITs and they're starting off at $35,000 to $45,000 a year. Most of them have never seen a $100 bill in all their natural lives. I told them if they wanted pilots they didn't have to get PITs out of the maritime academy. They could just go shake some coconut trees. Some of the monkeys will come down with the coconuts. Train the monkeys. We have pilots here that will actually train those monkeys. Do you believe that?"

These remarks went on all during the night. Since the smaller ships went through the canal at night, most of the PIT transits were at night. As a PIT Carl had hoped that he would get practice putting the ship in the locks and handling the ship. Instead, Wigwag did it all. He acted like he was such a hot shot! As Carl watched him operate, it became clear that he didn't need the tugboat on the stern of the ship. When Carl got to be a step 5 or 6 pilot, he never used a tug on the stern of a ship this size. This ship was only half loaded and handled like a charm. But Wiggars kept a tug on the stern. That's why they called him "Wigwag". He was calling out commands to the tug, "Stern to port. Stern to starboard."

The tug acknowledged the order with three whistles. "Pull straight astern."

One whistle. "Stern to starboard."

Two whistles. "Stern to port."

Wiggars wasn't going to take any chances of any damage; when he first came to the canal, he was told he would never make a pilot; his performance was so poor. Wiggars docked the S/S Cristobol at Colon—her last voyage to Panama. It was told by the ship's captain that Wiggars used over 54 engine orders.

Both the ship's captain and Wiggars were Dutch and spoke to one another in Dutch most of the time.

Wiggars told the captain, "When I got my American citizenship, I was asked, after I had been sworn in, if I had anything I wanted to say now that I was a citizen of the United States of America. I told them, 'I want you people in America to stop bringing in all these foreigners and taking our jobs.'"

Carl thought, "Can you imagine this turkey? What a piece of work!"

Anyway, they made it through the night in this fashion. When they got to Miraflores lock, Wiggars asked Carl for his performance report. Wiggars drew a diagonal line all the way across it and wrote, "This pilot does real good work. He worked all during the transit."

Carl knew this to be a damned lie, since he hadn't had the con at all. Wiggars signed the paper, and Carl stuck it in his pocket. At least he got credit for the transit. At the end of the transit, Carl went home. He tried to just wipe the insulting people out of his mind.

From that time on Carl had nothing to do with Wiggars, and he noticed that many of the other pilots also had nothing to do with him. He was always telling jokes, as though people were naïve and what he was saying was going over their heads. Some people laughed, but Carl never thought he was funny.

The next time Carl was called to work with Wiggars, he told the training officer at MTC in Balboa that he didn't want to ride with

Wiggars anymore. Carl told the officer that he had not been allowed to work at all and had been insulted all night long. He asked the officer to look up his performance report. The training officer agreed to put Carl with other pilots. He never had to work with Wiggars again.

5

1979 THROUGH 1986

Daughter Elaine

By March of 1979, a year after coming to the Panama Canal, Carl had advanced to the point that he was now piloting ships, not according to length, but rather by tonnage and beam. Therefore, he was no longer considered a PIT. He was a Step One Pilot. After this time he never saw a new hire PIT with an unlimited masters license.

In October Elaine, who had returned from Houston to live with her father in Panama, went to the housing office and looked over the quarters that were up for bid. When a civil service employee wants to move up to larger and more expensive quarters, he could put in a bid for the desired dwelling. Bids were awarded according to seniority. Elaine selected an apartment at 752B Balboa Road across from a restaurant. It was near the pool, movie theatre, library, post office, grocery store, and other retail establishments. Carl would have a convenient and more commodious place to live. Carl's bid was successful, so he went to Balboa and signed for the unit. Just before moving to the Balboa apartment Carl had a confrontation with his daughter. Elaine was 19 years old. She was out of high school and enjoying her freedom. She sometimes stayed out all night. Carl soon discovered that she had boyfriends in his home. She supplied them with his liquor. They supplied her with drugs. Carl caught her slipping out the door with her slovenly friends taking Carl's money and booze with her. While Carl was on a transit she and her friends trashed Carl's car. Half the time Carl didn't know where Elaine was. Carl confronted Elaine with her unacceptable behavior, telling her that when they got to Balboa she must start going to junior college, straighten out and fly right or Carl would have to ask her to leave and go back to the U.S.

On the day Carl and Elaine were to move to Balboa Carl slept late, until 10:00 A.M. since he had been on a long transit the day before. When he got up and went to the kitchen to make coffee, there was a note on the counter. It read, "DAD, Mom has sent me an airline ticket. When you read this I will be at the airport in Panama City. Good-bye." Elaine returned to Houston. Carl loved his children, but he was afraid that Elaine would turn out just like her mother. He determined that if she ever came back he would try again regardless of the pain and disappointment.

Ferrocarril de Panamá

When Carl moved to Balboa his furniture still had not arrived from the states, so he slept on the floor of the front porch. The porch was glassed in with jalousie windows. He would never forget the first night. At midnight Carl awoke to the sound of hollering, fireworks, and heavy traffic. He got up from the floor and looked out the window. Cachibachs (junk taxicabs) and trucks were filled with Panamanians jumping up and down in celebration. Carl had heard that the U.S. Army had offered to operate the trans-isthmian railroad for Panama. The offer was refused. Carl dressed and walked to the round house to take a look. Panamanian workers were swarming all over the locomotives painting "Ferrocarril de Panamá", railroad of Panama. Carl just stood and stared and thought about all the men, mostly from Caribbean countries, who had died horrible deaths building the railroad. Death toll estimates vary from 15,000 to much higher numbers. No accurate records were ever found. Dead bodies were stuffed in barrels of alcohol and sold to medical laboratories around the world. "Now street urchins can just walk in and take over," Carl thought. It was October 22, 1979, the very date that the Carter-Torrijos treaty provision was implemented, whereby Panama took control of the Canal Zone but not the Panama Canal. At this time Balboa and Cristobol Harbors were turned over to Panama. The Panamanians told the Panama Canal Company to move out. The Company complied and built a reporting station and pilot boat dock at Diablo, a point closer to Miraflores Locks.

In 1997 Panama sold the right to run container ports at either end of the canal to Hutchinson Port Holdings, a Hong Kong firm, for $22.2 million. Since this firm allegedly has ties with mainland China, U.S. conservatives fear this action will allow China to gain a strategic foothold in the Western Hemisphere.[i]

Daughters' IDs and Red Passports

In 1980 Carl had been living at 752B Balboa Road for about fourteen months. He was now a step 2 pilot. At the pilot office Carl applied for transportation to bring his two daughters to reside with him in Panama. His older daughter, Maureen was attending the University of Texas. His younger daughter, Elaine , who had lived with Carl for a short time in Coco Solo, was returning to live with Carl and attend the U.S. government junior college at Balboa, Panama. Carl had requested residency for his youngest child, Randle, but he did not come to Panama, stating that he preferred to stay with his mother and Uncle Jude.

Both daughters came to Panama and soon made friends with the local young people. One bright sunny afternoon Carl came home from a pleasant transit on the cruise ship Pacific Princess. He walked in the living room to find his two beautiful daughters in tears. "What is the world is the matter? You have found friends; you have my new, big car to drive to the beaches, shop and spend money."

"Daddy, your last statement hit the problem. We can't buy at any of the commissary stores or the military commissary. We can go in, but our friends have to pay for us. All our friends say that we are entitled to special ID cards and special passports," complained Elaine.

"I'm sorry, girls. I should have taken care of this as soon as you arrived, but you know I am working almost every day. There is a lot of traffic in the canal. I will get right on this problem for you," assured Carl. "Take your letter," he instructed, "the one you received in the U.S., along with a note I will write to the documentation center. They will issue you a special red passport, take your picture, and issue your ID Cards. That will get you in all the commissaries with purchasing privileges. Okay?"

"Oh, thank you, daddy," both girls chirped.

"Do you know where the documentation building is?"

"Yes, Ruth, my new friend knows and will go with us. Can we use the car?" asked Maureen.

"Why, sure; you know that we live in the middle of Balboa. A car and driver takes me to work and brings me home. I don't really need a car."

The next day Elaine and Maureen went to the documentation center, along with their friend, Ruth. They presented their papers to the documentation official and were promptly told that there were no orders to issue ID cards and passports to Captain Turner's girls. Carl came home from his next transit at 1400 and found two disappointed and crying daughters.

"What on earth happened?" Carl asked the two.

"Dad, we went to the documentation center. They treated us as if we were illegal immigrants!" sighed Maureen. Carl told them to wait right there; he would be right back. He went to the chief pilot's office and asked Mrs. Wright, office manager, if his children were entitled to ID Cards and red passports. She told Carl they were.

Then he asked, "Does the fact that I am now on the six-four plan have anything to do with refusing to issue the ID Cards and passports to my daughters?"

The pilots' association had recently made a contract with the U.S. Government called the six-four plan whereby a pilot could work six weeks and be off four weeks. This contract had been agreed to in order to make as many pilots happy as possible. Many pilot families did not want to live in Panama. With the six-four plan pilots' families could be repatriated back to the states at government expense, take up residence in the U.S., and have the pilots come home for a month every six weeks.

Union officials begged Carl to sign up for the six-four plan. Carl needed some additional transits, so he was reluctant to sign up for the six-four plan, since it would take him longer to make his needed transits. Finally he gave in to the pressure, however, and signed up for the six-four plan. After the vote was secured to ratify the contract, Carl went back to the regular plan which gave him an annual vacation.

"Captain Turner, everyone on the hill has been notified by the congressional committee that six-four pilots and dependents are entitled to all purchasing privileges, identification cards, and special passports."

"That's all I want to know!" Carl went straight to the hill, the Panama Canal Company's administrative office building. After the treaty was implemented in 1979, the Panama Canal company became the Panama Canal Commission. Panamanians began to assume administrative positions on the new Panama Canal Commission. At the main entrance Carl asked where he could find the documentation office. The guard told Carl to go to the second floor. Mr. Smith was the man Carl should see. Carl found the office, knocked on the door and went in. There were four or five men sitting around. Carl asked, "Which one of you is Mr. Smith?"

One of the men spoke up, "I am Mr. Smith."

"Are you in charge of documentation?"

"Yes."

"My daughters, Maureen and Elaine have been denied ID Cards and special passports. Why? They have all the paperwork issued by the

Panama Canal Commission and have been cleared by Panamanian Immigration for residential status."

Since Carl was wearing his pilot's cap, Mr. Smith did not have to ask if he were a pilot. "Captain, I wish I could get on the six-four plan. I'd like to take my family and travel domestic and foreign, lay around my garden and take it easy." The onlookers laughed.

"This is not the first time that I have run afoul of people like you," Carl retorted. "I went to sea and earned my masters license. I don't know your background, but I came here just a few years ago not knowing anyone. I want ID Cards and special passports issued for my children, and I want them *now*, or my next stop will be to General McAuliff's office!" General McAuliff was the canal's top administrator.

"Captain, you are just like a red ball going down a white carpet." He was referring to the fact that Carl was the first six-four pilot to apply for ID cards and special passports for dependents. Smith continued, "Take your girls to the documentation office at 1000 hours tomorrow morning. I will notify my staff to issue the ID Cards and official passports."

"Thank you." Carl left.

The next morning Carl and his girls went to the documentation office. Carl walked up to the counter, stated that he was Captain Carl Turner and that his girls were known to the person behind the counter. The Panamanian employee just stared blankly at Carl who blurted, "Well, get your asses in gear and issue these girls their ID Cards and official red passports!"

The poor man started shaking. He said, "Let me call Mr. Smith. I don't know anything about this matter."

"Mr. Smith told me yesterday that he would notify his staff, and for me to be here at 1000 hours this morning," Carl exclaimed.

A short time later the man motioned Carl over to the telephone and said that Mr. Smith wanted to talk to him. Mr. Smith's voice on the phone explained, "Look, Captain, I was called into an emergency meeting yesterday after you were in my office. I apologize for this, but I want you to stay off my staff's ass. They are just G1 and G2 minimum wage people. Let me talk to Jorge." Jorge spoke on the phone and then turned to Carl, "Captain, you do not have to stay here. We will issue the ID Cards here. I will take the girls over to Panama City Immigration and have their passports issued." Carl left the office.

The next day the girls were disgruntled and angry. "What's the matter? Didn't things go okay?"

"Look Dad," said Elaine, "These Panamanians are ignorant. They have my birth date on Maureen's passport and vice versa. I really do not want to go back to that office."

"Just a moment. I'll call Jorge. He seemed to be a nice person, not like his boss, Mr. Smith." Carl called Jorge and explained the mix-up.

"Oh, my God," Jorge exclaimed, "Let me call Panamanian immigration and see if they have finished filing their nails." Panamanian female office workers were famous for doing their fingernails and taking their shoes off and grooming their toenails while on duty. About ten minutes later Jorge called Carl back and told him that he would send a car for the girls and get them new passports. Carl repeated his address for Jorge and instructed him to park in back of the post office.

After this episode Carl was thoroughly disgusted with the chiefs who worked for the Panama Canal Commission—chief of the fire department, chief of transportation, chief pilot, chief of the motor pool, chief of swimming pools, and especially chief of documentation. It was obvious that these "chiefs" cared little about American canal workers. They knew Panamanian workers would soon displace all American workers. The "chiefs" will need the Panamanian government to secure their big, fat civil service pensions at the end of 1999. Some of these pensions would make a retiring U.S. Senator blush. The "chiefs" have been drawing civil service pay ever since they were teenagers, working part time while they were in high school. They got summer jobs if they knew the right people on the hill, at Panama Canal Commission Headquarters. To get a decent house in Panama an employee had to bid using civil service seniority. Because of this system the best and most beautiful homes were occupied by lock guards, mechanics, and others who had more seniority than new pilots who had been captains of ocean going vessels. Many captains quit because their wives and children would not live in substandard housing. At one time housing was assigned according to a person's salary. The "Zonies" had this changed, and no wonder! The Commission reserved beautiful homes within walking distance from the administration buildings for lawyers, doctors and other professionals.

Carlotta—The Beginning

In the summer of 1981 Carl acquired a girlfriend named Carlotta. His older daughter, Maureen, a student at the University of Texas, was with him in Panama during her summer vacation. Elaine had again gone back to Houston. The, swimming pool was less than half a block away behind the Balboa Clubhouse. She could walk across the street, go to the next street, walk less than half a block, and turn right to the swimming area. There were two big pools. Carl had never seen a pool any more beautiful than the government maintained Balboa pool. Included in the amenities were a high diving board, a special pool for children, luxurious dressing and locker rooms. Instructors were available to teach swimming. It was a big operation. Maureen went there frequently, swimming in the morning and sunbathing. One day she met a vivacious, bubbly, champagne lady, Carlotta. Carlotta introduced herself to Maureen, and they got to be real good friends. They swam, sunbathed, and talked together. Carlotta would frequently make a batch of cocktails and sneak them in to the pool where she and Maureen would have a couple of cocktails apiece. Carlotta asked Maureen one day, "Is your family here?"

"I just have my father here."

"Where do you live?" Carlotta's curiosity had surfaced.

"We live just across the street at 752B Balboa Road."

Balboa High School was only a block from Carl's apartment at 752B Balboa Road. On the ground floor of his apartment building were garages, laundry facilities and storerooms. Carl sometimes witnessed high school students hiding here from drug agents. The son of the resident in the apartment above Carl obviously either sold or used drugs. He was chased to his apartment by drug agents more than once. Unfortunately, when the family moved to the states, the youth ran a motorcycle through an intersection and was killed. In June of 1999 Balboa graduated its last class. The newspaper write-up quoted one student as saying, "We don't have fights. We do not have drug problems."[ii] Carl knew first-hand that this was not true. At this writing 752B Balboa Road is occupied by the fire department that took the entire building over.

"Where is your father? I'd like to meet him," Carlotta said to Maureen.

"He's busy all the time. He's a pilot."

Carlotta knew that pilots made pretty good money, so she said again, "I'd like to meet your father."

"After we finish swimming and get dressed, we can walk across the street, and I'll see if he is home. I think he went out on a transit real early this morning. It will be about 2:00 p.m. when we get through here, so he might be back in."

Carlotta spent most of the day in Balboa around the pool. She had her three children in Balboa schools; one in high school, one in junior high, and one in grammar school. Her family was fluent in both Spanish and English. Her father was a wealthy businessman who imported construction materials. He had given her a car and provided her with gasoline from the pumps at his business sites. Carlotta enjoyed her father's wealth.

Carl had gotten off his ship in Gamboa, so he got home about 1300. Maureen brought Carlotta over to meet her father who was mixing up a cocktail and making a few hors d' oeuvres when the two girls came in. Maureen introduced her father to Carlotta. Carlotta was the most beautiful woman Carl had ever seen in Panama. She had light brown, wavy hair, green eyes, honey-colored skin, an oval face, sensuous lips, and an alluring smile. She was five feet four inches tall and had a slender body shape that made all the male heads turn.

"What a gorgeous woman. I'll bet she is married with children. There is no way in the world I'm going to get anywhere with her," Carl thought.

Carlotta was bubbly and friendly. Her radiant personality would win over anyone in a matter of seconds. When Carl's son met Carlotta during a visit, he told his father, "Carlotta is like bubbly champagne. How did you ever meet this beautiful lady?"

She told Carl the history of her family. Carlotta's husband made a practice of humiliating her everywhere they went, calling her a whore, slut, and many other disparaging remarks. According to Carlotta, she had not had sex with her husband for a long while. A divorce was in the very near future.

Carlotta's father married in Panama during World War II. He met Carlotta's mother while he was in the U.S. Navy, stationed at Coco Solo navy base. The community consisted of docks for U.S. Navy ships, a commissary, PX, hardware store, a small hospital, and a high school. Coco Solo was beautifully laid out with many balconied buildings all along the main street, reminiscent of New Orleans. It was a pleasure to live there, except for the sand fleas Carl had encountered when he had his first apartment there. When Carlotta's father was discharged from the U.S. Navy after the war, he went back to Panama, married Carlotta's mother, and set up his import business importing building materials. He also owned stores where electrical fixtures were sold, as well as other business enterprises. Carlotta had been born with a "silver spoon in her mouth". Her mother was Panamanian.

On one occasion she told Carl that her father had bought her mother a new Lincoln Continental. Her parents owned an apartment on Coronado Beach on the Pacific Ocean. Her father was an officer in the Lions club. The first day they had the new Lincoln, her parents and Carlotta went to Coronado Beach for a Lions Club dance and dinner party. When they got outside they saw an Indian throwing rocks and breaking all the windows out of the new Lincoln. Carlotta's father turned to him and said, "Que paso?" ("What's happening?")

"Me Guami, me Guami," naming his Indian tribe, most of whom lived in the northern part of Panama.

Carlotta's father looked at him and said, "Why me? Why me?"

Every time Carlotta told Carl about this they laughed and laughed. That play on words always struck them funny.

Carlotta continued her conversation with Carl. She said, "Every afternoon I'm around here at about this time. If you don't mind I'll drop around and we'll have a drink together."

Maureen interrupted with, "That'll be fine, Carlotta."

Carlotta left to pick up her children and go back home. She lived way on the other side of Panama City on 75th Street, out near where the Union Club is located. The Union Club is a private club for Panamanians of means. Carl didn't see anything more of Carlotta for a couple of days, since he'd been making some pretty long transits at night.

He and Maureen were sitting in the living room one afternoon after Carl had arrived from a transit. Maureen needed him to help her go over her list of university expenses for the coming year. She was very liberal with her list. She was the vice president of her sorority and wanted several formal gowns to attend sorority parties and other formal affairs. Carl had already bought her a Pontiac Firebird, so there were automobile expenses as well. The total was an exorbitant amount. Carl was still paying child support for his younger daughter, Elaine, and his young son, Randle. In spite of that he wrote Maureen a check for the total.

It was soon time for Maureen to go to the airport to catch her flight to Austin. Carlotta offered to take her. Carl refused, saying, "No. I'm slated for a vacation soon. A government car is scheduled to take me to the airport for me to begin my vacation in the U.S. I'll give up this privilege so that a government car can take Maureen to the airport."

Maureen was eagerly awaiting her return to college as she finished her final packing. The government car came and she left for the airport. That left just Carlotta and Carl in his house. They mixed up a few more cocktails and then looked at each other. Carl recalled what Carlotta had said about her husband and their non-relationship. He asked Carlotta, "Doesn't your husband ever come home?"

"I never see him during the day. I take the children to school in the morning. Even if I come right back home I am there all by myself. I never see my husband."

"Well, he must come home sometime."

"The only time he ever comes home is when he shits in his pants. He seldom does that."

"Damn, Carlotta. That's pretty terrible. I'm single, and I'm a passionate old turkey."

They had some more hors d' oeuvres and a few more drinks. Carlotta liked Vodka with all kinds of exotic juices. She was a master in that kitchen. Her culinary arts could have taken care of any head of state.

The next day Carlotta came over after she took her children to school. Carl told her that he had the next day off. He had no job assignment until after 0600 the following morning. Carlotta came over on his day off at about 0930. She started mixing up drinks and naking hors d'oeuvres. Carl asked her, "At nine thirty in the morning, Carlotta?"

"Well, listen, it doesn't make any difference when you drink alcohol as long as you just don't drink all the time. These drinks don't know what time it is."

"Yeah, okay, mix them up. I don't go to work until tomorrow."

They had a few drinks. Carl walked by Carlotta's chair on his way to the kitchen. She just looked up at him with her big green eyes. As Carl passed in back of her chair, he let his hand touch her neck and slide across her shoulder and down into her blouse. He put his hand on one of her breasts and gave it a light squeeze.

She just looked down at the carpet and said, "We're just wasting time."

They went into one of the bedrooms where Carl had blocked out the light of the windows in order to sleep in the daytime. Pilots work a variety of shifts. Sometimes Carl had a night transit and worked all night, so he had to sleep during the daytime. They hadn't been naked in the bed but sixty seconds before they were making mad, passionate love. Carlotta responded eagerly to all of Carl's advances. He couldn't remember anyone so completely absorbed in the lovemaking process. It was rock bottom. They kept making love for a long time. Carl thought how lucky he was to have this beautiful, passionate woman whose husband never bothered her.

The Boat Launch

Carl had purchased an 18' fishing boat; he no longer used his "inner tube" boat. One lovely day Carl and Carlotta decided to launch Carl's boat and go to the beach at Toboga Island off the coast of Panama City. They fished and swam all afternoon. When they returned from fishing and swimming Carl got his car, a Pontiac Bonneville, and backed it down the boat ramp to pull his boat out of the water. When he got the boat on the trailer, he got in the car to pull the boat and trailer out of the water. The car's engine had stopped, and Carl couldn't get it started again. There was about a 21-foot tide in there that day. The tide was coming in fast. There were Panamanians all over the place with jeeps and trucks with four-wheel drive. Carlotta translated for Carl what they were saying, "Don't help them damn gringos. Let the tide get him. Let him get washed out of here. Let him go under."

Water came up so high that it began to cover the floorboards of Carl's car. Finally a large party arrived with a big four wheel drive pickup truck. There was one lady there from the government. They took one look and the lady in charge said to six of the men, "Get in line. We're going to help this American out!"

One gentleman in the lady's party spoke up and told the hecklers in a loud voice, "The lady that is helping the gringo is a government legislator. Stand back."

She backed her vehicle down; the men latched it on to Carl's car and pulled the car and the boat out of the water. She pulled them well away from the area under a big tree. Carl hadn't realized that she spoke flawless English until she spoke to him after the car had been pulled free. She said in perfect English, "I have assigned a person to tow your boat home. It is most vulnerable if left here."

The car had to stay there. Carl didn't think it would ever start again. The salt water had killed it. The legislator continued, "I will call for a wrecker to tow your car and have it repaired."

Carl was extremely grateful and thanked her profusely. The men disconnected the car from the trailer. The Panamanian legislator told some of her friends to tow the boat to Carl's home. She gave Carl and Carlotta a ride. He could see that not all Panamanians hate Americans, even members of the Panamanian government. The two Panamanian men who towed Carl's boat to his home asked Carlotta for her phone number and address. She let them have them after the boat was in Carl's garage. One of them asked her for a date.

One day Carlotta told Carl that she would prove to him what kind of a husband she had. "James, my husband, is out at the Union Club. He is one of the officials out there. My father is one of the stewards. That is a very exclusive club for wealthy Panamanians. The initiation fee is $40,000. Family background is also a requirement for membership. Not everyone can get in even if they have the money. I can go in because my father is next to the president of the club. Come on, we're going out there. I want you to meet this character that I'm married to."

Somewhat reluctantly Carl accompanied her to the Union Club. They sat at the bar and ordered drinks. The bartender brought their orders. James walked up and spoke to Carlotta.

"Well, what in hell is my God damn slutty whore doing here now?"

"Boy, Carlotta's right. I have never heard of a man talking to his wife like that." Carl thought.

When he walked away she said, "See, I told you how he talked to me."

The bartender set two drinks in front of Carl and Carlotta. He said they were "compliments of the house."

James would walk by once in a while. Carlotta would just sit there, nonchalant. Everybody in the club was very friendly to her. Carl thought, "She is one beautiful woman. I've never seen a woman more vivacious in public than Carlotta."

James came by one more time as they were leaving and said to Carl, "Well, enjoy my wife. She's a hot bitch. Everybody else is fucking her. You might as well too."

Carl was shocked. He had never heard a man talk like that in his life. He could hardly believe it.

"Carlotta, let's get out of here," Carl said as he turned to Carlotta.

"Yes, I agree."

On the way out Carlotta introduced Carl to some of the people in the club. One of the men was a well-known owner of a bakery. Carl remembered having seen his products in various places. Carl believed he must have been a wealthy man. Carlotta also introduced Carl to some of the Panamanian legislators and other important people. Even though they knew about her husband, they were just as friendly to Carlotta as they could be.

One of them asked her, "I see in another week or two Juan Iglesia is booked for the club. Are you coming down?"

"Sure, I'll be down. My mother thinks that man is absolutely out of this world. I'll be there."

"Good, Carlotta. Come on over. Don't forget to drop by our table and tell us 'Hello.'"

They left the club. As Carl drove back toward the Canal Zone, Carlotta said to Carl, "See, I told you. See what I have."

"Carlotta, how did you ever marry a man like that?"

"Before I graduated from Balboa High School, you know, the U.S. government operated high school, I got pregnant. I was a promiscuous young girl. I have a very dark-complexioned son. I knew that this baby was not going to have a father. My father knew James because he had been a policeman for the Canal Zone. He was a Panamanian of Dutch descent. His name is Pike. I met James and had an affair with him. He used to climb in the window and jump in bed with me with his shoes on. That was awful, but you know me, Carl. I'm a very passionate woman. It doesn't take much to turn me on. I was going with James. I liked him; he was a real friendly person. I didn't say anything about marriage, but he met my father and made a marriage arrangement. My father asked me if I would marry James if he asked me. I told my father that I would marry James. So we were married and had our two children, Elizabeth and Willie. They are very pale-complexioned like their father. Elizabeth is a pretty girl and a straight A student. They both speak fluent English and Spanish. Of course the first baby born had another father. I don't even remember who he was. I was going with more than one boy, then. I'll admit it."

Carlotta continued. "After awhile James left the Panamanian Police Force, since Panama was taking over and the people my father knew didn't look kindly on the people in the Police Force since they were employees of the U.S. government. My father bought James a fleet of trucks to travel up in the breadbasket of the country, in Chiriqui Province. He trucked fruits, vegetables, milk and other dairy products, and raw materials into Panama City. This proved to be a lucrative business. My father also bought James a gas station, also profitable. My father built James and me a big, beautiful home in an elite section of Panama City."

Carl was interested in Carlotta's story. He felt sorry for her situation at home. He thought, "There is more to happiness than having a good income." He thought over his own life, which confirmed his conviction. He continued to see Carlotta when she came to take her children to school and swim in the pools.

Suicide by Wine

Larry Moore, a friend of Carl's, lived close to his apartment on Balboa Road. Larry was a senior pilot; Carl was a step four pilot by this time and was assigned bow jobs with Larry as control pilot. One day while Carl was working in his yard, Larry' well groomed Pekinese dog relieved himself in the front yard. Although Carl was highly disgusted with the dog, he offered Larry some Cuban cigars. Carl didn't smoke, and Larry readily accepted the cigars, offering to pay for them. Carl refused the money, saying that they had been a gift, and James was welcome to them.

When Carl answered the phone one morning, MTC assigned him to a 2 pilot ship. At the pilot reporting station Carl called MTC for information concerning his transit. He got the needed information, hung up the phone, turned around, and noticed several pilots walking into the station. Paul Henry called, "Hi, Carl. Did you hear about Captain Larry Moore?"

"No," Carl replied, "What happened?"

"Larry died last Saturday. I'm surprised you didn't know since you live so close to him. Anyway, he drowned in his own body fluids. It seems that he passed out cold and vomited while he was unconscious. He apparently drowned on what he had regurgitated, which was about 90% wine."

John Green spoke up and said, "Carl, did you know he was married?"

"No," Carl answered, "Who was he married to? I thought he was a single man!"

"Carl, you won't believe this," Green went on, "He married that black lady, 'Miss Trinidad', you know, the cashier at the Canal Commission's commissary."

"Wow! I know that lady," commented Carl, "She is the one who continually bitches about her ancestors being robbed by the U.S. government when they were laborers building the Panama Canal. You remember the story of how the laborers were paid in silver and American engineers and skilled workers were paid in gold. She started a conversation with me one day while I was getting my purchases checked out. She asked me if I was a pilot. I told her that I was. She asked me, 'You pilots make a lot of money, don't you?' and then she started with the silver and gold tirade. I told her that her ancestors were illiterate, common laborers. The U.S. government offered them a contract for 10 cents an hour and they were glad to get it. That was back when you could buy a whole week's groceries for two or tree dollars a week. I also told her that Panamanians now have 95% of the jobs supplied both by the Panama Canal Company and the U.S. Army. She and her brothers and sisters are paid civil service wages and must make at least $5.50 an hour. Panama's minimum wage is 65 cents an hour."

John Green went on, "Carl, did you know that Larry died one day and was cremated the next day at Gorgas Crematorium? His ashes were scattered in Panama Bay. Now 'Miss Trinidad' has an annuity of $1500 a month, and all of Larry's furnishings, bank account, and other properties. It seems he was going to retire and stay in Panama."

Paul, another pilot who was standing in the group added, "You know that he loved his little dog, a Pekinese. He fed him specially cooked chicken breasts. I wonder what he will eat now? She has probably sold him or given him away."

All the pilots in the group soon went to their respective transits, wondering if Larry was a bit crazy, hiding his marriage and leaving everything to 'Miss Trinidad'. Carl wondered if Larry was trying to get even with the U.S. for giving away the canal and the zone. He wondered, too, if his widow would stop berating the U.S. for the low wages her ancestors had been paid. "Only time will tell," Carl thought.

Noreiga's Secretary Evicts Carl; Mary's Death

In January of 1982 Carl's elderly mother, an Alzheimer patient, came to live with him. He had been moved from the duplex apartment in Balboa to a big, beautiful home in Ancon overlooking Balboa so that his mother's twenty four hour a day caretakers could have a separate apartment. Manuel Noreiga was in power. His secretary wanted Carl's house. One day in 1986 Carl got a notice to get out of his home where his mother had been happy. He would have to live in a house in Panama City that had burglar bars on the windows. Although his special privileges were about to expire anyway, the notice said that he no longer had these privileges. While Carl was on leave and had flown to Houston, Texas to visit his daughter Maureen. Zelda, a cosmetologist who helped Carl's maid, Rose, with his mother's care, accepted the new house in Carl's name. Carl believed that he had no choice but to allow this takeover. It was some time later that he discovered such houses were to revert to Panama **only when they became available.** By this time it was too late to reclaim his home on Ancon hill. He was moved to a house at 3216 Empire Street, right behind the police station in Balboa. It had four bedrooms, three baths, and a small attached apartment.

When he returned to Panama, Carl signed the necessary papers and moved in to the new house. Mary Turner, Carl's mother, whose Alzheimer's disease was worsening, thought the burglar bars on the windows signified that she was in an insane asylum. She was very upset and was never happy in that house.

One evening when Carl had a transit, he told Rose she could go home to be with her family at the end of the day, since he would be home in a couple of hours after Rose had left. "Surely Mother would be safe for two hours," he thought.

When he got home Carl found his mother lying in a pool of blood. She had tried to escape from the supposed insane asylum and missed the 18" step between the kitchen and the utility room, causing her to fall on the concrete. Her arms, legs, and the left side of her face were scratched, cut, and bloody. Carl called for an ambulance, which took Mary to Gorgas Hospital.

Mary never used a walker again; she was confined to a wheelchair and was soon bedridden. Within a year and a half she died.

Carlotta—The End

In January of 1986 Carl was to go on leave in the States for three weeks. Before he left he went to the bottle store and loaded up the bar in his home with a case or two of vodka which came in half-gallon jugs. In Carl's bar was an ample supply of all kinds of booze. The captain of almost every ship he transited through the canal gave him a bottle of liquor until he had a supply that would rival most movie stars. He had every kind of beer one could imagine. When he returned from the States, Carlotta was there, and they continued their relationship. Carl had been damn good to Carlotta. On one occasion he won several thousand dollars in the lottery. With the money he bought her gold necklaces and expensive gifts. Many times he had gone to the commissary and loaded his trunk with anything Carlotta wanted. There were many items available at the commissary that a person just couldn't get in Panama, like big hams and Butterball turkeys. Goods there were at least 50% to 60% cheaper and of better quality than Panamanian goods. Carl had even given Carlotta an aquamarine stone about the size of a half-dollar that he had purchased in Sri Lanka on one of his sea voyages.

Zelda took Carl aside one day and told him, "I know you love Carlotta and hope she will get a divorce and you will marry her."

"I've thought about it," Carl answered truthfully.

By this time Carlotta had been coming over to visit Carl for five years. Carl kept asking her when she was going to get a divorce. She always said that it would be soon, but the divorce never materialized.

"Don't do it. I like you and I like your mother. I'm going to tell you some things about Carlotta."

Just then Carl's mother called Zelda to get her a glass of water. While Zelda was gone for the water, Carl put a tape recorder under the chair so he would have a record of what she had to say about Carlotta. In a few minutes Zelda was back. Carl sat in the chair in the bedroom; Zelda sat on the edge of the bed.

Zelda began her story, "While you were gone I saw Carlotta at the pool, half drunk, kissing the black man, Vonne, who manages the pool. One of the women at the pool told me that Carlotta had the hots for Vonne. She called me down there one time to come and look for myself. When I went, I saw them kissing. I don't know how he kept his job when he carried on like that, since he worked for the Panama Canal Company. I heard Carlotta call Vonne and tell him what time she would meet him at the Intel Parking lot. I saw her taking your liquor out of the house a few minutes before the time she had arranged to meet Vonne. I've gone this far, I might as well tell you the whole thing. During the week Carlotta goes over to Intel Parking lot. She parks there in her car. Vonne drives over behind her. She puts on a blond wig, gets out of her car, changes her blouse, and transfers into his car. They drive off to a "Pushbuttons", a motel by the highway on the way to Tocumen Airport that rents rooms by the hour. It has a big neon sign with hearts pierced with an arrow. People drive up to the office, pay the cashier, and park by the assigned cabin. Inside are porno movies, huge mirrors, lavish suites complete with showers. I've never been in one, but I've heard about them. They went to one named Dulce Sueno (Sweet Dreams)"

Carl had been getting more and more angry all the time Zelda was talking.

He told her, "Zelda, I'm getting sick and tired of Carlotta running around and cheating on me with that black man and her husband."

Zelda laughed so hard she almost hit the floor.

Carl checked out Zelda's story about Carlotta. What Zelda had said was true. Zelda had told Rose, Carl's maid, what was going on. Rose had also seen Carlotta taking liquor to Vonne. She overheard Carlotta making dates with Vonne. She hadn't told Carl because she was afraid he would be angry with her. She knew he loved Carlotta. Carl was hurt, angry, lonely, and sad by turns.

One Saturday Carlotta came over. She and Carl had dinner and talked. Carl knew it would be the last time he would see Carlotta. They went back in the back room and took off their clothes. Instead of the expected lovemaking Carl told Carlotta what she had been doing.

She screamed, "Liar, liar!" over and over again.

"It's not a lie. I saw you. I know what you are doing. I remember now that I saw you in 1980 when I first moved to Balboa. You were at the El Dorado shopping center at the casino. You came in there with Vonne. You were wearing a blond wig and buying him drinks. He was getting the drinks and you were playing the slot machines. You are that very same person. People know about it. I was told about it."

She said something to Carl that infuriated him, "You have a disease. You have herpes."

Carl told her he had herpes when he first met her, but he had always protected her. He gave her a whack across the head.

Carlotta ran naked to Rose's apartment screaming and crying, "He hates black people. He hit me."

Rose came to Carl and asked him for Carlotta's clothes. He gave them to her and told her to throw Carlotta out and never to let her back in the house again.

The next day Carl had off. He got his boat and went out to the farthest buoy in the Pacific anchorage and put the anchor down. It was late in the afternoon when he got to his fishing spot. He had his fishing tackle with him and was planning to fish, but he couldn't. He just cried his eyes out. It is pitiful when a grown man cries when he has lost a love like Carlotta. It was just like cutting off part of his body and casting it in the ocean. During the time he was in the boat he saw a huge whale shark drift up alongside the boat. The fish's eyes, situated almost on the top of his head, looked to be almost six feet apart. Carl was so depressed he wasn't even scared. The huge fish seemed to him to be offering companionship. After a while, he swam away. As the sun began to set, Carl crawled up under the small cabin in the front of his boat and went to sleep. When he woke up it was raining so hard he couldn't see fifteen feet in front of him. He didn't take up his anchor at this time because he couldn't see to determine the direction to shore. There were a number of big ships nearby, directed by radar. It is a wonder that one of them didn't run over him, but none of them did. He stayed there until the next morning. When day broke, the rain had stopped. He could now see the buoys, so he cranked up the motor and headed for home. His bilge pump ran for hours. There must have been a foot of water in that boat. It is a good thing that he had double bottoms built into that boat, or she would have sunk. Carl got back home safely and took a shower. He got breakfast and then called in to transit to see if he had a job that day. He had a transit scheduled for early that afternoon. He dragged around and pined for his lost love the rest of the day. He wouldn't drink; he didn't before going on transit. He just didn't do it. It is a policy he adhered to. It was too dangerous to do otherwise.

Carl never told Carlotta about the tape recording, but he did play it for her brother. He just looked at his feet and shook his head. Carl never heard from any of her family after that. Carl only saw Carlotta one or two times more when she drove the car around the block. He was tempted to tell her to stop and come in, but he didn't.

Submerged Stumps

During the time when Carl was a step seven pilot, he was piloting a fruit boat through the canal, doing about 17 knots up Tabernilla Reach when he saw some speedboats racing across the lake. They were cutting across Gatun Lake out of the channel on the east side, in an area which contained submerged trees from the time Gatun Lake was flooded behind Gatun Dam. Just the top of some of the trees could be seen while others could not be seen, since their tops were just below the surface. Five or six people were in the boat. Carl called the captain.

"Captain, come over here and take a look at this." As the captain came over to look, Carl added, "The submerged trees outside the shipping channel are solid as rocks as though they are petrified. Look, there he goes!"

The boat struck one of the trees. It shot up twenty feet in the air, came back down, and hit the water upside down with a mighty thud. People were scattered all over the place. They weren't moving and appeared to be unconscious. There was no way Carl could get into that shallow area, full of submerged trees, with his large ship. There were large patches of aquatic weeds and stumps making it almost impossible for a lifeboat to get through. By the time the crew could have put a lifeboat over the side and got to the boaters, they would all have been drowned. Carl used his transit radio and told MTC, "Some speedboat has been racing over the lake east of Tabernilla Reach. It hit submerged treetops and flipped in the air. I don't know if anybody is still alive in the water or not. I don't see any movement out there. If they are still alive, they might have been able to grab something and hold on to it. You better get an emergency crew and a military helicopter to come out here and see what you can do."

"Okay, Captain Turner. We'll call the military and call Panama and let them know about this accident," came the reply.

The captain commented, "I can't imagine anyone not knowing about these trees. Panamanians surely know the history of this lake, how this area was flooded and became Gatun Lake when Gatun Dam was built. Surely everyone is aware of the trees just below the surface. Why, you can see the tops of some of them sticking just above the water. Many of the limbs are still visible a bit."

At 18 knots it didn't take very long before the ship was around the bend into Buena Vista Reach. Neither the ship's captain or Carl ever knew what happened to the boat's occupants.

"Holy mackerel, I did see this sort of thing happen once before near Barro Colorado Island. Although nobody was hurt in that boat, the bottom was torn out and the boat sank. Some military personnel took the boaters back to Gamboa. I used to fish near Barro Colorado Island and the other small islands on its south side," Turner recalled.

Champlain and Champlane

Two days before Christmas in 1984, Joe Champlane piloted a Panamax tanker through the Panama Canal. The skipper, Bob Champlain, was a good friend of Carl's. They used to drink together at the Peek-a-boo Lounge next door to the Master Mates and Pilots Union Hall in Houston. Although they had both been skippers of ocean going vessels, they had never sailed together.

The pilot Joe Champlane was friendly when he was sober. He was blond, 6'3", a muscular, heavily built man with a reputation for beating the hell out of anybody who gave him any problem. When Carl went to Panama he did not know Champlane's reputation. When Champlane and Carl were both control pilots, every time Carl would do something, Champlane would ask, "What causes it to do that?"

Carl would answer, "Well, I guess the water is pushed against the quarter and causes the ship to go in that direction. When I make a turn, there's pressure on the rudder."

"How about that? How'd you know that?" Champlane would say.

Such remarks went on and on. He acted like a big shot, all relaxed and tough. After a while, after Carl had transited with Champlane a few times, they got to know and respect each other's abilities. Carl began to like the ornery pilot, although Champlane didn't want any PITs working with him. It was below his dignity.

On this particular December 23, when Carl had a few days off during the Christmas holidays, both skipper and pilot with names that sounded alike, Bob and Joe, came ashore on the pilot boat. Joe had piloted for Bob. They were intrigued by the similarity of their names and became friendly during the transit. Joe had asked Bob if he knew Carl. Joe responded that he did and invited Bob to come ashore with him in the pilot launch and then in the jitney to his home for some Christmas "cheer". They went over to Williamson Place, a huge apartment complex.

Carl's phone rang. It was about 1900 hours It was the captain, Bob Champlain. "Hey, Carl, this is your old shipmate from Houston, Bob Champlain. What's happening?" he began.

"I'm over here in my apartment, Bob. I have the day off."

"I'm over here in Joe Champlane's apartment in Williamson Place. I transited the canal today, and I was ordered to anchor for a few days and await further orders. Come on over and have a beer with us. Joe has a beautiful wife, and his maid has laid out all the trimmings. We can talk about old times and celebrate Christmas."

"I'll be glad to reminisce with you, Bob. I'm just a few blocks away, so I'll walk over. Which apartment is it?"

"It's apartment 254. Come on over, Carl."

Carl walked down Balboa road, turned on Amador Road, found building C and apartment 254. Joe answered the door and Carl went inside. The two men had obviously been drinking for some time. Bob and Carl had a good time laughing and talking about their shipboard experiences in the U.S. Merchant Marine and about old times together at the union hall on Broadway Street in Houston. Looking back on it, Carl guessed Joe felt left out of the conversation. The more Joe drank the angrier he got. After about an hour he began to crush beer cans and throw them all over the apartment slamming some of them against the wall. Finally he bellowed in a red-faced rage, "I'm the pilot here! I'm the best pilot in the Panama Canal! Me—just me! When I'm in the wheel-house, all the mates and ships' captains have to take my orders. I can put my feet on any ship that floats and automatically know everything about that ship. You sea captains think you're something special because you sailed the oceans, but just remember, I'M THE BOSS HERE!"

Oops! There went another crushed beer can and then an empty whiskey bottle shattered against the bar. Bob sat very still, petrified, as though frozen in his chair. Seeing the violence rising to a fever pitch in this man, Carl wished Bob and Joe a "Merry Christmas", excused him-self, ducked another beer can, and left. He thought of the quotation, "Better now to run away and live to fight another day".

The next day Bob called Carl. He asked about Joe Champlane. "Is that guy crazy?"

"Well, you have to be a little bit crazy to be a pilot. He's been piloting the canal ever since he was young. He thinks he owns the damn place, but he's not as good a pilot as he thinks he is. I've known three or four times when he's had damage done. He's over confident. He comes into the locks too fast. Lately he's had more damage. Other pilots have told me that when Joe first came to Panama as a pilot he was a fine pilot and did excellent work, but today he doesn't respect ships like he should. He must be in his sixties now, so I guess he's slippin'."

"I hope I don't get him on my ship as a pilot anymore. I think he's kind of crazy. You better retire and get away from these crazy people. The government puts the pilots on ships. Some of them are damn fine pilots, but you never know what you're going to get," added Bob.

About twelve years later, when Bob and Carl were both retired and were in the states, Bob called Carl. "I hear you're retired now, Carl. Is that right?" Bob began.

"That's right. I'm in Houston staying with my daughter, Maureen, for a few weeks; then I'll go back to my condo overlooking the Atlantic Ocean at Daytona Beach, Florida."

Bob asked for Carl's address, which Carl gave him. Then he said, "If you don't have anything else pressing, I'll pick you up in my truck. We can take a drive to Freeport to visit a bar and have a few drinks where a friend of mine used to hang out and live in a trailer in back of the bar. You probably remember him—Herman Highman."

"Yes I remember him. I'll be ready when you get here," Carl agreed.

Bob showed up as he said he would. The two men talked about the "good old days" on the way to Freeport. Soon the subject of the Christmas of 1984 and the episode in Joe Champlane's apartment came up. Bob asked Carl if there were many crazy drunks like Joe in the pilot force in Panama. Carl told him there were not many; none like Joe Champlane. "Let me tell you something about him and you will understand his character," Carl went on, "Two of my friends were in a restaurant on Front Street in Colón when Joe Champlane came in. He'd been drinking, so he was looking for a fight. My two friends were big, burly guys, just the kind Joe chose to fight. They weren't interested in fighting, and they convinced Joe to leave the restaurant. Nevertheless, Joe was still looking for a fight. He drove to Gatun Landing where there were pool tables and a bar. Joe went in and started playing pool. There were also some Green Berets, who were stationed at Camp Davis, drinking and playing pool. At times soldiers of the 508 airborne and Rangers undergoing jungle warfare are housed at Fort Davis not far from Gamboa. Joe didn't like what one of them was saying, so he went over and took a swing at him. The soldier floored Joe with a cue stick he had taken from the rack. Joe was all bloody and looked all broken up. The next thing he knew he was in the hospital at Coco Solo. When he awoke he was told that he would have to stay awhile. He had been so badly hurt that silver plates had to be put into his head. He recovered, however, and went back to work. His transit didn't get a pilot until the next day. I heard several different stories about this incident, but knowing Joe, I believe this one. Panama pilots seemed to get away with anything. None were ever fired that I ever heard of. Maybe that's because they were under civil service."

"Obviously Joe didn't learn anything from that fight," Bob remarked. He just shook his head.

"Joe is a good pilot to ride with, but any time he is drinking, I just get up and leave, as I did the day we were at his home at Christmas time. You know, Bob, he's still piloting in the Panama Canal. He must be past 70 now."

The two men stopped for lunch on the way back to Houston. Bob told Carl that he was undergoing treatment for cancer. Ever after that Carl scanned his Master Mates and Pilots paper to see if his name appeared under the "Passed the Final Bar" column, but he didn't see it.

Jitneys and Commissary Privileges

By 1985 there were between forty and fifty Panamanian pilots employed in the canal. These included PITs up to step four pilots. Panamanian pilots expected the jitneys to pick them up at their homes and take them to the pilothouse in the same way they had for American pilots. The only difference was that the Panamanian pilots lived mostly in Panama City, far from boathouses, while the American pilots lived near the boathouses in military housing. At the most it was a ten-minute ride from the American pilots' homes to a boathouse. The feeling of the Panamanian pilots was that if they couldn't have a privilege, no one should have it. Because of the controversy, the Panama Canal Commission ruled that every pilot had to use his own transportation and drive to the boathouse. Panamanian pilots were always complaining about the free housing, utilities, yard maintenance, and free access to all the military PXs and commissaries which the American pilots received for five years after October, 1979. In October of 1979, when the Panama Canal Zone was handed over to Panama, all the Panamanian Canal Company department stores, sports stores, and grocery stores closed. Merchandise had been sold at huge discounts of 25 to 75% off the original prices. The U.S. military was out there in trucks and bought out those stores. U. S. citizens stocked up as best they could, because they knew that in 1985 they would have to buy from Panamanian stores. All the huge stores were emptied. After that U. S. canal personnel could never enter a U.S. commissary, shoe store, garden supply store, furniture store, or any other store operated by the U. S. military.

However the package stores stayed open to Americans. Panamanians threatened to leave the package freight on the dock. The Panamanian government stated that civil service workers were not entitled to buy from the U.S. Department of Defense package stores. All the big honchos from the states and Panama Canal administrators got together and told the Panamanian leaders, "Look, you have approved recreation facilities for these civil service people until the year 2000."

Panamanians argued, "Whiskey stores are not recreation."

"It's been listed as recreation since the first spoonful of dirt was shoveled out of here and that is the way it is going to stand."

"Our longshoremen will not unload the whiskey." the Panamanians threatened.

The government loaded the whiskey stores on air cargo planes, unloaded it at Howard Air Force base, and trucked it to the package stores for distribution. Panamanian longshoremen complained they were losing jobs and money, so they relented and allowed longshoremen to unload booze, candy, and other party items for sale in package stores. In this way the American civil servants, which included pilots, kept their package store privileges until December 31,1999. Carl used to get Carlotta anything she wanted in these stores. This was against regulations, but he had a hard on for the Company because he saw that whatever Panamanians wanted, they got, especially "Big Dog Panamanian military". They got privileges before 1979 and after 1985. Carl was also angry with the Company because of the way his children had been denied ID Cards and special passports which would allow them to buy goods at the Panama Canal Company and U.S. military stores. Carl had to personally make 2 trips to get this straightened out. Carl had the biggest Pontiac the company made and he loaded it down with as much as it would hold for his house and all that Carlotta wanted.

Pheneus Grog, the Flying Ship Pilot

Carl was a step six pilot in 1988 when he first piloted with Pheneus Grog. Pheneus had been hired in 1966, so he was a senior pilot by this time. He was of Norwegian descent, tall, blond, and muscular, and had immigrated to the U.S. and become a naturalized U.S. citizen. Although he had the reputation of being one of the Panama Canal's notorious drunks, he was an excellent pilot, especially when he had a couple of sheets to the wind.

The day Carl rode with Pheneus who had first control, Carl relieved him at Gamboa. Now that he was something of a passenger Pheneus began to hit the bottle heavily. He did not appear on the bridge when called to assist through the locks. Carl didn't think this was a problem since only one pilot was really needed to lock down and proceed through the locks; he could just as well let Pheneus sleep down below in one of the cabins.

While in the last chamber at Miraflores Locks Pheneus came to the bridge and demanded that the captain get him a bottle of Scotch whiskey. The captain went below and brought up a full bottle of Scotch and a shot glass. He placed them on the wheel house window sill. Pheneus opened the bottle and asked for a water glass. He gave the shot glass back to the steward. The steward gave Pheneus a water glass. Pheneus poured himself a water glass full of Scotch and drank it as though he were drinking iced tea on a hot summer day. He drank a second glass. The ship's captain looked at him and said to Carl, "This man is sick. He needs to be in a rehab center. During his turn as control pilot he does a very fine job of piloting even though his breath would knock you out if you stood very close to him. If I drank that much alcohol at one time I would drop dead! I have transited this canal many times, but I have never witnessed a man drink like this."

Pheneus continued to guzzle booze. He got his radio out of his pocket and began to speak to other pilots. His speech was so slurred that Carl warned him to get off the radio or MTC would know he was drunk. Besides, in ten minutes his pilot boat would come alongside to take him to the Balboa pilot station. Pheneus continued to talk unintelligibly on the radio. When the vessel cleared Miraflores Locks, Carl could see the pilot boat approaching. The captain told Pheneus, "Here. Take another bottle; you need it more than we do. Be careful. God help your family."

Carl turned to the captain and instructed him, "Please take up the pilot ladder. Just leave it on the deck ready to go over the side for me when we get to buoys one and two. Put out the accommodation ladder for Pheneus or this man will get killed trying to use the pilot ladder." The pilot ladder is a long rope ladder with wooden slats for rungs. It is put over the side of the ship to the pilot boat.

"Captain Turner, I have already thought about this a long time ago. The accommodation ladder is ready. Just say the word and I will have the officer on deck lower it down. I don't want Pheneus on it too soon."

"Sure, captain. The pilot boat is almost alongside, so lower the ladder now."

Pheneus Grog got off as though he had never had a drink in his life. If Carl and the captain had not seen him with the bottle of Scotch, they would never have suspected he had been drinking. Carl asked the captain if he could blow the whistle signal used at sea for good-bye. "Sure, pilot, go ahead," consented the captain.

Three long blasts on the whistle signaling good-bye, good luck. The pilot boat repeated the blasts. Carl blew again-one short blast. The pilot boat repeated it. Later when Carl arrived at the reporting station everyone laughed and asked, "What was all that whistle blowing about?" Pilots would not know the meaning of the signals unless they had gone to sea.

Pheneus owned an airplane and flew from the island of Contadora to Paitilla Airport in Panama City. When Pheneus got his radio message from MTC telling him when to report for pilot duty, he would fly directly through the flight pattern of Tocumen Airport in Panama City. One afternoon in May Pheneus was flying from Paitilla airport to Contadora Island. A Braniff flight was making its landing approach. The co-pilot of the Braniff flight said to the pilot, "Captain, I see a small engine plane heading this way. It looks like he will pass through our approach pattern. I feel sure it is the same plane that has given us many frightening moments on this run before."

The captain called air traffic control on his radio, "Tocumen traffic control, this is Braniff 3261. Repeat, Braniff 3261."

"Come in 3261."

"Tocumen, we are aborting landing. We are climbing. Give us an altitude to circle and keep this small craft on radar. When he is clear, give us another okay for landing. Tocumen, we can now identify the small craft. It is NC491, the same craft that frequently crosses our flight pattern. Please report these incidents to the proper authorities."

"We will radio headquarters." Responded the tower.

"This pilot should have his license revoked. We have 190 lives aboard this flight. This continual occurrence is preposterous."

In a few minutes the tower called the Braniff flight again. "Tocumen to 3261. The area is now clear. You may once again land. You are clear to land, 3261. A report will be filed. This will not happen again. Tocumen, out."

"The co-pilot again addressed the pilot, "Captain, look how that character is flying. I wonder if he will make it to Paitilla. He sure is flying erratically. Man, he is sure some turkey.""

"I would rather see a feathered turkey flying a plane. This turkey seems to be flying without a tail."

Later, after the Braniff plane had landed, the co-pilot again commented to a crewman, "Did you see NC 491 hit the ground? He was bouncing up and down like a rubber ball."

NC 491 taxied to a hanger and stopped. Pheneus got out and staggered about. A crewman said to Pheneus, "Here comes the airport manager, red faced. I'll bet he heard the radio transmissions at Tocumen."

"Pheneus, give me your license! There will be a hearing tomorrow at 1000 hours. Be there!" Pheneus tore up his license and threw it on the ground, saying to the airport manager, "Fuck you," and walked away.

The next day Pheneus put his airplane up for sale.

6

EXPERIENCES AS A SENIOR PILOT

In minimum time Carl advanced through the various stages to become a senior pilot qualified to take any ship through the canal regardless of its size, beam, or tonnage. A pilot could become a senior pilot after eight years of experience. Carl became a senior pilot in 1986.

The Crocodile

One time Carl was launching his fishing boat at Gamboa. He planned to go fishing on Gatun Lake about halfway between Gamboa and the Gatun Locks. He knew that if he gave one of the Panamanians a few dollars, he would launch the boat for him. The Panamanian would put Carl's boat alongside the dock, unload his gear from the back of his car, and place everything in the boat. Carl walked a few yards away while his equipment was being put in the boat. He noticed a crowd gathering. Carl went over to take a look. There was a ten-foot crocodile all tied up to a tree. He turned to Jose, who was loading the boat, and asked, "Where in the world did this crocodile come from, Jose?"

Jose told Carl, "They caught him under the dock. Some fellow had a big hook on his fishing rod. He put a fairly large fish on the hook and threw the line under the dock. The crocodile took it. It was hooked in the mouth. Even though it was a fairly strong line, it broke, but everybody could see what was under the dock. Someone had a VHF radio and called the military. The people from Barro Colorado came over and captured the crocodile and tied it to a tree. They didn't bring enough equipment with them to take the crocodile back to Barro Colorado, so they're coming back to put him on the island and turn him loose in the wildlife refuge near there. On Barro Colorado they breed and rehabilitate animals and scatter them all around Central and South America to keep them from becoming extinct. It is a game and plant preserve run by the Smithsonian Institute."

"That is a huge crocodile. I can't believe it. Kids are swimming all around where boats are launched. The children who don't go fishing hang around and go swimming," Carl said to Jose in amazement.

That devil had been living under the dock and probably under the big boathouse next to the dock. The lake is just loaded with *sargentos* and peacock bass. Some of the fishermen come back with from 10 to 100 fish. They pay Panamanians ten cents a fish to fillet them. The Panamanians throw the backbone, head, and what's left from filleting the fish over the side. The croc was living the life of Riley on the bass too small to keep; heads, fins, guts, and other fish parts discarded in the filleting. The croc was fat as a butterball. Carl knew for sure that children swam all around the boat ramp and dock the day the crocodile was caught. Dependents of the military were swimming there, too. Carl wouldn't swim out there. No way! To his knowledge there is no record of any human ever being attacked by a crocodile in Gatun Lake.

When Carl went fishing on his inner tube raft in the vicinity of Colon Beach and across the lake from there, he often saw cayman and crocodiles. He just tossed them a big fish or two and they were happy; eventually they just swam away. He also spotted large snakes along the shore. He did the same thing. A fish made them happy. While fishing from his little inner tube raft, he just became part of the tranquil scenery. Carl continued this practice even after he bought a larger boat.

At times both large and small birds came very close to Carl. The water was very clear in this area; there were no boats or ships. Once Carl spotted a very large turtle near Colon Beach. He told his neighbor about the sighting. "You're a liar," the neighbor accused.

Carl thought, "Well, he's a graduate of the California Maritime Academy. These characters think they know everything. I'll just think nothing of it."

The Blonde and the Mestizo

This is a story that Carl heard from another pilot, Steve Hancock, while the two of them were having refreshments on Carl's patio.

One bright and sunny day in May, Steve arrived at Cristobal Boathouse. The dispatcher told him, "Good morning, Captain Hancock. We have a pilot boat waiting for you. You are going to South 10, right?"

"Yes, that's right," Steve answered him.

"Captain, we have a passenger who needs to board N-9. It appears she missed her ship at Balboa, but it should be here in about thirty minutes. Could you put her on board the Sea Splendor, N-9, for us when the pilot debarks?"

The next thing Steve knew, here came this beautiful blonde running down the dock. She was tall and slender, bronzed in the sun, blue eyed, and willowy. She looked Scandinavian and spoke excellent English. She sure was a gorgeous creature.

"Do you have any objection, Captain Hancock?" asked the captain.

"No, I've no objection. But I would rather take her on a transit and then to my house in Balboa."

Steve noticed that the blonde gave him a big, beautiful smile.

Steve addressed the blonde, "You speak English, I see."

"Yes sir, I do," she replied.

"In that case, let's board the pilot boat. Your ship is in the lower chamber at Gatun Locks."

Steve and the blonde got on the pilot boat. Steve knew the pilot boat captain, John, very well. He was a handsome-looking Panamanian *mestizo*, part Indian, part Spanish with a bit of Negro blood also. He was a ladies man. "I see we have a beautiful passenger this morning," John commented.

"That's right," Steve replied, "Take her to N-9. It should be here in about 30 minutes."

The blonde boarded and took a seat on the launch. John told her, "If you want to get back out to your ship, there has got to be something in this for me, or I'll take you back to the pier. Do you have any money? They don't pay us much here."

Hancock knew this to be a lie. Everybody who worked in the canal was on civil service pay system and was paid at least $10 per hour.

"No, I don't have any money with me. This is a U.S. government boat. Do I have to pay, Captain?"

"In order to ride my launch you must have official approval from the U.S. Government or one of the federal agencies to take you to your ship. I haven't seen such approval," John bluffed, "I'll just take you back to the landing."

"Well, what do you want from me, Captain?"

"If you want to go back to your ship, you will have to go down below and give me some action."

"I have to get back on my ship," she said nervously.

The young lady looked at Hancock and asked, "Do I have to go below with him?"

"You don't have to do anything you don't want to," Hancock assured her.

She smiled broadly, turned to John, and said, "Let's go."

Hancock started up the pilot boat and steered it toward the rendezvous point. Down below, John and the blonde eyed each other as they sat on the bunk. John bent toward the girl, kissed her with open lips. She kissed him back. She was having as good a time as the pilot boat captain; that was for sure. He caressed her cheeks and neck with his lips. Slowly, savoring with his eyes and touch the smooth, silky skin and long hair of his prize, John unbuttoned her blouse and felt for the breast beneath. She took off his shirt, then took out the combs in her hair, letting the long, blonde hair cascade on John's bare torso. They felt the warmth of each other's bodies as they felt their way down each other's thighs. Completely nude by this time, John felt for her opening, which was moist and ready. As he entered her body, she began to move, slowly at first, then pulsating, matching his rhythm. Hancock could hear their heavy breathing and low moans. When they were finished they came up to the pilothouse deck. The blond was all disheveled, but bright eyed with a big grin on her face.

The phone buzzed on the control panel. John answered, "Would Captain Hancock mind picking up Captain Travener from N-9 for us?"

"I heard the request. The answer is yes," Steve spoke into the phone.

"Thank you, Captain."

North 9 was soon spotted; she was slowing down in the basin. The pilot boat pulled alongside and Captain Travener climbed down the Jacob's ladder over the side of the Sea Splendor and boarded the pilot boat. Then the lovely blonde ascended the same ladder and boarded the Sea Splendor. On deck she turned, and, with a last smile, shouted, "Thank you for everything, Captain, and I mean EVERYTHING!"

"Good bye, bon voyage," John called.

On the pilot boat, Spencer Travener asked Steve Hancock, "Who was that beautiful blond you had on board?"

"I don't know her very well. You'll have to ask Captain John."

Hancock told John to call South 10 and have the captain heave up the anchor, since the pilot would be boarding in about fifteen minutes. At the boathouse Travener debarked. He had been on an all night transit. As tired as he was, he said, "Steve, tomorrow I will be at your house at about 7:00 p.m. You must tell me about that girl. I am sure she was a movie star."

"Have a good ride home," was all Steve would say.

Just as Steve started to board S-10, he told John, "I wish I had been the pilot boat captain today."

A Colombian Ship Goes to Scrap

One afternoon about 1700 hours Carl got a call from MTC. He had worked the previous night and slept during the day. "Can you take a transit for us this evening? We have a ship that's been turned down by any number of pilots, but we've got to get it through. Will you take it?"

"You know," Carl replied, "I'm not supposed to take any ships through that don't meet certain standards. Besides that, I'm not supposed to take ship assignments after 0900."

"I know what they said. Everybody's turned this ship down, but you are the next one in the rotation according to your union contract. When your name comes to the top of the list, you can accept this transit if you will volunteer," was MTC's answer.

"I don't know about that. That's going to cause a lot of trouble. You know how pilots are. We get paid for each start, and money is money."

Carl knew he'd catch flack from the other pilots by taking a ship that they had turned down, especially so late in the day.

MTC pleaded, "I don't want that boat to stay at anchor here until it rots and sinks to the bottom. Hardly anything works, but we think you can get it through for us. We've had the port captain look at it more than once."

"Well, okay, assented Carl, "I'll go down and take a look at it and see whatcha got."

Carl went down to the ship and looked at it. It was a shambles. It was all rusty with holes in the deck. Boards had been laid across the holes in the decks to keep people from falling through. It was an old World War II Knott ship that flew the Colombian flag. After it unloaded its cargo, it would be going to scrap. Carl got on board and picked his way across the deck to the wheelhouse. He addressed the captain, "What in the hell have you got here?"

"We'd like to get back to Colombia, unload and then sell this ship for scrap. Then the crew can get their wages. We've been at sea for six months. It looks like every pilot is going to turn us down."

Carl knew what it was like to have been to sea for many months at a time. If he didn't take this ship through, no telling when the crew would get home.

"I guess I can give it a try," Carl told the captain reluctantly.

The captain informed Carl of some of the ship's deficiencies, "I can tell you now that whistle doesn't work."

"Captain, put the telegraph on standby, then," Carl offered.

"The telegraph doesn't work either. I have to use the voice tube. Here's the latch with a spring on it. Push it down and blow in the mouthpiece. They'll hear you whistle in the engine room. One of the men in the engine room will push down on his latch at the other end and you can talk to each other. I guarantee I'll have a man in the engine room to stand by the voice tube at all times, so your orders will be heard and carried out," the captain assured Carl.

"Okay, I know how a voice tube works. I guess that'll work. How well does this ship steer?" Carl queried.

"It will steer up a gnat's ass."

"How about going astern?" Carl wanted to know.

"Well, we have a problem there. It takes a long time to get it to go astern. When you approach a lock, you'll have to stop the engine and drift into the lock."

"Man, I don't know," Carl worried, "Everything I see here is against the Federal Code of Regulations. Will the anchor heave up?"

"Yes, the anchor will heave up," the captain assured Carl.

Carl thought about what the captain had told him, and he believed he could get the ship through, so he told the captain, "Well, heave up the anchor. Let's go."

Carl put the engine on 'Dead Slow'. The captain was right about the way the ship steered. He wouldn't need a locomotive until it was completely stopped. Carl never gave the order to go astern the entire way through the canal. He eased through all the locks, put it "Full Ahead" across Miraflores and Gatun Lakes. When they got to the other side, the captain put two bottles of Johnny Walker Black Label in a green garbage sack and gave it to Carl. He was extremely grateful.

When Carl got back to the reporting station, he ran into a bunch of mad pilots. One of them slammed the door against Carl. Angrily he accosted Carl with, "We don't need people like you down here."

"You're just a little junior nothing," Carl defended as he pushed on the door, "I'm a step eight pilot. Get the hell out of my way!"

The other pilot released the door and let Carl pass. He walked in and asked the dispatcher, "Where's the jitney going to the other side?"

One man popped up and said, "Well, they left you. The other guys don't want to ride with you. YOU STINK!"

The dispatcher assured Carl that there was another jitney waiting for him. Carl saw it just coming in the drive, so he went out, got in the jitney, and left. When he got home, some pilots called Carl on the phone and asked him why he took that boat through. Carl explained to some of the ones who were reasonable that the union contract allowed for this assignment. They understood. He just hung up the phone on the unreasonable ones.

Canal History

Carl was piloting during a transit through the Panama Canal with another pilot named Rodriguez.

"Good morning there, Rodriguez. How you doin'?"

"Okay, Carl. I guess I'll be riding with you today."

"What have we got?"

"We have north 7 and we're gonna get off at Gamboa."

"That's pretty good if somebody doesn't come in here and take our transit away from us. Transit has been changing things around on us."

"No, I don't think so. I called in. This one is set in concrete."

"Hey, Carl, I heard you talking the other day with Perez about all their Panamanian ancestors who raced over here when they smelled the miners' gold in 1849 and now the American dollars. I understood that crossing the isthmus was a short route to the gold fields in California. Do you still think that way?"

"I'll tell you. Here's the story. I've read several books on the Canal and its history back to 1552 when a Spanish priest, Francisco Lopez de Gomara, wrote about digging a canal, naming Panama, Nicaragua, Darien, and Tehuantepec as the best choices for a location. His book was ignored until the gold rush gave people the incentive to take a serious look at a shortcut to the California gold fields. Crossing the isthmus without a canal began in 1849 when all these routes were used. Some foolhardy souls hacked their way through the jungle. Some of them hired Indian guides who just left them and disappeared in the jungle. Those poor suckers never got out. Some other groups made it, though. You can still see the Cruces Trail they took. It is barely three feet wide. Tourists hike through it now, just for the fun of it.

Most North Americans thought the best place for a canal was through Nicaragua. Going through Panama all started with the 1846 Bidlack Treaty in which Colombia gave the United States the right to transit the Isthmus of Panama, using any existing or future mode of transportation. In return the U.S. guaranteed neutrality of the isthmus and Colombia, then called "New Granada". The 1846 treaty made the building of the trans-isthmian Panama railroad possible. The first railroad was begun by a group of American business men in 1850 and was finished in 1855. While it is probably exaggerated, there was a saying that there was a dead body for every railroad tie that was laid."

"I've heard about the stories of cholera, yellow fever, and malaria killing a lot of people before the mosquitoes were wiped out. What did they do with all those bodies, anyway?" asked Rodriguez.

"So many people died without any way to identify them, other than a first name, and the land was too swampy for burial underground, that the dead bodies were pickled in real big barrels and shipped to medical schools and hospitals all over the world. The money they got for them paid for the hospital in Colón.

"How did the Panamanians figure in this?" interjected Rodriguez.

Carl continued, "The Americans broke the Bidlack treaty. Instead of protecting Colombia's sovereignty, they recognized the sovereignty of a little puppet government in Panama, then a province of Colombia. The Panamanians wanted independence from Colombia. The United States gave Panama the same rights that Colombia had given to the U.S. Not only that, but Teddy Roosevelt covertly supported a revolution to see that the Panamanians got independence from Colombia. Colombia already had signed a treaty with France, the Turr Syndicate, in 1882 that gave France exclusive privileges for 99 years to construct a canal across the isthmus. The French had to deposit right away 750,000 francs in a bank in London for Colombia to show their good faith.

After the construction period, supposedly 17 years, Colombia was to get five percent of the canal tolls for the first 15 years, six percent for the next 25 years, seven percent for the next 25 years, and eight percent for the final years of the concession. The minimum payment was never to be less than $250,000, the same as Colombia's share of earnings from the railroad. You don't think that's enough money for people to start climbing in here from Spain and Cuba? They smelled all that money; sure they did. I heard Panama even had a Cuban president.

Of course we know that France failed in their canal building effort, but she still had all her equipment there and just a token force to keep some of the equipment in working order. Ferdinand de Lesseps successfully built the Suez Canal, so he wanted to build another sea level canal here. In Panama there was the continental divide to cross as well as jungle, Indians and disease to contend with. Another Frenchman, Nicholas Lepinay, recommended a lock canal, but he was paid no attention at a Paris conference on canal building in 1879. Ferdinand de Lesseps changed the name of the company from Associado Seville Internacional De Canal Interoceana Que de Gallien to Compagnie Universelle du Canal Interoceaniquede Panama when he bought out the Turr syndicate. Colombia didn't have a contract or treaty with anyone in France to change to a different company. They only had a contract with the one original company. The result was that Colombia really had no agreement whatsoever with France. Colombia could have told France to get its equipment out within a specified time, perhaps six months.

The United States actually stabbed Colombia in the back. Even though the Colombian government was dragging out the time to sign a treaty with the U.S. after France's attempt to build the canal failed, I think that the U.S. could have been more patient and made an agreement with Colombia. They were getting a good deal from Colombia. I think they got a better deal than with Panama because Panama was just a rag tag, renegade government. They had the American military and naval forces on their side."

"What about the Panamanians? Didn't they help to build the railroad and the canal?" Rodriguez wanted to know.

"About one fourth of the workers on the railroad were white. Three-fourths were black. It was the same on the canal construction. The blacks were mostly from the Caribbean, working for sometimes as little as 10 cents an hour. There were some Chinese, too, but no Panamanians. When the French engineers under Ferdinand DeLesseps were getting ready to come to Panama they were told, "You better bring everything you will need with you. When you come to Panama you will find nothing except jungle, heat, and mosquitoes. Do not depend on anything local."

"Well, that clears up a lot of things for me. Thanks, Carl."

"We're about to Gamboa, so we better get ready to debark. Here comes the pilot boat with our relief."

The new pilots came aboard; then Carl and Rodriguez debarked, went to the pilot station, took the jitney, and went home.

Transition of Panama Canal from United States to Panama

The Carter-Torrijos Treaty of 1979 provided that Panamanian pilots be employed at the rate of five percent per year from 1979 through 1999. This would make the pilot force 100% Panamanian by the time the Panama Canal, and all U.S. military installations, are totally turned over to Panama at noon on December 31, 1999. The Panama Canal *Zone* was turned over to Panama in 1979. Sometimes, when qualified Panamanians cannot be found to fill the available positions, the Panama Canal Commission hired third nationals to work in the canal because of their skills and education. Most were bi-lingual. They paid neither American nor Panamanian taxes. The president of Panama wanted to deport them, but the U.S. government was still responsible for the smooth operation of the canal, so they stayed. Panama wanted to tax their incomes, but could not.

In 1985 the U.S. Government raised pilots' pension percentage and gave them free housing to encourage them to stay and train Panamanian pilots. Before 1985 pilots paid for their own housing and electricity.

Transit with Captain Flowers

By 1988, when the Carter-Torrijos Treaty had been implemented by phases for nine years, it was apparent that renovations were under way on the canal, including locks, locomotives, and all other facilities and equipment. One morning as Carl began another transit, after he had ascended the pilot ladder and made his way to the wheelhouse, he greeted the ship's captain with, "Good morning, Captain. Thank you for having my bags brought up."

"They do it, anyway, but you're welcome," responded the captain.

Carl knew it was standard procedure for a member of the crew to tie a line to a pilot's bag and hoist it up to the deck of the ship, but he wanted to start this transit with a friendly greeting. He introduced himself with, "I'm Captain Turner."

"I'm Captain Flowers. Glad to know you. When are we gonna get under way?"

"We have about an hour wait. I believe I'll get another cup of coffee."

"Sure. There's fresh coffee just behind you on the table."

On nearly every ship there is fresh coffee available on the bridge, as well as cookies or crackers. "By the way, Captain, how do you Americans feel about the Panamanians ripping off this canal from under you? It looks like you have to fix everything up and put it in new condition. If they don't like the way it is, they won't sign for it. Is that right?"

"Yeah, that's right, Captain. We have to restore everything to new condition. The Panamanians have to sign for everything. You know, our president, Jimmy Carter, the peanut man, he not only gave the canal away, but he has given the Panamanians everything they wanted, and we must comply with his wish or quit and give up our pensions. I guess it will cost hundreds of millions of dollars to fully implement the treaty for the twenty year period from 1979 to 1999."

"Yeah, well, pilot, I didn't mean to insult you or anything, but you got it coming. You know the state department under Eisenhower put the pressure on England and France to get out of the Suez Canal, but we got our money out of there, but I don't think you'll ever get your money out of here."

"Well, I agree with you, Captain. We had it coming. We got three branches of government, the executive, legislative and judicial. Our State Department in the executive branch has to be the most over educated, dumbest group of people in the whole world. I don't know if it is true or not, but I've heard it from many quarters. I had an uncle who was a colonel and was stationed down here for a number of years. He said that when the Hay-Bunau-Varilla Treaty was negotiated on November 18, 1903, the Army Corps of Engineers was to build this canal, which they did. I heard that advisers begged the State Department to eliminate the treaty provision to pay Panama $250,000 a year as an annuity. I can't prove that, of course, and I know that it only took 40 minutes to negotiate the treaty, so it may well be just a false rumor. Those annuity payments have come back to haunt the U.S. They surely have done that. You can hear the hue and cry, 'We can't help it if you have built condominiums on our land. Get out! We don't want your rent any more.' Paying an annuity each year has given the Panamanians a foothold to claim ownership of the canal. That's exactly what happened, Captain.

Well, here we are, Captain. It's going to be a beautiful day. I don't feel badly about the situation. It doesn't upset me any more. As we transit today, you can knock the canal situation any way you want to. I came down here at age fifty-five, and I've only got a few years to go in order to retire with fifteen years of service. That ain't bad! Total pension-$32,000 a year. By the time they take out American taxes and an annuity for my wife and I'll probably take a $64,000 lump sum. They'll take another big whack out of that. I will most likely wind up with $1700 a month clear. But that's okay; I can take the lump sum and invest it and make a whole lot more than if I don't take a lump sum."

Such conversations were frequent on transits and at "watering holes" among pilots, ships' captains, and others. Seamen liked to "drop anchors", as their wives called it when they swapped stories and opinions on the current situations and past histories of the canal.

By this time, the hour of wait time had passed, so Carl gave the order, "Okay, Captain, get your men up there, and let's start heaving up the anchor. Has all your engine equipment and everything all been tested out?"

"Yeah, Captain, everything's ready."

"Captain, you need to put some flags up. Run up the pilot flag over the number seven. We're north seven today. You'll see the other ships coming down with all even numbers—two, four, six, eight, they're southbound. The northbound ships are all odd numbers one, three, five, seven. If you have any dangerous cargo, explosives, firearms, chemicals or the like—"

"Yeah, Captain, we got about 200 tons of black powder in number four hold. It has been labeled 'Dangerous Cargo' and inspected by the Canal Commission."

"Okay, Captain. Run up your red flag, your baker flag, to signify 'Explosives on Board.'"

"Okay. Good luck, Mr. Pilot, on your canal. It's too bad you weren't around when they first dug this canal."

"Thank you for that, Captain. Coffee's damn good. Here we go. Have a good day. We'll be talking later on. Half ahead, starboard ten."

Transit with Captain Menendez

"Morning, Menendez," Carl greeted the captain. "We have a southbound today. We're south eight; that's not so bad. This is a passenger ship, so we're not going to get any delays, I can tell you that. They're going to fireball us through. They don't have many ships today, only about 60 ships to go through counting both north and south directions."

"Okay, good morning, Carl. I've already told the steward to get us some lunch ready at 1000 hours."

"That's fine. Thank you."

"Well, Carl, I heard you talking the other day about Phillippe Bunau-Varilla. Nobody here in Panama likes him. Now I hear people bad-mouthing him all the time. But you seem to think he was just about the right man to negotiate the treaty in the canal for Panama in 1903."

"That's right, Menendez. I said that and I still say it. Phillippe Bunau-Varilla was the chief engineer for the French effort in building the canal. He was around to negotiate for Panama. This place would have exploded with hatred if they had put an American in there. He was the only one who was qualified. Panama only had one engineer and who knows what school he went to. He didn't have any background for negotiating a treaty. They didn't have anybody here in Panama. Some of the Panamanian legislators were educated in Spain and had only a twelfth grade education, but they didn't have any diplomatic experience with treaties and in technical engineering expertise. Anyway, Bunau-Varilla graduated from a polytechnic institute, a very elite school in Paris. He appointed himself as French ambassador to the U.S. He and General Amador from Panama hatched a scheme to get Teddy Roosevelt to back Panama's revolution from Colombia. Then Bunau-Varilla worked with Secretary of State Hay on a treaty with Panama and a sale of the French company's holdings to the U.S. I think he did a good job. I really think he did! He got Panama $10,000,000 upon acceptance of the treaty and $250,000 a year annuity. Of course he also got $40 million for the French. He pocketed a lot of that, I think. Panama agreed to give up the ten mile wide Canal Zone to be ruled by the United States as if sovereign in perpetuity. Then the U.S. had to pay all the people who owned private lands in the zone a total of $5,000,000. I don't hear any Panamanians saying, 'Here is your $5,000,000'. At that time five cents would buy a loaf of bread. Shucks, man, how much would that be today? There's no telling. The Americans should really say, 'Hey, we want all our private land back that we paid for in cash to private Panamanian citizens. If Panama wants to keep the land in the zone, she is going to have to find some money somewhere to repay the U.S. government.' But nobody is asking for it, so I think the man did a good job and you people are coming out smelling like a whole sack of roses."

"Okay, Carl, let's just go ahead and make our transit. We all know it's a political deal and you people have sovereignty over land that's right in the middle of our country and that's not right."

"Well, you have a point there, but I've got my point, too, so let's not argue about it. Let's make a good transit today. I don't have any hard feelings. Here we go. Captain, how about getting some fresh, hot coffee up here, please?"

"Sure, pilot. Here's a dish of doughnuts and some cakes over there and fresh coffee. If you need anything else let me know. I'll send this man on standby to get whatever you need. You got your bags up here okay?"

"Sure have, Captain. Thank you very much. Okay, Captain, let's heave up."

Transit with Captain Green and pilot Geoff Jones

When Carl boarded this day's transit and reported to the wheel-house, he greeted the captain, who introduced himself as Captain Green. Captain Green inquired as to when the ship was due to get under way. Carl replied, "Now. I will be your first control pilot. We will get our second control pilot aboard in about 30 minutes. Leave the ladder out for him and for the canal seamen who will board just before we arrive at Gatun Locks. Hoist the pilot flag over the number 10. We are South 10 today. If you have any dangerous cargo aboard, hoist the baker flag. Captain, let's heave up," Carl ordered.

"Where's my transit bag?" Carl asked. "Oh there it is, on the table."

Carl took out his radio and switched to channel one. "Transit, transit, this is south ten for a radio check."

"South ten, this is transit. You will have the west side at Gatun following south six. Your locomotives will be back at 1300 hours. Your tugs will be Goethals and Amistad."

"Thank you transit."

Carl called on his radio, "Goethals, this is south ten. Where are you?"

"We're at the landing. Do you want us come to you or wait for you here?"

"Wait at the landing. You'll be on the stern."

"Roger."

After the ship had been under way for 20 minutes, a pilot boat delivered Carl's old friend, Captain Geoff Jones to the ship to serve as the second control pilot.

"It looks like I'm going to make a transit today with an Americano, one of our most senior pilots. How ya doin' Geoff? You look a little tired. I guess the climb up to this light ship will wind anyone".

"No, Carl, I didn't get any sleep last night. One of my dogs was very ill."

"Have a cup of coffee. It's the best I've had in a long time. Maybe that will perk you up," Carl offered.

"Thanks, but no. I'm going below to the pilots' room. Call me when you get to the locks."

"Okay," agreed Carl.

Geoff went below. After clearing the three locks at Gatun Carl called MTC to tell transit that he had cleared Gatun Locks.

"Roger, south ten. You will have the west side at Pedro Miguel following south six. You should have your locomotives at 1900 hours."

"Thank you, transit."

Carl never called Jones to assist at Gatun; he just let Geoff rest. Carl felt that Jones needed his rest so that he could make it to the year 2000. Carl thought of Geoff as a good friend. They had met when Carl was a PIT. Both men had met their wives while sailing aboard the Pioneer Reef when it was on an Australian run. Jones' diabetes had worsened over the years. He still drank a glass of Scotch after taking his insulin shot. That's the wrong way to go for longevity, Carl thought.

Carl let Geoff sleep all the way through Gatun Lake, past Gamboa, and through the Gaillard cut. Just before entering Pedro Miguel Lock Jones came to the bridge.

"Well, Geoff, you look more rested now. Maybe you will make it to 2000 after all."

"With help from brother pilots like you I will, Carl. I can take it from here."

"Are you sure? I'll take it through Pedro Miguel if you like."

"No, I've got it, but thanks," Jones replied.

"Your tugs are Trinidad on the stern and McAuliff on the starboard bow," Carl informed his friend.

"Okay, Carl. Captain, will you please get me a shot of scotch? I would appreciate it."

The captain assented, "Sure. Mate, take these keys and bring up a bottle of Black Label."

"Yes, sir."

The captain called Carl in to the chart room and asked him if Jones could handle a shot of Scotch.

Carl answered the captain's query this way, "Captain Jones comes over to my house and polishes off a fifth in one afternoon. Sure, let him have it. He is one of the best pilots on the canal—drink or no drink."

The mate put the bottle on the window ledge. Jones took a glassful and downed it without making a face or sound.

"You know, Geoff, you really ought to get off the booze. You are drinking really too heavy."

"I know it. Don't start that. I know it. I'm fighting my wife over that too. I drink, and I'm always going to drink."

"Okay. Well, looks like you're taking out your needle to give yourself a pop in the arm or the hip with your insulin. As far as I'm concerned you're one of the best-qualified pilots in this canal. I don't know of anybody who has kept on top of his profession the way you have. You can name almost every star that's used in navigation. Gee, I wish you would watch your health and stay with us a while, Geoff."

"Yeah, go ahead. I'll stay here until the year 2000 and watch all the fun."

"What kind of fun is that, Geoff?"

"The fun is going to begin at noon on December 31, 1999. The Panamanians will start fighting over the spoils. Land, housing, jobs, pay equal to that of the U. S. government's civil service pay. A lot of the Panamanians who worked for the U.S. government before the treaty was implemented in 1979 will retire in 1999. When December 31, 1999 comes, they will take the civil service pension and retire. It's gonna leave a hell of a vacuum here. The Panamanians who hired out after October 1979 will receive their pensions from the Panamanian government. I've been told that the maximum is $1,000 a month regardless of what they made on the job. They are really bitter. I don't know how many will remain on the job."

"Well, Geoff, I'd like to stay here until 1999 and watch all the fun and all the fireworks. You know Panamanians are about the luckiest people in the world. Just think of all the sickness and death of, I guess 45,000 workers who died here building the railroad and canal, including the various surveyors and engineers, the French effort and the American completion. All they have to do is stand by until Dec. 31, 1999 rolls around, and everything falls right in their laps. Between the French and the U.S. at least a billion dollars must have been poured in. I hear people say how stupid these Panamanians are. Hey listen, they aren't stupid. I don't know of any Panamanians who suffered or died during the building of the canal. They sat on the bank and sold the workers bananas and pineapples and all kinds of concoctions contrived by the local markets. They made all kind of money directly and indirectly off of this canal and now the whole thing is going to drop right in their lap. That ain't being stupid, is it?"

"No, Carl, I don't guess so. Let's go ahead and have a good trip. It makes me sick to think about it."

"It doesn't bother me because I came down here at 55. I figured if my health would hold up I would get in ten years, and here it is nearly fifteen years. I went to sea all my adult life except for 18 months in the 508 army airborne unit. I am grateful that I will be able to spend my remaining years ashore in this beautiful country."

"All right, Carl, don't rub it in."

After clearing Pedro Miguel and crossing Miraflores Lake the steward came to the bridge and picked up the glass and bottle of Scotch. Jones jumped up and said in a stern voice, "Put that bottle down! I will tell you when I am finished."

Then he downed another glass full. After clearing the two locks at Miraflores the captain told the steward to put a bottle of Black Label in each of the pilots' bags. Then he said, "I see your pilot boat is in the channel and is coming this way."

"Thanks, Captain. Will you have a sailor take my bag down to the ladder?" Carl asked.

As the captain and Carl walked down the stairwell to the deck, Captain Green remarked, "You were right, Captain Turner. Jones is a damn good pilot. I have been through here a number of times, and he is the best I have seen yet. No offense."

"None taken, Captain Green. Thanks for a good transit. Have a good voyage."

Carl debarked and took the pilot boat to the Balboa boathouse. Jones continued with the transit under the Bridge of the Americas and on to Pacific Sea Buoys one and two.

On the way home, Carl thought about other pilots he had become friends with since he had come to Panama. He remembered Paul Simon, his mentor when he first arrived at Coco Solo. After Carl's furniture arrived from the states, Paul often came over for coffee and conversation. Paul talked about his time in the Merchant Marines during World War II. Paul had completed college in three years, so he became a third officer at age twenty. He had married a pretty, young redhead from Arkansas. Paul had wanted Carl to invest in Arkansas real estate, but Carl refused because he had heavy expenses, paying for his eldest daughter, Maureen, in college and child support for the younger two children. Paul drank a full pot of coffee and smoked a large ashtray full of Camel cigarettes on every visit. He was a chain smoker. One time when he was leaving Panama for California for Christmas, on his four-week vacation time, he asked Carl to keep his new Ford car for him. Carl agreed, so the car was parked behind Carl's apartment in the parking lot. At this time the Panama Canal Commission was in charge of the police and security for the Canal Zone, so the car would be safe. When Paul returned, he wanted to borrow $5,000 from Carl. Carl told Paul, "I don't have it, Paul. You know I have a daughter in college and two other children to support. I still am a PIT without overtime."

Approximately nine months later Paul came to see Carl and told him that while he was on his Christmas vacation with his family in California, he passed out on his way to the bathroom. He was taken to a hospital, where he was operated on. He had a brain tumor. But now he was ready to go back to work piloting. He was still smoking one cigarette after another. After another six months, Paul's friends came to Carl's home and told him that Paul had cancer in both lungs. He was not expected to live but a very short time. Carl had wondered why he had not seen Paul in the canal. By that time both Carl and Paul were at step four.

When Carl went to visit Paul, his ex-wife (he had divorced the Arkansas redhead) came to the door and told him in no uncertain terms that no visitors were allowed. In a few days Paul passed away. Trouble had just begun for his new bride. Paul had not paid his income taxes. Carl remembered Paul's request for a loan, and was glad he had not loaned him any money, for he would have lost it all. Both wives were in trouble with the IRS, since they had also signed Paul's tax returns. Paul's two wives had not paid any attention to the tax returns, trusting Paul was doing the honest thing, so they were caught with a big debt to pay. It seems that quite a number of pilots had not paid their income taxes, claiming that they were exempted from paying income taxes according to a provision in the 1977 treaty. The U.S. government stated that the treaty provision pertained to paying Panamanian income taxes. These pilots had to cough up all their back taxes, along with late payment penalties.

Equipment from Scrapped American Ship

One morning Carl was to pilot on a Panamax ship that called for four pilots. As Carl reported to the wheelhouse after boarding at Balboa, he found the other control pilot, Johnson, already there.

"Good morning there, Johnson. How are you doing?"

"Oh, pretty good, Carl."

"I'm going to get off at Gamboa."

"That's right, Carl. Everybody says you have pull with the administration up there on the hill. Everyone else has to make the complete transit, but you get off at Gamboa every time."

"No, that's not true. I get my assignments off the telephone just like everyone else."

As soon as the ship was under way, the two pilots starting "dropping anchors" as usual. One of them began to tell a story of a ship being towed through the canal. When pilots are on a dead tow of any description, they only take the ship half way, so the two pilots were to get off at Gamboa. Transit Operations would have a car and a driver to pick up the pilots no matter where they are put off. They are taken to the pilot stations or to the ship to which they are assigned for the next transit. This service costs the pilots absolutely nothing; they merely get their wages. "Hey, Carl, I hear they got a couple of pilots on suspension. They are in real hot water," Johnson began.

"Yeah? What happened?"

"They had this ship they were towing through the canal. The pilots got together and said to each other, 'Why let the Chinamen in Khoushung have all this beautiful equipment? Since it's going to the scrap heap, let's help ourselves. We can outfit our bars at home with nautical antiques.' So they proceeded to take off the brass clock, a beautiful magnetic compass, in fact the entire binnacle, a lot of brass voice tubes, a barometer, and the steering wheel. They got to Gamboa where both pilots were relieved, because the transit was so slow with a ship being towed, that the transit took too long, way over eight to twelve hours, for just one set of pilots to be on duty during the entire time. When they got off they hoisted their loot down to the pilot boat and went ashore. They approached the jitney driver to take them and their confiscated articles to their homes, but the jitney driver wouldn't do it. He told them that he was authorized to take them to their homes and that was all. One of the pilots turned to Bill Thompson and asked, 'Bill, you have a truck, don't you?' 'Yes, I have a truck. I'll call my wife to come and pick us up.' The wives were called. They were getting ready to load up all their loot on Thompson's truck when the FBI and CIA arrived and arrested them. All the items were picked up by the government and hauled off. The pilots had to pay several thousand dollars to have it crated and shipped back to its rightful owners. The pilots had to go to court. I tell you, I don't put my hands on anything on these ships that doesn't belong to me. How about you, Carl?"

"No, not me. I don't take anything. Now I'll accept a gift if it is given to me, but I don't take anything from any of these ships. They can keep all this stuff. All I have in my bar is all kinds of good liquor like Johnny Walker Black Label and good premium beer, Carlsberg and you name it. Well, here comes my lunch. I'll go get it and get off and go on home. I'll probably see you in a day or two. We should come up in the rotation pretty close because there isn't anybody getting off in the canal now just you and me. They gotta make the full transit. So we'll probably work together again tomorrow. Take it easy."

"Sure, Carl. See you."

The VIP Entourage

Another time Carl was assigned to the ship called The Pacific Princess. She was a beauty, not very old. Transit informed Carl that he would have some courtesy passengers board at Gatun Lake. He was to wear his white Panama shirt and dress slacks. He boarded the ship at the Cristobal anchorage. He had his friend, Mather, with him. He called in to transit, identified himself as South six, and called for the usual radio check. He was to make sure the proper gangway was put out to insure the VIPs' safety, as they were U. S. Senators, their wives, and entourage. They would be going all the way to Balboa, where they would disembark.

"Yeah, transit, okay." Carl responded. He knew that he didn't have to let them on the bridge of the ship, since they could interfere with its smooth operation. However, Carl was feeling magnanimous that day, and allowed the guests to come to the bridge when the officers were not too busy.

When they cleared Gatun locks, they were ready to take on the guests. This ship had a side port with watertight doors. When the side port is opened, there is only about 3 or 4 feet to the water. When the ship goes to sea, these doors are closed. There are only two steps from the pilot boat onto the ship. The captain sent some officers to help the guests aboard. They didn't come up to the bridge for some time, since they were having breakfast. Shortly after breakfast the ship passed Mamei curve and headed into Gamboa Reach. Then the senators and their wives streamed up to the bridge, about nine people in all. Along with them was a general, the administrator of the whole canal dressed in civilian clothes. He was very courteous and accommodating. All of the ships' officers and the pilots were especially well dressed for the occasion. The general knew who Carl was, since he had checked out the personnel before he came aboard. He said to Carl, "Good morning, Captain Turner. I see you are senior pilot in first control."

"Yes, sir, I am, General." Carl replied.

The general introduced Carl to the senators, their wives and friends as the senior control pilot. The ladies oohed and aahed, asking, "Oh, is he the senior control pilot in the entire canal?"

"Oh, no, Captain Turner is the senior control pilot on this ship for this transit through the canal," the general informed them.

The ladies would not or did not understand the distinction, so they fawned over all the officers on the bridge. The captain had the stewards standing by to get anything anyone wanted. The ladies looked pretty bleary-eyed from too much booze and too little sleep. The senators were standing by the windows.

"Would you ladies like a cocktail?" Carl asked.

"Oh, yes, we would like that," one of them answered.

"Captain, can you get these ladies some cocktails?" Carl asked the captain.

"Why sure, pilot, whatever they would like," the captain answered and then turned to the ladies, "Would you like hors d'oeuvres with it or possibly some champagne? Our bartenders can fix you up with anything you would like."

"A glass of peach champagne would be lovely," one of the ladies cooed.

Other ladies ordered other drinks, bloody Mary, grasshopper, whiskey sour, and the like.

The captain turned to his steward with these instructions, "Get some of your page boys and bring up three bottles of champagne and a pitcher to shake up the bloody Marys and whatever else is needed to fill the ladies orders."

The general was absolutely white-faced. He knew that drinking on the ship's bridge was forbidden. Drinking on the bridge was **not allowed**. He approached the captain about this. The captain answered him, "Look, general. I'm not drinking; my crew's not drinking. The pilot's not drinking. The passengers are not going to fall down or get hurt. We have another six to eight hours. It's only about 2100 hours now. We have a long delay at Pedro Miguel locks. If they want to have a drink, it's all right with me. If you say no, since you are the superior officer and administrator, then that will be it."

"No, no, captain, that's all right. Whatever they want is fine."

The general gave Carl a bad look.

The ship proceeded to Gamboa, arriving at noon. Captain Masters, another senior pilot, relieved Carl as control pilot. Carl went down below. He didn't know when the visitors left the bridge. They were on the bridge drinking when he left. The ship's captain gave Carl his card, which allowed him to get anything he wanted by showing the card to the ship's personnel. His requests would be charged to the ship's bill. Carl thanked the captain and assured him that he wouldn't abuse the privilege. Carl went to the first class passengers' dining room and had a beautiful lunch of filet of sole and a variety of steaming vegetables served in covered dishes, complete with a bottle of wine. Since he wasn't on the bridge or on duty at this time, he enjoyed some of the ship's fine wine. He was pretty sure that none of the guests would come in there. But lo and behold, who should come in but the general with the whole entourage. He saw Carl with that bottle of wine on his table, as well as the bottle of wine he had placed in his bag, but he did not say anything. They all went by and dined in the first class passengers' dining room. Carl finished his meal and left.

Carl thought to himself that one glass of wine would not do him at all, so he decided to go on the stern where there was an outdoor smorgasbord. There was a big dance floor and barbecue as well. He went back on the stern and crawled up on a barstool. He ordered a beer. He had not been there thirty minutes when here came the general and all the others trailing right behind him. They walked right past Carl on their way to the smorgasbord. He just knew he would get his ass fired. He would get canned!

Well, anyway, the transit went on smoothly. Carl went on up to the bridge and assisted Captain Masters through Pedro Miguel lock. They crossed Miraflores Lake. The visiting guests asked Carl all kinds of questions. They were all so happy, and Carl met some friends for life. The ship went on through Miraflores Locks. When the passengers debarked at Balboa, Carl got off too, since Captain Masters was to take the ship from Balboa under the bridge of the Americas right out to the Pacific. Then a pilot boat would take him to the pilot station on Naos Island.

On the pilot boat Carl was with the group of special visitors and they got to chatting. The general was friendly. Carl was invited everywhere by the ladies in the party. Everything was just "hunky dorey". Carl went home and thought to himself that the general was just putting on a show in front of all the big shots and Carl was going to get fired for drinking aboard ship. But you know, about three weeks later he went to the mailbox. There was an official looking envelope. He knew it was from "the hill" as the headquarters of the Panama Canal Commission was called, since it sat on a knoll above the Prado, an avenue of palms exactly the size of a lock chamber. He opened the envelope. It was a letter from the general. He complimented Carl on his appearance, seamanship, and the manner in which he handled the ship, and stated that he was a good ambassador for his country. Carl breathed a sigh of relief. He wasn't fired after all.

A few weeks later Carl was called in to the chief pilot's office. He was handed a check for $1500 for outstanding performance. He knew where it came from, because, prior to this transit described above, the general didn't know Carl from a cabbage in a whole field of cabbages. He got $1500 and had a wonderful time. That's the way it goes sometimes.

The Goldonski Incident

"Good morning, Captain Peterson," Carl greeted the ship's captain as he entered the wheelhouse accompanied by three other pilots, "My name is Carl Turner. I will be your first control pilot. Have you been through the canal before?"

"Good morning, Captain Turner. Yes, I've been through here many times."

"We have three other pilots here; Mr. Bowes is a senior pilot. Captain Bowes will take over at Gamboa. Then I'll assist him. The other two pilots are Hank Spears and John Daley. They'll be our bow pilots, working only when we go through the locks. You know the routine. We have had an hour and a half ride over from the Pacific side and an hour wait in the boat house. Do you suppose you could arrange breakfast below for the three pilots and find a spare room for them to rest in? I'd like my breakfast here on the bridge." Carl requested.

"Sure thing, pilot. Breakfast is being served now. The steward will show these gentlemen their quarters."

"What time do you think we will be at Gatun Locks?"

"One moment. Let me get my radio out of my bag and I will give transit a call."

Carl got his radio out and called the transit office.

"Transit, transit. This is south ten for a radio check."

"Good morning, Captain Turner. You will have the east side at Gatun; when N-29 clears at 0930 your locomotives will be available. Your tugs will be the Goethals and the Amistad."

"Okay, transit. Thank you. What time do you have us clearing Miraflorcs? "

"You should clear at 1830."

"Did you get that, Captain?"

"Yes, pilot."

Carl would be taking the ship through Gatun Locks and on to Gamboa. The ship was heading south, going from the Atlantic side to the Pacific. It would have to wait for the locomotives to return from taking a ship heading north through the west side of the lock chamber. Waiting was a large part of the time it takes to go through the Panama Canal, since the locomotives must return from their current assignment in order to take the next ship through the locks. Often there were several ships waiting alongside the canal at each set of locks. He would put the ship in the first lock and use a single culvert. Water fills the lock chamber through 18-foot culverts located in the center and side walls of the locks. From these, the water flows through smaller culverts which open into the floor of the lock chambers. By using only a single culvert, it would take about 25 to 30 minutes to fill the chamber. This is a slow lockage. With the cattle boat, on the other hand, a fast lockage was desired, so a double culvert was used in order to fill the chamber rapidly.

While Carl and Captain Peterson were having breakfast on the bridge, Peterson remarked, "Mr. Pilot, I was through here about three or four months ago. Lord, we had a pilot on here—. We had an investigation."

"Whew! Man, that's bad. Who was the pilot, Cap?"

"Let's see. Yeah, I remember his name. It was Goldonski or something like that. He was a Polish guy from Germany. He was something terrible. His English was very broken and I lost confidence in that guy when he had been here for only ten minutes. You know it was a four pilot ship, 792 feet long, with 106' beam and loaded right down to 39.9. It was a bulk carrier. The SS World Glory was a good ship and would back to port even when fully loaded. Her engine responded very quickly. He would order, 'Hard to port, hard to starboard' in rapid succession. I couldn't understand why Goldonski was so nervous. What could I do? Your government pays for any damage caused by lousy pilots. You know that this ship is 792 feet long and has a 106 foot beam. It was loaded to 39.6 feet just as it is now. This man should not be a pilot anywhere."

"Yeah, Captain. I know this guy. The Commission has tried hard to just make him go away, but somehow or another these pilots who trained him are carrying some hatred against the Commission for this treaty. Some of them think they're not treated right. They think they've been done wrong, and I agree. A lot of them have, you know. But, anyway, I know this guy you're talking about and I'm sorry. Dead slow ahead, Mr. Mate."

The mate relayed the order to the quartermaster. "Dead slow ahead, sir." The quartermaster complied.

"Well, we were alongside the center wall moving toward the entrance of the lock, west side. We had center wall number one and number two fast, center wall number three fast. He let go the stern tug. All of a sudden I heard, 'Center number one and number two slack'. You know what happened! The bow came off the wall and we hit the knuckle opening up a gash about 14 feet long on the starboard bow."

"Whew," Turner whistled. "It sure is important to keep the bow in close to the center wall when you are entering any lock, but especially at Gatun. Fresh water is spilling through the locks into the Atlantic Ocean. This works against the ship, forcing it away from the center wall and into the knuckle. All pilots should know that. I remember that was stressed when I was a PIT. So what happened then, Cap? Did you transit on through? Were you taking any water?"

"No, we weren't taking any water. The gash was about ten feet above the water line. It was a terrible hole. It makes you kind of sick when you feel your ship being torn up. We continued the transit after anchoring in Gatun Lake. The port captain came aboard and cleared the ship to continue the transit. We had to go to the shipyard in Balboa and have the necessary repairs made to make the ship seaworthy. After the investigation we were told that this pilot needs a long signal when he meets another ship in the canal."

Carl remembered another incident with Goldonski as pilot. "About a year or two ago, I think he was just a small ship pilot then. This is what I heard about this collision. I was not at the investigation, nor was I a witness to the collision. Anyway, he gave the quartermaster the wrong signal. He sank a ship right there in San Pablo reach or close to there.

Hardaway, pilot of the other ship, gave one whistle to pass starboard to starboard and come right. Goldonski gave no signal, turned unexpectedly and came right striking Hardaway's ship amidships. Hardaway's ship was carrying bayroid, a very heavy oil drilling material."

The captain went on, "I am sure that the poor captain aboard the other ship was just at the wrong place at the right time. My last memory of Captain Goldonski was 'hard to starboard, hard to port.' There were so many telegraph orders to the engine room that the chief engineer thought we had a bunch of children playing in the wheelhouse. When the quartermasters were relieved they were exhausted. Hard to starboard, hard to port, 'midships—my God! What a day! I would have hated to have been the captain whose ship got sunk."

"Yeah, just prior to the investigation," Carl recalled, "my cousin was down here visiting me. He was a cracker jack sailor and boat builder. We were in a big shopping center in Balboa. We were shopping when Goldonski came rushing up to me and said, 'Hey, Carl, I sunk a ship, I sunk a ship.'"

I kind of felt sorry for him; he used to bring me a cup of coffee and the paper every morning. I told him, 'My God. Don't tell people that. There will be an investigation by the board of Inspectors. Don't tell everybody *you* sunk a ship. Let them have their investigation and don't admit anything. Let then prove who sunk the ship. Calm yourself. Control yourself. Take it easy, and, when you go into the investigation, we'll see what happens.' Would you believe, Captain, Hathaway was held at fault because he didn't give two whistles and pass port to port. He was a retired navy captain. He did just about what I'd have done. He was trying to give the guy room. He was cutting across his bow. He had no idea in the world he was going to pull a hard over wheel and come back and let him chop him in two. The commission tried for weeks to move the sunken vessel out of the channel to no avail. There was a British salvage ship at sea not far away with the needed equipment. The Commission contracted with it to move the vessel out of the channel for $3,000,000. The salvage company put cables under the vessel, broke it in two, placed more cables under the vessel with huge barges on each side of each half and floated it out of the channel. I think that was fast money for a few days work."

"What happened then to Goldonski?" the captain questioned.

"Goldonski just went on back to work for the U.S. government. Everybody in the administration knew what kind of pilot he was and that he shouldn't be here, but he's back. Pilots take him out and give him check rides, and since the pilots hate the Panama Canal Commission so much, they pass him again. Then the government rules and regulations say that they have to put him back to work. So he goes back to work. I don't know what happened to him. Nobody wants to work with him, but he's here and he won't go away. My cousin must have thought that half the pilots here are incompetent."

"I don't know, man. He must have a pair of balls the size of footballs or basketballs to stay here and face fellow pilots and captains," the captain commented.

By this time the ship was turning the corner into San Pablo Reach. Carl thought he would have time for just one more story before they reached Gamboa. "Captain, I remember when Goldonski was with me on another transit," he began. "I was giving him a check ride for his 225' pilot license. He couldn't get the ship off the dock, as there were some other tuna boats around his ship. I called the port captain and had the ships that were docked abreast moved. Then Goldonski asked me to take the ship off the dock and into the channel, in spite of the fact that I was not supposed to do any of the pilot work. I felt sorry for him, so I called for a small workboat to assist putting the boat in the channel. After the ship was in the channel Goldonski cried out, 'I am the pilot. I am the pilot. I want to work. I want to work.' I told him 'okay' and let him take the con. We went on to Miraflores Locks. In the approaches he turned the vessel completely around and almost hit the soft nose. The captain on the ship said to me, 'Please do not let this idiot wreck my ship.' I stayed in the wheelhouse and gave all the orders with my radio. We had four locomotives (mules) when Goldonski ordered, 'Center One, coil in.' I would have said, 'Center One release.' You do not need locomotives to assist putting a small boat into the lock, only to keep her in the middle of the chamber. This went on throughout the transit. Goldonski never knew that I was giving all the orders—poor soul. I could hear the locomotive operators laughing. They can hear your orders but can't talk back. They can only ring the locomotive bell to let you know they understand and will comply."

"Well, captain, here is my relief. I'll see you at Pedro Miguel lock. The steward has saved me a special dinner down below."

Carl took his leave of the captain, ate his supper and boarded the pilot boat to disembark in due time.

Twinkle, Twinkle, Little Star

One dark, clear night during the dry season, Carl had the good fortune to pilot a beautiful diesel ship called the Indian Crescent. It was 675' long, with a beam of 78'. If a ship had a beam of 80' or more, it would have required two pilots. It was a beautiful ship with six hatches, a German built vessel with an East Indian captain. He had his wife and five-year-old daughter on board. The ship tramped around the world for a year at a time without stopping at its home port. During this period cargo and crew were picked up and dropped off at various ports in a large number of countries.

As Carl gave the order, "Starboard 10°," the bow would rise slightly, then settle on the new heading just as pretty as you please. The Indian Crescent handled so easily that Carl absent-mindedly looked at the stars and listened to the hum of the finely tuned diesel engines as the ship glided along Peña Blanca Reach. Carl sat near the steering station on a high pilot chair, the seat of which was about 5' above the deck. In the dark Carl felt something moving along his leg. He asked the captain to turn on the light in the chart room so he could see what was going on. When the captain turned on the light, Carl saw a beautiful little girl at his knee. Her hair fell in ringlets as though her mother had put them up in rags the night before. Carl thought she looked like a brown skinned Shirley Temple. She held up her arms for Carl to lift her up on his lap. As he did so, she looked up at him with large dark eyes that looked like they had been set in a pool of white marble. Her large eyes and her innocent look reminded Carl of his daughter Elaine when she was about five years old. His heart ached at her lost innocence. The little Indian girl pointed her tiny finger up at the overhead and began to sing,

Twinkle, Twinkle, little star.
How I wonder what you are.
Up above the world so high,
Like a diamond in the sky.

She had a sweet, high, clear voice, very pleasant to the ear. Then the little girl recited Humpty, dumpty and other nursery rhymes. She sang and spoke perfect English. Carl was amazed! She slid off Carl's lap, went over to a deck officer, and carried on a conversation with him in Greek. Then she turned back to Carl and asked him if he would like a cup of coffee. Carl said he would, so she turned to the steward and spoke to him in Arabic. The steward replied in Arabic and left the wheelhouse, soon reappearing with the tray of coffee, sugar and cream. "Where did that child learn to speak English, Greek, and Arabic? Is there any language she doesn't know?" Carl asked the captain.

The captain was a tall, dark skinned Indian, his uncut hair wound under a white silk turban, identifying him as a member of the Sikh religion. He was dressed in his officer's dress uniform. He was very friendly and offered this explanation, "My daughter, Sasha, travels with my wife and me. She seems to pick up languages very easily. Whenever we take on a new crew member who speaks a language with which she is unfamiliar, she makes friends with him and learns to speak his language. Her native language is Hindi, of course, but she also speaks Greek and several other languages. She wanted to show you that she knows English as well. My wife and Sasha have been traveling with me for five years. Sasha is a very bright child. How many languages does she speak? I really do not know, many, I am sure. My wife and I have taught Sasha on board ship. Soon my wife and Sasha will get off the ship and return to India where Sasha will attend a regular school. Then I won't be able to have my family with me except in the summer and when I go home on vacation."

Sasha walked over to her mother who was standing off to one side. Her mother wore a softly draped pink sari, edged in gold. She wore the red dot on her forehead signifying that she was married. She was slender with the same large dark eyes and winning smile as her daughter. The whole family was very hospitable. As Carl looked back on this experience, he would count it as one of the most pleasant times in all his fifteen years of piloting the Panama Canal.

Carl Meets Yolanda

It was February 1988. Carl had not remembered he had a birthday coming soon until Rose, his maid, told him that she and Maria had planned a birthday party for him at Maria's home near Old Panama. Carl told Rose, "Rose, I do not like birthday parties. I don't like to think about them or how old I am unless I am asked for some official purpose."

Rose went on and on, "Maria loves you an awfully lot. You are lucky because she is a virgin! If she does not marry, she is going to become a nun."

Rose's last statement finally convinced Carl, "Wow! In that case I must go."

Immediately after Carl accepted the idea of a birthday party in his honor, Rose added, "Captain, could you get all the drinks and mixes, potato chips, nuts and mints at the package store at Rodman Naval Base? We will pay you for them."

Carl agreed, but thought to himself, "Well, if they do pay me, it will be the first time a Panamanian ever repaid me for anything. I know they will never pay me. I will be financing my own birthday party! Anyway, I guess it will be worth it. It's not every day that a 22 year old girl is in love with a 65 year old man."

The 26th arrived; party goods were purchased. Rose and Carl were driving toward Old Panama when the realization that he was 65 years old struck him. Piloting here in Panama had made time stand still for him. He did not feel or think like an old man.

They arrived at Maria's home about 1700. It was a beautiful, clear night. A gentle breeze was blowing and all the stars were out, shining brightly. In Panama during the dry season the sky is clear; it appears that you can just reach up and pick a bucketful of stars—romance for sure.

After unloading all the "loot" with the help of the other guests, the music started. Beer cans and soda pop cans popped all around; scotch and soda flowed freely. Maria's father was an alcoholic, but a very likeable, jovial, and honest person. Carl liked him best of all the male guests. Later Carl found out that he died a few years later. He was a fairly young man.

Maria had a cousin staying with her whose name was Yolanda, a very pretty young woman, 26 years old, dark skinned. Like many Panamanians, she was part Spanish, Indian, Chinese, and African. She had a lovely, slender, figure and a bright smile. Things went very well until Maria and Yolanda continued to find every excuse to sit next to Carl. Whenever Maria got up to dance, go to the powder room, or to see to the other guests, Yolanda took the seat next to Carl. The two women glared at each other.

Yolanda asked Carl if he had ever been to Davíd, a city of approximately 50,000 people in the northern province of Chíriqui. Carl told her that he had not. Yolanda had been raised by her father in a small town near Davíd. When Yolanda was five years old, her mother had an accident. The medical attention she got at the Social Security Hospital was so poor that she died. Yolanda said her older sister, Aida, became the mother she never had. Aida worked and did whatever she had to do in order to send her siblings to school. She paid for their schooling through grade 12 and sent Yolanda to college in Davíd. There she studied journalism for three and a half years in the evening and served as a governess for two boys during the day.

There are many horses in the province of Chíriqui, where Davíd is located. The pasture grass there is much like the blue grass in Kentucky, so many race horses are bred and raised there. Some Kentucky Derby winners have come from Chíriqui. Yolanda had a boyfriend for eight years whose family was wealthy and had many horses. Jorge and Yolanda took many a horseback ride together. They decided they wanted to get married, but when Jorge asked his parents for their blessing, they refused. His father told Jorge that Yolanda was not from a well-to-do family and that her skin was too dark. If Jorge married Yolanda, his family would disown him. Sadly, Jorge told Yolanda that he could not marry her. Heartbroken, Yolanda went to Panama City to visit her cousin, Maria.

Yolanda invited Carl to go to Davíd for a visit and stay with her family. He told her that he would finish his work cycle in about two weeks and then he could go. Maria, sitting on the other side of Carl, piped up, "Yolanda's grandmother is a relative of mine. My mother and I would like to go to Chíriqui when you go."

"Okay," Carl agreed.

The party ended quite late. On the way home Carl sorted out his feelings about the two girls. There was no doubt about it. He liked Yolanda much better. It was really no contest in Carl's mind. The two weeks of his work cycle soon passed and he prepared for the trip to Davíd.

When Carl went to pick up Maria and her mother, there were four people packed to go, Maria, her father, mother, and sister. Carl's Montero was loaded with soda pop, beer, whiskey, peanuts, potato chips, and other groceries. Carl knew Yolanda's family was not well-to-do and would appreciate these items. This is just one of the many ways that Carl's generous nature manifested itself.

They traveled through the countryside of rolling hills, with large trees and mountains in the distance. It took most of the day to cover the approximately 300 miles to David; then on another 10 miles or so to Yolanda's home. It was a small house made of concrete blocks, stuccoed and painted white. It had a corrugated zinc roof, no ceilings, and polished concrete floors. The windows consisted of perforated concrete blocks. There was an apartment size gas stove and one small cupboard in the kitchen.

In the narrow living room was a small table, four chairs, shelf unit with tape player, TV and other small items, loveseat and chair. There were no rugs in the house. In the yard were many banana and plantain trees. Yolanda picked cilantro growing under the banana trees.

Yolanda assigned Carl a bedroom, while she and Maria slept on the floor in sleeping bags. Maria could have stayed with her mother's relatives, but she did not want Yolanda to win Carl in her absence. Carl enjoyed his visit. Everyone in Yolanda's family was friendly and gave him a warm welcome.

Yolanda told Carl that the university in David was small and that she needed to attend six months of classes in Panama City to finish her degree, but she had no money for supplies or lodging. Carl told her that his mother had died a year ago, that he had a very large house with an attached one-bedroom apartment. "If you will come and stay with me, I will help you finish your college degree," Carl told her, but he thought, "Little Red Riding Hood and the big, bad wolf."

Yolanda said she would have to talk it over with her father and she would let Carl know. On the return trip to Balboa Maria and her family were very cool. Carl took them home; they did not even say "Thank You."

Two weeks later Yolanda called and told Carl that she would like to come to Panama City to stay with Carl and attend college, but she had no money for busfare. Carl sent her $400, but it never left the Balboa Post office. However, Aida got Yolanda a ticket; she arrived in a few days.

A few days after that Yolanda's sister, Nelda, arrived. Carl let her stay with Yolanda. Nelda attended the YMCA school to study English. The two girls redecorated Carl's house, cooked and cleaned. Rose quit. Carl gave her $2,000 for her loyal service.

7

BEFORE THE "INVASION" OF 1989

Ethnicity of Canal Builders

Groups of pilots enjoyed getting together on their days off. They often gathered at one of the pilot's homes. The party was held in the back yard, all strung with lights. There was music playing on the stereo and dancing on the patio. One day a number of pilots were discussing canal building history, wondering what the impact of total Panamanian takeover in 1999 would be on the continuing operation of the canal. Carl enjoyed reading about the history of the canal. He was a relative newcomer compared to pilots who had been on the job for many years, and he wanted to be cognizant of the backgrounds of the people, their ethnic traits, their present impact and future prospects. He enjoyed offering facts that he had recently read in several books.

"I wonder why there are so many different kinds of people here in this little country. I can understand the Spanish being here. Panama was settled by the Spanish just like the rest of Central America. I know there are basically three groups of Indians here as well, the Guami in the north, San Blas off the coast of Panama City, and the Choco group, those primitive ones in the jungles of the Darien Peninsula. Where did all the rest of them come from?" inquired Bill Thomas.

Carl thought he knew the answer. "According to the records ninety-seven countries were represented in the canal building work force. Skilled craftsmen, professionals like engineers and doctors, and unskilled laborers were needed. Chinese labor gangs were brought in until China stopped allowing them to come, fearing that their own source of cheap labor would dry up. Southern congressmen in the United States objected to southern blacks working in the canal for the same reason. John Stevens, the railroad construction expert, imported Spanish groups from the Basque region in northern Spain. He liked them best, since they were hard workers and intelligent men. But so many workers were needed that recruiters went back to the Caribbean. So many Jamaican blacks suffered and died working for the French that few of them would work for the Americans.[iii] The Jamaicans who came to Panama did so of their own free will and were mostly skilled technicians. The Americans recruited almost twenty thousand workers from Barbados. About 7,500 men came from Martinique and Guadeloupe. They were given a contract, free passage to Colón, and free passage back home if they wanted to go. The U.S. didn't leave anybody stranded in Panama. Workers' relatives and descendants couldn't scream and holler that the Americans were a bunch of bastards who only paid ten or fifteen cents an hour and worked them like dogs all day. This might be true, but they came of their own free will and they didn't have to stay. They talk about white, skilled workers being paid in gold and unskilled blacks being paid in silver. It was easy to pay in silver coin, worth about half that of the gold coin, when the unskilled workers were being paid ten or fifteen cents an hour. The engineers, crane operators, surveyors and highly skilled workers in the machine shops would have had to have a sack to haul off all the silver coin they were due, so they were paid in gold."

"I guess that explains how we got such a mixed up group of people here. From what I can see, they all intermarried, so now a lot of the people are a Heinz 57 mixture," Bill remarked, "I heard that stories went around about schoolteachers and skilled craftsmen doing unskilled work like serving steaks to engineers. I also heard that blacks almost never got to be a supervisor over white men. Sounds like South Africa. What do you say about that, Carl?"

"Yeah, I read about that. If you were black whatever skills you had were ignored. You just loaded and unloaded cement or carried lumber or delivered messages or waited tables. But in a way, you can't blame those in charge entirely. I read about three men loading a wheelbarrow. When it was full, two of the men loaded it on the back of the third man who carried it away."

All the pilots laughed at that one. They all got another round of whatever they were having. About that time some of the wives came by. "I can see you guys are 'dropping anchors' again. Don't you ever get tired of telling each other about the transits and sea voyages you've made?" Carol, Bill's wife, asked.

"Honey, this time you've got it all wrong. We were having a sophisticated discussion about Panama Canal History." Bill stuck out his chest, put his thumbs under his armpits, and strutted.

"Okay, okay, but you usually are not only high, but also on the high seas somewhere. It's a wonder you ex-sea captains ever came ashore." Carol defended.

"It's just for such juicy, soft things as you that I came ashore," Bill intoned as he pulled Carol on his lap.

"Carol, how about a dance?" asked one of the other pilots who wasn't much interested in the canal's history.

"Sure, Andy. Okay, Bill?"

Bill nodded his head, released Carol, and continued his conversation with Carl as Carol and Andy whirled away to the music. Carl had been thinking about the Panamanians' role in running the canal. Then he said, "To my way of thinking the American government made a grave mistake when they hired Panamanians to run the canal. They didn't hire any of them to speak of to build it because they were worthless, skinny, weak, lazy, and spoke only Spanish. Professionals and skilled labor was European, and the biggest part of the unskilled labor force came from the Caribbean. Virtually no Panamanians worked to build the canal. You could set them all down at your dinner table and have room for more; that is about how many Panamanians worked to help build the canal. A guy named Robert Wood made a report about the canal builders. He wrote that the bulk of the building work on the canal was done by West Indian carpenters, masons and painters. Stevens changed the diet of the West Indian blacks from rice and yams to more nourishing food. Then they were better workers. In the meantime the Spanish from Basque had trouble with the heat. Near the end of the construction the West Indians worked just as well as the Spanish or Americans."

"If you know so much about it, Carl, tell us about the houses the canal builders had. I heard living conditions were pretty awful, especially for the blacks," said Hank, another one of the pilots.

"Okay, Hank. It just so happens that Robert Wood wrote about that, too. He wrote that during construction days quarters were issued to the workers, one square foot for each dollar he earned. The wives got one square foot per dollar earned by their husbands. You can see, Bill, that the blacks, who were paid much less than the whites, had very little space to live in. If they were single, they lived in barracks, just a string of cots, double deckers, with no screens on the windows to keep the malaria and yellow fever mosquitoes out. Married blacks found shacks in the jungle. For a long time how much you made determined what kind of house you lived in. Somewhere down the line the Zonies had this changed. When I got down to Panama, the person with the most seniority, regardless of occupation or pay, could bid on the best house he could find. I was brought down here as a pilot and put in a little two room apartment in Colón, while big, beautiful houses on the waterfront were mostly occupied by truck drivers and other people paid a lower wage. I think it was wrong, but that was the way they did it. This was sure the reverse of the way it was while the canal was being built.

After it was completed the U.S. should have only hired foreign nationals, not Panamanians to work in the canal. They needed to repay the people from the Caribbean, Jamaica, Trinidad, and other places, for their loyal service digging the canal. All they had when they hired Panamanians was a bunch of foxes running around in the Panama Canal chicken house. It pleased the Panamanian government not to hire people from the outside."

Carl went on, "Panama is out to get all it can. The Panamanian government took advantage of the United States to get the Carter-Torrijos treaty through. I think Panama blackmailed the United States with Russia, Cuba, and Nicaragua and threatened another war like we had in Vietnam. They pushed the new treaty because our government was embarrassed over the children being shot up in Vietnam. But, believe me, I was in Saigon when the Tet offensive occurred. I saw soldiers walk down the street and have hand grenades thrown at them by kids seven, eight, nine, ten years old. I think they went overboard to shoot up tiny children, but it was nothing for children to be Vietnamese in the daytime and be big, bad Viet Cong all night long. In every deep-water port I saw children no more than 12 years old with rifles and hand grenades as part of the Viet Cong. You didn't know what their loyalties were and children were involved in the war. When the war ended, the Viet Cong didn't surrender. The Americans just backed out and left all their equipment to the South Vietnamese army. In one respect the Americans actually won the war because the spread of communism throughout all of Southeast Asia was halted. Look at them now; there is no threat from anybody. The countries are all turning toward democracy."

"Yeah, I was there too and saw what you saw. Well, let's think of happier things. The evening went on in a similar fashion until the wives finally called a halt and asked to go home. A few of the pilots had an early morning transit and had to get some rest. The party broke up and the sober ones drove the party home.

Panama as a State

In 1989 there were two Panamanian pilots on a Scandinavian Panamax ship, a big bulk carrier nearly 950 feet long with 106 foot beam requiring four pilots. The Panamanian pilots were Eckert and Marino, along with another pilot named Jerry Murphy, and Carl Turner. The ship was in Limón Bay, loaded to the gills, waiting for the word from transit to proceed through Gatun Locks. Carl always enjoyed getting on Spanish, Portuguese, Japanese, Chilean, and Ecuadorian as well as Scandinavian ships. Shrimp, Carlsberg beer, and fine wines are served on these ships. They have some of the finest restaurants in the world on board. Carl enjoyed the wonderful food. Jerry and Carl were talking to Eckert and Marino when the subject of canal ownership came up. Murphy asked, "How come the Americans didn't take over Panama and make it one of the United States when they had a chance to rather than giving Panama its independence?"

Carl recalled another conversation with another pilot about the same subject. "We were talking to Kincaid. He was laying it on about how the U. S. didn't want Panama and how his grandfather got 10 cents an hour for his labor during the building of the canal. Kincaid thought that Panama should have had the canal a long time ago since the U. S. didn't want to make Panama a state. The U.S. held on to it. What do you think about that, Jerry? You were there."

"Yeah, that's right," Jerry agreed, "You remember from reading books about building the canal and the conditions in Panama when gold was discovered in California. A whole bunch of Americans came through here and found the streets barely above water and filled with raw sewage, garbage, and swamp water. Dead cats and dogs were all over the place. Buzzards were circling overhead. The stench from unwashed bodies as well as that rising from the streets was appalling. Who would want to have a country like this? This was way before the Americans got involved in Panama. The first railroad had to be completely rebuilt by

John Stevens after the U. S. took over. I don't know why anyone would stay here longer than to rush across the isthmus. I guess their greed for gold in California fueled their energy and determination. Did you read about this, Carl?"

"Yes, I read about it. I read about the poverty and disease; yellow fever and malaria were the worst in addition to typhoid. There was even an outbreak of the plague. I didn't hear about the native Panamanians dying of these diseases, but I'm sure they did. When the U. S. started negotiating, they didn't want to own Panama. They just wanted to put a canal through here and clean up this stinking mess. They offered Colombia $10 million for the right to dig across their country, but Colombia wanted more money, so they wouldn't agree. In the meantime the French Canal company was in financial trouble and was accused of squandering the money until it finally went bankrupt. Ferdinand de Lesseps was accused of fraud, but he was old and sick, so he never served time. Phillippe Bunau-Varilla, the main French engineer, appointed himself as French ambassador to the United States and met with Amador."

"Who was this Amador, anyway?" Jerry wanted to know, "I know there is a tug and a road named Amador."

"Well, he started out as Doctor Manuel Amador Guerrero. He was chief physician of the Panama railroad. He came to New York to arrange for a revolutionary Panamanian takeover. Amador and Bunau-Varilla met. Bunau-Varilla wanted to sell the French Canal company and recover the money he lost in the French effort. Amador wanted Panamanian independence from Colombia. Teddy Roosevelt was livid over Colombia's refusal of the $10 million, but wanted a canal dug because he was convinced of the importance of sea power after his experience in the Spanish-American War. Amador and Roosevelt met; Roosevelt agreed not to oppose a Panamanian revolution. In fact, he stationed American gunboats at the entrance to Colon and Panama City harbors.

Even when the Colombian General Esteban Huertas surrendered his troops for $65,000, paying each man $50, half of them went back to Colombia, but the other half stayed here and became Panamanian citizens. The general was all decked out with turkey feathers in his hat, about two pounds of gold chains draped across his uniform, gold epaulets on his shoulders, shiny black boots halfway up his legs, a long sword dangling at his side. He was just a short, little guy, strutting around. I bet he looked silly. Anyway, Huertas and Amador had agreed to this arrangement and that the revolution was to take place on the afternoon of November 3, 1903. The only casualties were a donkey and a Chinese shopkeeper asleep in his store. After the revolution, Roosevelt told the Secretary of State, John Hay, to meet with Amador and draw up a treaty. The result was the Hay-Bunau-Varilla Treaty of 1903 which gave Panama $10 million and the French government $40 million for purchase of the French Canal Company. I understand that a lot of that money went into Bunau-Varilla's pocket. Then Amador was elected President of Panama. Don't talk so much about what a Panamanian patriot you are, Eckert. The Colombians are your ancestors. They betrayed their own country and stayed here for money. Anything you want here you can get it if you have money."

Carl was fiercely loyal to his native country, the United States. Neither Eckert nor Marino had said anything during this verbal exchange. They couldn't get a word in edgewise if they had wanted to. They were loyal to Panama and wanted their country to own the Panama Canal and the Panama Canal Zone. Because of the canal's importance to international shipping, they knew the canal and zone to be very valuable assets, which would put Panama in the forefront of the world stage. They knew they would be pilots long after Carl Turner and Jerry Murphy had retired. They just exchanged knowing glances and grinned.

"I think Kincaid was right. I don't think the negotiators wanted to annex Panama to the United States and make a state out of it. It would have been bad politics for the rest of Central and South America. But you bet it was filthy," Jerry agreed.

Carl recalled another conversation with Kincaid, "The captain of the ship I was transiting said, 'Every time you turn around these Panamanians are rioting in the streets and burning things down, warring against each other and the United States. Why do you suppose they renamed the Thatcher Ferry Bridge? It was the name of the ferry that went across the place where the new bridge was built. It was an historic name."

Kincaid answered in an irritated tone, "We didn't want it named after that ferry. It was France and the United States that dredged the channel through the area where the bridge presently spans. Before the channel was dredged as part of the canal for ocean going vessels, there was nothing but a shallow channel crossed by Thatcher's ferry in that place. If the channel hadn't been dredged, we wouldn't have needed a damn bridge. Besides, Bridge of the Americas is a better name. Panama is one of the Americas just as much as the United States. Remember that."

"Well, let's get on with this transit. Captain, are your engines all tested?" Carl asked.

"Yes, Mr. Pilot. We're all ready to go."

"Put your pilot flag up over 10. Do you have any dangerous cargo on board?"

"No, we have a full load of grain."

"Well, that's fine, Captain. Tell the chief mate to start heaving up. We're going to get under way here. As soon as he has his anchor up, let me know."

Carl spoke into his radio, "Transit, transit, this is south 10 calling for a radio check."

"Good morning, Captain Turner. You will have the west side at about 1100. Your locomotives will all be back. Your tugs will be the Goethals and the Culebra."

"Okay. Thank you very much."

Colombia and France

Carl was living as 3216 Empire Street, Balboa. The Balboa Yacht Club was on his way home from the pilothouse on Naos Island. He often stopped there and enjoyed a beer or two with some of the other pilots. On one of these occasions he was at the bar when one of the pilots said, "The only thing that struck me was this deal with Colombia. The United States signed a treaty with Colombia in which Americans were granted equal rights and free transit across the canal. The United States was to respect and protect Colombia's sovereignty. Hey, Carl, you've read about this. What do you say about it?"

Carl was glad to oblige. He told the group, "The very beginning was in 1870 with Ferdinand de Lesseps, the French engineer who had successfully built the Suez Canal. His company ran out of money and had all kinds of trouble with disease, equipment that was too small, trying to make a sea level canal in mountainous country that has to cross a continental divide, as well as other problems. His company was about to go under. Finally, on October 20, 1894, the French incorporated a new company, Compagnie Nouvelle du canal de Panama in order to comply with the provision that the Wyse Concession would be extended until 1903. The Wyse Concession was the agreement with Colombia that gave the U.S. the right to construct a canal across the Isthmus of Panama. Some of the big American financiers figured this new organization was nothing better than an assembly of crooks. Colombia had a contract with the original French company, but now the agreement has been broken because the company was no more. Everything should have reverted back to Colombia rather than having been put up for sale to anybody who would buy it. That's not good business, I don't think. All the time the Panamanians were trying to build a country in preparation for seceding from Colombia; they didn't have anything. I think Teddy Roosevelt secretly ordered the U. S. Navy to support the little Panamanian revolution. He knew what was coming. There is nothing on record anywhere saying that Roosevelt supported the revolution, but after Panama said they had broken away from Colombia, the U. S. quickly recognized their sovereignty. It was the Americans, not the Panamanians who took control, including the railroad. They had cut off the Colombian military by sending all the trains to the other side of the isthmus, leaving them in Colón. The generals were taken to Panama City and locked up. Colombia's general and colonel and military personnel were paid off in American dollars to commit treason against their own country."

United States Treatment of Panama

"How do you think the U.S. has treated Panama, Carl?" asked Joe, another pilot, "There is a lot of resentment built up against U.S. citizens."

"Every conceivable concession has been given to the Panamanian people at the expense of the United States. The U.S. paved the roads; Dr. Gorgas spent a year and a half exterminating the mosquitoes and making the country healthy and sanitary, built hospitals and housing. The U.S. brought Panama up to date largely through the efforts of the military organizer Lt. Colonel George Goethals. Why, we even taught them how to pasteurize milk and then gave them the equipment and all the cows to do it with; then we bought milk from Panama. Why, do you know that since World War II Panama has been one of the countries that has gotten the most money from the U.S. in grants? My girlfriend's aunt got a grant from the United States to build her family a little house in a little village near Davíd. I'm glad she did; all the family had before that was two little buildings made of bamboo with outside plumbing, cooking pit, and oven. They are mighty grateful to the Americans and have a good attitude. I wish all Panamanians were like that, but unfortunately there is a lot of resentment toward Americans on the part of many Panamanians. The money that the military personnel spends down here sure benefits the economy! What do you think about that, Joe?"

"I don't really know. It seems to me that when politicians want something, they will make most anything go their way whether it's right or not."

"Yes, Joe, I guess that's about right," agreed Carl. "You see what their ancestors were and what they are today. They'd commit treason and God knows what all to take over this canal."

The group was left with various opinions about the rightful ownership of the Panama Canal, the Panama Canal Zone, and the entire country of Panama. In addition they all wondered about the future of the canal, the politics and economy of the country, the impact on world trade, and future relations with the United States.

Illegal Free Zone Purchases

There were two port captains who complained continuously from the time Carl was a P.I.T. until the time he retired. As soon as they could they worked themselves into official jobs in the canal. In 1987 it was rumored that they used government cars to go into the Free Zone in Cristobol, under the guise of making purchases for the Panama Canal Commission, while, in reality, they were taking the goods they bought to Balboa and selling them on the black market. Then, too, they had their sisters and other relatives peddle some of the goods in the offices where they worked.

It was also rumored that the top officials on the hill were importing luxury foreign cars, such as BMW's, Mercedes Benzs, and Volvos duty free. They resold them at a staggering profit. Although Carl had no proof of these practices, access to the Free Zone is now highly restricted. He thought of the saying, 'Forty thousand Frenchmen can't be wrong'.

Russian Tankers to Nicaragua

One morning during the rainy season, which lasts in Panama from December through May, Carl looked out his window and saw his jitney parked in his driveway. When he opened the door to get in, he saw his old friend, Jerry, inside. The two pilots greeted each other, "Good morning, Carl."

"Good morning, Jerry. It looks like we got a good one today."

The pilots had heard from MTC that they would be transiting a new ship.

"Yeah, I hope so. There's a whole lot of rain falling in that canal, though. The skies were just black when we passed over the Bridge of the Americas. I could barely see Miraflores Locks."

"I guess we will get over to Cristobol. They have had a bit of trouble. A helicopter hit some wires and the army blocked off the highway for awhile."

"I heard the highway is open now. I guess we will get started this morning at about 1000 and we should be home at 2000 or 2100 or 2200 tonight."

"Yeah, transits are good when you have a friendly pilot and captain- somebody you like and you get along fine. No matter how rusty the ship is, or how dirty or grimy or grouchy people are, we're happy. Isn't that right?"

"Yeah, Carl, that's right. This is a good ship. We should be able to just play with it and have a wonderful day."

The jitney ride would take an hour or so, since it had to cross the entire isthmus to get from Balboa to Cristobol. On the way Jerry asked Carl, "Say, listen, didn't you hear about the latest big whing whang up there on the hill?"

"No, I haven't heard a thing."

"They say it is on the hill, but I don't think it's gone anywhere except just among the pilots. President Reagan ordered the port closed. He had it mined and had the U.S. Navy stand offshore so that he could put an end to the contras. When he gets through with the contras, he is going to go for Cuba and the rest of these communist nut, fruit cakes around here. I even heard that when Castro came to Panama he went to see the president of Panama, Arias. They had a discussion in which Castro told Arias, 'When are you going to kick all these gringos out of here?' Arias replied, 'Just as soon as you kick them all out of Guantanamo.' Anyway, a Russian tanker struck a mine and killed a Russian sailor. Guess who was running the ship? By golly, he was a Panama Canal pilot. You've got it right. His name was Harris, one of my worst enemies. When I was learning piloting, he was a nasty son of a bitch. I hated to even see him."

"Yeah, I know him. You know the Panama Canal pilots are working for the United States government. Why would they take Russian tankers to Nicaragua?"

"Well, Carl, they are given something like $8,000 to $15,000 to make each trip. It takes only about a week. That's a lot of money. That's more than they can make here by far. They just take time off from working here in the canal and run those ships up there."

"Well, greed is greed. I think it is un-American, myself."

"Yeah, me, too."

"Thank you, Jerry, for that information."

When the jitney arrived at Cristobol, Jerry and Carl boarded a new Colombian ship built in Poland. It was about 700' long and had a lot of power. It had thrusters and was easy to handle. They just played with that boat and had a wonderful day.

By the time Carl got off that ship in Balboa he had made up his mind what he would do with the information Jerry had given him. He was disgusted with American pilots, making $100,000, or even more with overtime and start bonus pay, betraying their country for extra pay. Pilots' pay had been greatly upgraded since Carl started piloting in 1978. Pilots were scarce and essential to operate the canal.

The next morning after he got his job call and had his assignment to go out at 1700 hours the next afternoon, he got in his little Montero and immediately went to the American embassy. Across the street and a block or so down from the ambassador's home are the consulate offices where Panamanians line up around the block for visas and the like. There was a sort of "bull pen" downstairs where people get visas to go to the states for fifteen to sixty days. There were many Panamanians working in the embassy. Carl showed his passport to the marine guard in a bulletproof glass cage. Carl told him that he was a Panama Canal pilot and that he thought it was very important, even urgent, that he talk to the chief consulate or to the ambassador or members of his staff.

Carl didn't have to stand in line, but was shown right in. He was checked through the metal detectors. Then he went upstairs to one of the inspection cages and told one of the Panamanian girls who was clerking there that he had some information that would be extremely embarrassing to President Reagan. She called for the consulate who came out and asked Carl, "Who are you?"

"My name is Carl Turner, and I am a Panama Canal pilot."

"Do you have any identification?"

"Yes, I do." Carl gave the consulate his identification.

"You just come with me."

He led Carl into a big conference room with comfortable chairs.

"Would you like any coffee?" he asked.

"No, I'm just fine."

Carl must have been in there for at least twenty minutes. Then about ten or fifteen men came in and introduced themselves. The chief consulate was there, another consul, the secretary to the ambassador, and other people with recording equipment.

"Why have I been sitting here waiting for so long?" Carl asked.

"It's routine. We know all about you from the first day you went to sea. You were in the airborne army, in the merchant marine for 32 years and have been piloting here for ten years. You are a senior pilot. You have an absolutely immaculate record. That's why all these gentlemen are here. They know this is very important and there is not going to be a lot of superfluous nonsense. Okay, now tell us what you got."

Carl reported what he had heard concerning the story about pilots taking Russian tankers to Nicaragua. He told them that the pilot Harris and six others were boarding Russian tankers in Panama and piloting them to Nicaragua and assisting the ships to be moored in Nicaragua and assisting them to pump their oil cargo ashore in Nicaragua. They were running the blockade that Reagan had set up through the minefields. A day or two ago one of the tankers struck a mine and killed a Russian sailor. Carl told them he got this information through the grapevine from another pilot friend of his named Jerry as they were driving in the jitney to Cristobol. Carl also told them, "I know who these pilots are and I know where they get their jobs. It's ESSO. They have not changed their name to EXXON. They are right over here on the highway in a big beautiful building on the left. They have a big blackboard in there where they get jobs for Panamanians and other foreigners on ships. They import oil for Panamanian civilians and for the Panamanian government. They have a big tank farm near here. Something ought to be done about it."

The diplomats were absolutely flabbergasted.

The chief consulate addressed Carl, "Captain Turner, we thank you and your government thanks you. This matter will be taken care of. We can assure you of that. Can we have a car and driver take you home or wherever you want to go?"

"No, thank you. I have my own car here."

"You will never hear about this again, and no one will ever know that you were in this building today," assured the consulate.

"Thank you, I appreciate that. But I hate this Harris so bad that I wouldn't care if he did know it."

"We don't operate that way. There is a lunchroom here. Please feel free to be our guest to make yourself a sandwich and have a coke."

"No, I gotta get back home. I got a transit this afternoon. I'm glad I came here. I feel a lot better about it."

"Well, we are certainly glad you came here."

Carl shook hands with the gentlemen and went home. He didn't hear anything about this business until a week later. He was again riding with some pilots to the pilothouse. There must have been about eight or ten pilots waiting for their launches to go out and board ships at anchor. Carl heard them talking.

"Hey, Smith, did you ever hear about the pilots who have been taking ships up to Nicaragua?" asked one of the pilots.

Everybody knew about it.

Smith answered, "Hey, man, look, the United States government, big powerful consulates, and ambassadors they got 'em all up there in front of the commissioner and all the big shots up on the hill. The way I understand it, and I got it from Jeffries, he said that they told them 'If you take one more ship up there and run the Nicaraguan blockade, you're going to lose your job here.' They answered that they were American citizens. But I know that Harris was a naturalized citizen. How he got his U. S. citizenship I don't know, but he came from Iceland. The pilots asserted that they were free American people, not Russians, and they would go ahead and do it anyway. Then they left."

Carl heard no more about it until he found out that there were seven pilots on suspension. The gossip was that it was not known whether they would be fired or not, but they sure were on suspension. A week later they were back working in the canal. The word was, however, that the pilots were told, "This is for real! If you take one more Russian ship or, for that matter, any foreign ship anywhere, you won't be on suspension. You are an employee of the United States government. We will terminate your employment here. You will have to face a good many complicated charges as well."

That did it. That was the end of the blockade running. No one says anything about the incident. They just go quietly about the business of piloting ships through the Panama Canal. Carl was so happy. Just before he retired, he told everybody, "I turned them in. You bet it was old Carl Turner. I'm glad I did. Anything else that I find out that will affect my country adversely I will report that any day in the week."

Carl knew how Harris got to the United States. He used his sea time on foreign ships to qualify him to go to the Coast Guard and set for an American license provided he is a citizen. He got to be a citizen by marrying an American girl. As soon as he got his American citizenship, he kicked the American girl in the street and then sent for his foreign girl-friend and married her. Lots of men did this. There were about 10 or 15 pilots in the Panama Canal who had never sailed aboard an American ship.

The Guide's Information

Early in 1989 Carl was piloting a passenger ship, one of the "Love Boats." They came up Gatun Reach approaching Gatun Locks. To the right is a narrow river that looked a lot like a canal leading off into the jungle. A tourist guide on the bridge was on the speaker telling the passengers all about the Panama Canal and announcing points of interest. Carl pointed toward the canal-like river and told him, "Do you see that little strip of a canal over there to the right? Fifty thousand people died digging that canal."

Carl was just joking with the guide, but do you know, the darn fool piped that false information over the loud speaker.

Six Months Before the "Invasion"

In 1989 General Manuel Noriega was in power. His predecessor was Omar Torrijos, the same man who had signed the Carter-Torrijos treaty of 1977. Torrijos died in a freak plane accident in 1981. It was rumored that Noreiga had a bomb planted in the plane. In any case, from the time Noreiga seized power until December 20, 1989, conditions in

Panama consistently worsened both for the Panamanians and the Americans. Under Torrijos the country went into debt. The debt worsened under Noreiga. The "Guardia", as the National Guard was called, Noreiga's 'Dignity Battalions', or 'dignidads' (the American military called them 'dingbats'), and other government workers were paid with checks dated six months in advance. The Guardia acted as a national police force and pulled over people, especially Americans who had more money than Panamanians, for any traffic infractions they could dream up, real or imagined. Several times Carl was pulled over. Most of the time he was allowed to proceed by giving the Guardia money.

One such instance occurred in November of 1989. Carl was heading down Balboa Road when he sighted a serious traffic situation. To avoid the jam Carl cut through a parking lot in front of the port captain's office building. Just after he crossed over a set of railroad tracks, a Guardia pulled him over. He just stood and looked at Carl without saying anything. Carl asked him what the problem was. He just kept pointing at the traffic light. Carl started to leave. The Guardia officer pulled his gun. Carl stopped. The officer held out his hand, but still he said nothing.

Carl had been to a casino the day before and had a roll of quarters in his car's glove compartment. He handed the officer the roll of quarters. The officer unrolled the wrapper and examined the quarters. Carl told him in Spanish that there were no more quarters, "No mas."

The officer motioned Carl to go. Carl went. Although Carl had $100 in his wallet, he had determined that the officer had gotten all that he was going to get. At this time the U.S. sanctions against Panama were really hurting everyone who needed cash. The Guardia could draw food from the warehouse, but no one else could get any. Therefore, the people with guns were fed, but the poor people had very little. The U.S. put economic sanctions in place against Panama to pressure Noriega. Since currency in Panama is the American dollar, stopping the flow of American dollars worked a hardship on many people.

Paying off the Guardia on the spot didn't always work, however. Several times, Carl had to go to court. When his name was called, he answered by calling out, "Aquí es Carlo Dinero." (Here is Carl Money.)

A chuckle invariably went through the crowd gathered in the courtroom. Everybody knew just what he meant. He was there to pay a fine. The money would allow him to leave.

The Guardia also confiscated farms, cars, private property and businesses by saying, "Give your new business partner, Colonel Gonzales half of what this property is worth." Any name was used to get the property.

A Panamanian friend of Carl's told him that someone had stolen his new Mitsubishi Montero. He went to the Panamanian police at the motor pool across the street from Noreiga's headquarters. There he talked to a Guardia captain and told him that he had spotted his Montero in the corner of the yard. The Guardia officer told the car owner to prove his ownership. Carl's friend went to the Montero, lifted the carpet and showed him evidence of his sole ownership, his name engraved in the metal, just as he had reported it. The captain called soldiers and had the Montero owner thrown off the lot. The captain told the Montero owner that if he ever came back he would be shot. The captain emphatically stated, "This is **my** jeep, you understand!"

U.S. Military Guns Muzzled; Officers Shot; Wives Raped

Carl went to the commissary at Fort Clayton one day. When he arrived at the gate, he could not get in due to a crowd of Panamanians blocking the entrance. They had large Panamanian flags and threw rocks at the guard shack. The captain called for more guards. They appeared and blocked the Panamanians' forward progress.

The captain ordered the crowd, "Stand back. If you come any further, I will order my men to open fire. The treaty calls for the U.S. military to be present to protect the canal."

The crowd continued to hurl insults and rocks. The American soldiers moved forward with bayonets drawn and backed the crowd into the street. Nothing else was done. The United States government had muzzled the military. They couldn't do anything. They were kicked around and spit on. Just before the war a couple of the officers got shot, Carl heard it was in the back, running a road block hastily thrown up by Panamanians on a main street going to Panama City. Everyone seemed to be bending over backward to do nothing to aggravate the Panamanians in spite of the fact that they had violated the treaty. The treaty said that military people could go from post to post without being harassed. General Woerner, commanding officer of the Southern Command, or South Com, didn't do anything about it. He was drinking cocktails and entertaining the colonels and Panamanian higher ups. They were going to dances and social parties. All his officers got commissary and PX privileges that pilots didn't have. The government was bending over backward to make Panama happy. Never mind what it took to make them happy.

On another occasion, several naval officers were taking their wives to Panama City to a restaurant to have dinner and get off the naval base. They were in a downtown area in Panama City called Chorrillo, close to Noriega's general headquarters. Calle Balboa was a main thoroughfare going past there. A person wouldn't know it was a military complex if he hadn't lived in Panama City. The naval officers were stopped and pushed around. The story Carl and other pilots got in the Canal was that the officers were pulled out of their automobiles and shot. Their wives were also pulled from their automobiles, dragged into the street, and raped by Panamanians. The pilots had no proof of that, but from the hearsay, they believed that it actually happened. This helped to set this war off, in addition to the fact that Noriega got up on his podium, banged a machete on the table, and declared war against the United States.

In September 1989, Carl was on his four-week-off-period. He had flown to the United States and was staying in his condominium on the ocean at Daytona Beach, Florida. There he heard the news of the naval officers being shot and their wives raped. His brother-in-law, a retired U.S. Naval officer, warned him that a war was coming, and he had better get back to Panama and protect the girls in his home. Carl took the next flight out to stay with Yolanda and her sister Nelda. Carl flew out on the last plane that left Miami before hurricane Hugo struck. He could see the eye of the hurricane from the plane window just before it hit mainland Florida. As soon as he reached Panama, he stocked up on water and groceries, filling the cupboards.

School Bus Incident

One day in November of 1989 a school bus full of children was on its way home from U.S. schools in the Zone to Panama City. Many members of the U.S. military forces lived in Panama City, since there was not sufficient housing for them on military bases in the Zone. In addition, a good many Panamanians paid to go to the American public schools. The buses took the children home. One day the Guardia stopped this bus full of school children. They jacked up the bus, hooked a tow truck to the front of it, towed it to a Panamanian military base in Panama City, and held all the children in the bus. The children screamed and cried.

The American military was informed about the situation. A U.S. army major, his driver, and some military police went to the Panamanian military base and ordered the Panamanian colonels and army personnel to release the bus. They refused. The American officer in charge told the Panamanian colonel to either release the bus or he was going to call for some heavy back-up. He didn't care whether General Woerner was "in their pocket" or not. He would ignore the directives that had muzzled the American military from taking action against the Panamanians. He would show them they had gone too far. They had stepped over the boundary when they commandeered the bus. The colonel refused to release the bus. The major called for reinforcements. A huge helicopter armed to the teeth was dispatched. It flew to the site and hovered over the Panamanians. Its laser beam locked on the Panamanian military personnel. It was poised to open fire on the major's command. The major assured the Panamanian colonel that there would be nothing left. The colonel told his men to stand back and release the bus. The tow truck was disconnected from the bus. The colonel told the bus driver to go on his way. The major and his driver followed the bus until all the children had been taken home.

Plight of Zonians

When the Zone was turned over to Panama in October, 1979, the Panamanians turned on the Zonians. They had to go into Panamanian territory to buy food and all their services. The only thing that was open was a bottle store. Everything else had to be bought from Panama. Americans were not promoted anymore; at least that was the impression the pilots had. Panamanians were placed in charge. It looked like the Zonies got the worst treatment. Many of the Zonies had married Latinos from different countries—Costa Rica, Colombia, and others. Some of these women had passports from about three countries, Colombia, Costa Rica, and Panama. They got Panamanian passports from being married to an American working in Panama and another country because they had a parent born there. Even these people didn't like the Panamanians.

Female Officer Arrested

During this period of general harassment by the Guardia and "dignidads", a female U.S. army lieutenant had to fly to Panama to take care of the funeral arrangements for her father, a U.S. army colonel. She went to the U. S. consulate on Balboa Avenue alongside the bay. Because she was in uniform, the Panamanians arrested her. When the Americans heard of her detainment, they got her out of jail and told her that Americans were not allowed to wear any kind of military uniform on the streets in Panama City even though soldiers in uniform from all other countries could go all over Panama without incident. The treaty regulations stated that U.S. military personnel in uniform could go from base to base in military vehicles, but they were constantly stopped, dragged out of their cars, and shoved around.

The female lieutenant was forced to buy civilian clothes before she could complete her father's funeral arrangements. She then took his body back to the U. S. with her to be buried in Arlington National Cemetery. In Carl's opinion the harassment was completely uncalled for, as well as being cruel and unfeeling.

The Waitress Incident

Carl heard of a case of extreme cruelty when he and his new girl-friend, Yolanda, were having lunch on a Saturday at a beautiful club on a very high hill overlooking the Chagres River near Gamboa. It was really beautiful up there with all the greenery and the jungle. There used to be a thriving restaurant there until the Zone was turned over to the Panamanians. Now there were only three people in the entire restaurant. The quality of the food had gone down to the point that it really was not good any more. There was a waitress there with whom they began to talk. She spoke fluent English. They started talking about the treaty. The waitress said she was working there using an anonymous name. Her husband had actively worked against Noriega. One day some of Noriega's goons captured him, then came to his house and took her and the children out into the jungle. They dug a hole and buried her husband alive and forced the family to witness this. Noriega committed some horrible crimes. Carl had no proof of this story, but he had no reason to doubt it.

During a visit in 1999 Carl wanted to revisit the restaurant. There is a fence and sign at the bottom of the hill leading up to the site of the former restaurant. No one is allowed admittance. The sign says that the site is being used as a rain forest preserve. Carl thought this was just another way of saying that the Panamanians were letting it just go to hell.

Es Semafóro Todos Verde

During the period when Panama was taking over parts of the administration of former U.S. functions in the Panama Canal Zone, there were many instances of either inefficiency or incomplete learning. Carl witnessed an example of this one day when he was walking north along Balboa Road. He heard a loud noise, then another, and still another. Two cars had plowed into a bus, and another had run off the road. Right at the intersection of Amador Road and Balboa Road the traffic signal was green on every side. Cars were crashing right and left in the intersection. Carl ran over to the Balboa police station, which was just to his right. Carl burst into the police station and told the captain behind the desk that there was an accident at the intersection and about the traffic light. The police captain stood up and shook his finger in Carl's face and shouted, "Habla en Espanol—GRINGO!"

Carl answered in Spanish, "Señor, el semáforo todo verde. Muchos golpes accidentes! Verde, verde, verde, verde, todo, todo, todo, todo," Carl pointed upward in all four directions as he turned around, "Vaya, vaya rápido!"

The police captain jumped over the desk, hit the door running, and called for other police officers. They had wreckers tow the cars away. Carl wondered whether the poor victims should wait for the Panamanian government to pay for the damages or just go ahead and get their own cars repaired. Personally, he would opt for the latter. It would be an interminable wait for the government. Most likely there will never be any payment for damages.

The next thing Carl knew nearly all the traffic lights in Balboa became flashing yellow lights. Now, in 1999, they can signal red, green, and yellow, but they sure couldn't then.

Strikes, Riots, Traffic Tie-ups

Many times Carl was unable to take the jitney to work because of strikes, traffic problems, riots against the U.S. The U.S. government withheld income tax from Panamanian workers in the canal and gave the money to Panama. The U.S. tried to break Noreiga by refusing to turn the money over to Panama. Months before the invasion Noreiga's dignidads were starting to take Panamanian houses away from their owners for non-payment of income tax. Riots broke out to pressure the U.S. to turn the collected income tax money over to Noreiga's government to prevent the seizure of homes from private citizens. Carl had never before heard of a government withholding income tax from citizens of another country. Very little or no provocation would set off a riot. If it looked like a good day for a riot, people would riot. Carl suspected people were paid to riot against the United States. Carl had to take a pilot boat to bypass the congested area or areas. A two-hour ride on a pilot boat in both directions added to the total transit time and often made for 16-hour days.

Nidia and the Vicious Dogs

Yolanda had some distant relatives who lived just a few blocks from Old Panama, or Panama La Vieja. This section of Panama is several blocks wide and quite a number of blocks long. It is the ruins of the oldest part of the city which the pirate Morgan burned in 1668. Near there is the Saint Joseph Church, commonly referred to as The Church of the Golden Altar. The legend declares that the altar was gilded in solid gold in 1666. Figures of thick gold were encrusted in the carvings. News of the arrival of Henry Morgan was rumored everywhere. Morgan was a fugitive Saxon who had been enslaved; he joined a band of buccaneers, became their chief, and invaded ports of the Antillas and sacked them. In June 1668 he took the city of Portobelo, south of Cristobol, by surprise with 460 men and nine ships. Soon he appeared at the Chagres River and proceeded toward Panama City. A lay brother called Brother John organized priests, lay brothers, and other workers to save the golden altar. They pulled out the four gold columns, the principal baroque style ornaments, the top of the main altar, as well as the table of the altar itself, put them in launches, and submerged them in the Bay of Panama. The rest of the altar was painted with whitewash and other paints to hide the treasured gilt underneath. When Morgan arrived, Brother John received him very courteously; the priests and others had all fled. Brother John showed Morgan the incomplete altar and asked him for 1,000 ducats to finish the wooden altar. Morgan laughed and said, "You are more of a pirate than I am."

Morgan commanded that Brother John be given the ducats. After Morgan left, the paint and whitewash were removed and the "sunken treasure" was retrieved and set back in place.

One of Yolanda's relatives, Nidia, knew some of the Guardia officers who had horses stabled in Old Panama. They also bred and raised guard dogs to be vicious animals. They had nearly 100 such animals. There were a great many horse guard units as well as heavy equipment in the area with the guard dogs. The building that housed them was like the tall shell of a huge church. Perhaps it had been a government building, but it looked to he hundreds of years old. Carl, Yolanda, and Nidia were there, talking to the Guardia. They said they hated Americans and how they were going to cut them down. They said they were just waiting for their chance. Nidia told them in Spanish, "Yo creo que ustedes quieren morir, porque si ustedes tienen una confrontacion con los americanos, ello van acabar con ustedes en cosa de minutos." Yolanda translated for

Carl, "I believe you like death, because if you have a confrontation with the Americans, you will die in a matter of minutes."

The Guardia just laughed and frowned at the three visitors. At that time the Panamanian Army, the Guardia, and Dignity Battalions absolutely despised Americans.

Story of the TV "Repair"

In November of 1989 Carl and Yolanda took his television set to Panama City to have it repaired since he no longer had purchasing privileges in the Canal Zone. He had to have all repairs on radio, television, or office machines done in Panama City. They were told that the best repair technicians were in a section called "Hollywood." Carl wondered why they called it Hollywood. It was just a shantytown with poor people living there. Many remains of demolished apartments could be seen. Shacks were made of thatch and anything else the residents could get their hands on. It was a very, very poor area. There was one place where there were a few buildings. Nobody was in the buildings anymore; they had moved away. As they made their way further back through the rubble they found a place where some Panamanians had set up shop in a little hole that still had a roof on it. They found the place where the recommended technicians had their shop. They repaired slot machines, pinball machines, televisions, and radios for the Panamanian government. Carl gave them his TV. While they were there, Carl's girlfriend, Yolanda talked to these boys. She translated to Carl, who was never very fluent in Spanish, what they were saying, "Americans will do just about anything they want to in the Canal Zone and in Panama because of the Hay-Bunau-Varilla treaty of 1903. That's not right. It is time for them to go, and we are going to have to throw them out."

Yolanda told them in Spanish, "Hey, look, the United States is a world power. You are going to get hurt real bad. You might even get killed. Why do you want to attack these Americans? Don't you know you people have been shoving the U.S. military around, attacking them and their wives, and violating the 1977 treaty in every way you can think of? You're going to get hurt. The Americans are not going to stand for it. You're breaking this treaty over and over again. If you keep it up, there are going to be a lot of people die here. You are very young. Why do you want to die so young?"

They answered her, "We don't care. If it has anything to do with throwing the gringos out, we're willing to die. Now the United States rules the canal with an iron fist and collects all the transit fees and sends all the money to the U.S. When Panama gets control of the canal, we will have enough money to build good homes for every Panamanian family that needs one. They will all have swimming pools—maybe even some tennis courts."

"Dream on! Dream on! The United States has to pour money into the canal every year for its upkeep and repairs. Transit fees have never paid for the canal's operation since it was opened in 1914. You are in for a big surprise! Are you members of the civilian military group called the Dignity Battalions?" Yolanda asked.

"Si, estamos dignidads." They answered.

"I think you're making a bad mistake. If anything happens here, you'd better go home and take care of your families. The United States has the power."

The dignidads were adamant, "Yo no creo eso. Nosotros tenemos 18,000 a 20,000 personas en Panama que están dispuestos a morir peleando. Deja que los americanos empienzen la confrontacion."

Yolanda translated for Carl, "I don't think so. We have 18,000 to 20,000 people in Panama who are willing to die fighting. Let the Americans begin the confrontation."

That's just exactly what happened to them. In spite of this conversation the technicians agreed to repair the television. One of them came over and shook hands with Carl. He spoke to Carl in Spanish, which Yolanda again translated for him, "We don't bother anybody who works in the canal. We know you are a pilot. We are going to need pilots in the canal when we take over its operation. We won't bother you pilots. It's the damn military that we want the hell out of here so this canal will belong to Panama."

The men shook hands. Carl ended the conversation with, "Bueno suerte. (Good luck.) I hope you make out. I'd sure hate to see a confrontation. Su muchachos son muy jovenes." (You boys are very young.)

They drove away.

Carl and Yolanda drove to Central Street to have Carl's Remington electric typewriter repaired. The technician agreed to repair the typewriter. Yolanda was given a tickct for the machine, and she left the machine there.

The Crippled Pilot

In about 1984 some local toughs, either Noriega's "dignidads" or just plain criminals accosted a step two pilot, bent him over the hood of his car and beat him so badly that he had to be hospitalized. He was injured so badly the he could never pilot again. The Panama Canal Commission gave him the job of hiring all the new PITs.

8

THE DECEMBER WAR

Military Build-Up

Heavy equipment for the Canal is located in the little town of Gamboa, the halfway point in the Panama Canal. Most of the tugboats that work the Pacific side are docked here. In addition, there are the enormous Bucyrus floating cranes, the Hercules, Samson, and the Goliath. The Goliath was the largest floating crane in the world for a very long time. Only since the advent of offshore oil drilling rigs did the world see cranes that could lift several times the weight that the old Goliath could take. Just before the war U.S. army helicopters landed at Gamboa during military maneuvers. Panamanians got used to them and paid no attention to them.

Although General Woerner had taken no action against the Panamanian "dingbats" when the naval officers got shot and their wives were raped, evidence began to be seen of an American military build up.

War appeared imminent. In the fall of 1989, President George Bush replaced General Woerner with General Fuhrman, an old war-horse of a general. Under this new command, a few of the guns were unmuzzled. Americans began to enforce their privileges in the treaty. The situation did not improve.

Although personnel carriers with rubber tracks instead of wheels had brackets on top for machine guns and arms, they were not armed. They moved in a convoy, two or three at a time, down Amador Road, through Balboa, through the American housing area to Amador. They parked in the parking lot next to the Amador Officers Club. The Amador Officers Club was located at the end of Amador Road just at the beginning of the causeway that leads to Naos Island. They opened the back doors. No one remained there except the driver. Panamanians who were in the area, school children, and others sang the Panamanian national anthem and waved the Panamanian flag. The Panamanian newspapers, controlled by the Noriega government, had photographers taking pictures. The next day a few more personnel carriers were added to the parking lot. Each day the drivers opened up the back of the personnel carriers and tanks and showed them to the Panamanians. This went on for a number of days until nobody paid any attention to them anymore. Soon, however, more troops arrived as well as arms and ammunition. By late afternoon on December 19 there were 25 or 30 personnel carriers filled with American troops armed to the gills fully armed and ready for combat. The troops stayed inside. Noreiga had fortified the interior of Perico Island, one of the islands on the causeway. U.S. troops discovered this munitions storage area. At about 2200 or 2300 hours the troops took up their positions and captured the Perico Island Fortress.

Destruction and Casualties

Carl knew that when General Noreiga stood up behind his podium at the Amador Officers Club, banged his machete, and declared war on the U.S., war would soon break out, but he hadn't expected the invasion to start this early. Shooting the Naval Officers did the trick. It was the straw that broke the camel's back. Just before midnight on December 20, 1989 the shooting started. Everyone in Carl's house was asleep. Personnel carriers opened their doors; troops poured out. Huge helicopters hovered over the three or four buildings in the Panamanian police station and locked on military equipment. U.S. troops ordered

Panamanian military personnel at the military complex in Amador to come out with their hands up. Nobody came out. The personnel carriers brought up their artillery pieces and opened fire. Panamanian soldiers in Amador's military barracks ran to the Canal and jumped in. They left their hats, shoes, and other clothes behind. Navy personnel from Rodman Navy Base came out in small craft, picked up the swimmers, gave them dry clothes, and took them prisoner.

Carl's home on Empire Street was about a block from the police station, right in the center of downtown Balboa. Bombs fell. Yolanda, fully awake by this time, wrung her hands, frightened, and went into another room. Her sister Nelda, terrified, hid in a closet in a back bedroom. Carl foolishly stepped out into the front yard to watch the action. Bullets hit the coconut tree across the street. Carl looked toward the Balboa Police Station. Incendiary bombs looked like a million sparklers exploding. Carl ran back in the house, turned on the TV, and, behold, the war was on TV. He lay on the sofa, drank beer, and watched the armies go at it. He saw Noreiga's headquarters go up in flames. Noreiga's war machines raced down the streets to Amador Road and around Balboa Boulevard along Panama Bay. Americans were firing at them. They'd miss. Then every once in a while they'd get one. Then POW! A tank would explode. Carl and the girls could hear gunfire coming from every direction. The sky lit up periodically. The girls didn't know what was happening. They feared for their lives.

Huge helicopters came over Carl's house and hovered over the Balboa police station. Loud speakers blared from one of the helicopters, in both Spanish and English, "Salgon con los manos sobre la cabeza. Get out! Come out with your hands up. Walk out into the yard. Cross the street to the YMCA. Gather there and we will come and pick you up and take you to a compound."

Some people did come out, but the people in the YMCA across the street said that the Guardia shot any Panamanian policemen who tried to surrender. American gun ships in the Pacific anchorage lobbed salvos into the Balboa Police Station. A helicopter opened fire and burned the buildings to the ground. Only one building was left untouched at the far end of the field in a grassy area. The guardia captain ordered all his men to stay and fight. After the shelling ceased, there was nothing left of that police station except for portions of a few of the walls. The place was cremated. Ashes stood in piles. Bed frames were hanging from beam fragments. Only twenty feet away was a nativity scene made from plywood panels. None of them was even turned over. They were still standing the next morning when Carl and Yolanda saw them.

Helicopters took over Gamboa in an hour. Panamanian military housing and installations were obliterated in less than 60 minutes. About daybreak things quieted down except for sporadic firing. Carl went through nearly a case of beer, so it was easy for him to fall asleep on his sofa. At about 1000 hours a loud speaker blared, "The town of Rio Hato has fallen."

Rio Hato is a little town about 60 kilometers southwest of Panama City, located on the Highway of the Americas. Rio Hato has a big airfield. Along one side of the highway, next to the airport was strung about a dozen houses and other guardia military installations. They were all brick and fortified. After the war the airfield was abandoned. Today there is nothing standing but a few tattered walls. On the opposite side was a big fort area. There was no damage done here since the guardia came out and surrendered. The Americans had built this airstrip for the military use of the Panamanians. It had been turned over to Panama. Carl was sure that airstrip had been used to bring drugs into the United States. One seldom if ever sees any planes landing there anymore. It is pretty well dead, but the airstrip is still there. Carl has passed it many times on the way to David and he has never seen any aircraft there.

About a week later Carl was at the enlisted men's club drinking with soldiers of the 508 parachute infantry, his old regiment from World War II. Members of the regiment told him that the U.S. army dropped several concussion bombs from stealth bombers at Rio Hato. When the U.S. soldiers arrived they told the Panamanians to put up their hands and surrender, but the disoriented Panamanian soldiers just stumbled around in their underwear. They could not hear because of the loudness of the concussion bombs. Later the army artillery destroyed the fortifications and other buildings. No Panamanians were killed, just dazed, and confused. Carl was told that no firepower was used west of Rio Hato; just a lot of surrendering went on.

A pilot named Milton, who had transited with Carl as a PIT, lived only a few blocks from Carl when he lived on Ancon Hill. They sometimes had coffee together. Milton had been a chief petty officer in the U.S. Navy. He was selected as a Panama Canal pilot because he had applied as a navy pilot. Carl recalled that Milton said one afternoon, "Pilots have the rank of generals here in the canal. They are completely in charge!"

"If you park your car in a general's marked parking spot, just see how fast your car will be towed," Carl burst Milton's balloon.

Milton told Carl that on the night of the invasion Navy seals boarded his ship while it was at anchor during its transit. They burst into the bridge and covered everyone with automatic weapons. "Hit the deck face down everyone!" a seal ordered.

The ship's captain, his officers, and the quartermaster all hit the deck immediately. Since pilots are the absolute authority in the canal, Milton not only did not lay face down on the deck but remained defiant. "I am in command here. I don't hit the deck for anyone."

The next thing Milton knew he did indeed hit the deck with a seal's boot in his back. "SHUT UP!" the seal commanded.

Milton told Carl that he was sore for about a week. Milton spent the night on his transit. MTC told him to proceed the next day.

The Canal was closed for one day.

By late afternoon most of the fighting had died down. Only spasmodic firing was still going on. Ten hours later, the "war" was over.

There was no further Panamanian resistance. The American military was in control.

Two days after the invasion Carl took his pilot's hat and radio and walked to Amador where the U.S. MPs stopped him from entering the military section that used to be the Amador Guardia Headquarters and barracks. When he told the MPs he was a Panama Canal pilot going to work, Carl was able to pass the U.S. military police and look through the barracks the Panamanians had abandoned during the night. He really was not on his way to work since he did not have a transit scheduled that day. He was just curious. There were a few military personnel there, a couple of half-tracks, and a few personnel carriers with machine guns on top. American soldiers had been through the buildings and taken whatever they wanted as souvenirs. GIs had ripped the badges off the guardias' hats that were lying around. Most everything of any value had been stripped. However, Carl spotted a pistol on one of the ledges. He just left it there; he didn't want any part of it. He wished he had a camera, but he didn't. Carl could see where some of the guardia had hastily abandoned their coffee and partially eaten meals and jumped in the canal.

He walked on through the buildings to the causeway that had been built from island to island—Naos, Culebra, Perico, and Flamenco Islands. The Americans had built the causeway connecting the islands when they built the Canal. There were beautiful plantings of trees and green lawns alongside the road, which Americans had planted. On one side were the Bay of Panama and Panama City. On the other side was the Panama Canal. It was all open water, and you could see all the way to Taboga Island, 12 miles away.

At the beginning of the highway connecting the islands was the Amador Officers Club. This is the place where the personnel carriers gathered on successive days in preparation for the war. Now it was closed up tight. Behind the club were six beautiful homes for high-ranking officers, majors, colonels, and civilian technicians. Carl walked through these houses. The GIs had already taken what they wanted. Partitions had been knocked out. Carl later learned that in one of the closets he didn't look in was $6 million in U. S. currency right out of the Bank of Panama. The bank bands were still around the money. Perhaps some GI knew it was there and was coming back for it later. Two or three days later the army came back through, found the money, and took it away. When the GIs searched these houses, they *really* went through them. The jitney drivers kept saying, "Oh, man, $6 million in that house. We drove back and forth past that house, taking pilots to work every day, and wish we hadn't passed up $6 million. Oh, God, help us!"

Carl didn't grieve over it too much. He knew that the army would shake these places down more than once. If a person had tried to get that money out of there, he would have been in trouble. The army kept a pretty tight watch over everything.

Down at the end of the road overlooking Panama Harbor was where General Woerner's house was. It was a large home reserved for a general. His top staff of aides and colonels was housed in a row of about six houses along a semicircular road. Just before the road forks off to the right to the officers quarters, the officers' wives had built a huge sign and stuck it in the ground. It read, "A Job Well Done. Thank You."

After Fighting Ceased

Chorrillo

About three days after the war people again began to more around, assuming their normal activities. Carl's girlfriend Yolanda, her sister Nelda, and Carl walked down Balboa road, across the Fourth of July road, and into Chorrillo where Noriega's headquarters had been. Chorrillo has many low-income high rise apartments. Some were still intact. Some were destroyed; some were partially destroyed. The guardia and dignidads paramilitary army had fired on the U.S. army from the apartment buildings. The Americans returned fire. Carl heard from many sources, even the Panamanian pilot boat crews, some of whom lived in Chorrillo, that U.S. soldiers were receiving fire from the roofs of the high rise apartment buildings. Panamanians who lived in these apartments could not stand Americans. A great many of the U.S. army's problems stemmed from this district. The infantry lieutenant in charge was ordered to return fire but refused. Carl could only guess what happened to that lieutenant.

The Prison

Off to the left is a large three-story prison which housed malefactors from throughout the city. Soldiers told Carl that the prison had not received any fire; no one was injured there. Carl could see the prisoners hanging out the windows. The soldiers told Carl and Yolanda that the Panamanian people have to bring prisoners their food. The government won't feed them. They'd starve to death, but their families can be seen going in there all the time with baskets and packages of food for them.

Noriega's Headquarters

Noriega's headquarters, a fairly large building, was heavily armed. On this day they were still digging in the rubble of the motor pool across the street from Noreiga's headquarters. Carl asked a soldier, with a colored band on his arm, "What is this terrible odor? Are they bringing bodies out of there?"

He answered, "It's either people or dogs. You make up your mind. I'm not allowed to say anything."

Across the street was a big warehouse complex. Carl, Yolanda, and Nelda walked around the warehouse and saw body bags being brought out of the warehouse. Carl thought there was no telling how many Panamanians were killed in that war.

Under all the rubble covering the motor pool area were the dreaded water cannons used to break up street riots. The Panamanians called them "carrobomba." They had cartoon characters painted all over them like Mickey Mouse and Donald Duck. Panamanians were glad to hear that the water cannons had been destroyed. There were also tanks, personnel carriers, jeeps and cars the officers used. Many of these cars had been seized from civilians on the street. Army personnel simply forced the car open and drove it away without asking anybody anything. If anyone spotted his car in the army lot and went to get it, he was told to get out of there or he would be arrested. That is what happened to the new Montero belonging to a Panamanian friend of Carl's. When the American army hit they caved that place in. It took a real pounding. Carl felt sure they thought Noriega was in there when they hit it. This is the area where the people obeyed the army without question. Whatever the army told them to do, they did it. If the army said, "Riot" they did. If the army said, "Destroy" or "Rob" or "Steal" they did. The Panamanian police just stood by and encouraged the hatred of Americans. This is the area where the American naval officers and their wives were driving through when they were shot and raped, not knowing the intensity of the hatred Panamanians felt toward the American military. There was no sign to indicate this was the location of Noreiga's headquarters. It was an open road through the main part of town.

Refugees

On the morning of December 20, after the Panamanian garrisons were destroyed, especially Noreiga's headquarters and the entire Chorrillo area, refugees flooded the street Carl lived on—Empire Street. They knocked on Carl's door and asked for food, water, and to use the telephone. Residents had been instructed not to open their doors to any Panamanians, so no one gave them anything, nor were they allowed in any houses on Empire Street. U.S. army helicopters dropped pamphlets with instructions telling the refugees to go to Balboa High School. They were homeless because their apartment buildings in Chorrillo had been destroyed. A tent city was erected for them in the athletic field behind the school. The U.S. army provided food, water, blankets, and portable toilet facilities. Later new apartments were built and the apartment tenants were moved in and monetarily compensated for their losses. Now these apartment buildings are painted in bright pastels and are located along the Bay of Panama within sight of the causeway connecting Amador with the several islands, Naos, Culebra, Perico, and Flamenco.

U.S. soldiers went up and down the street, stopped at each house, and knocked on each door. They entered each house and searched thoroughly for Panamanians. If no one let them in, they broke the door down. The soldiers complimented Carl and the girls on their preparedness for war. They said, "Very good, plenty of food."

The soldiers were about to break his neighbor's door down when Carl asked them to stop. Carl told the soldiers, "My friend has left his key with my girlfriend. He is on vacation in the U.S."

Yolanda got the key, gave it to the soldiers, and went with them through the house to see that everything was intact. They were satisfied and soon left. During the searching of the neighborhood armored personnel carriers moved up and down Empire Street. Carl ran inside and put on his confederate cap and waved his confederate flag. Most of the troops were from the south, and they enjoyed the show. They shouted, "Atta boy, Reb. Long live the south. We will rise again."

Irate Store Clerk

On December 23, 1989, the U.S. Government opened all the military stores to U.S. civil service employees. The shopping areas in Panama City had been either looted or destroyed during the "war" of December 19 & 20. U.S. civil service employees were allowed to purchase a limited supply of goods from the commissary and PX.

Carl bought over $100 worth of groceries and received a very nasty letter from the Commission. His privileges were cut off. He filed for foreign hardship on his next income tax return. It was denied, and Carl was ordered to the consulate. He had to pay an additional amount of income tax plus a penalty for late filing.

An additional incident occurred in relation to a PX. Carl was met at the door by a Panamanian store clerk who stopped him and said, "No more to Panama Canal Workers! GET OUT, GRINGOS!"

Panamanians were employed by the U.S. Department of Defense to run all army facilities from cutting the grass to repairing and painting the buildings, clerking in the commissaries, and the thousands of other jobs required to run the military operation.

TV and Typewriter Lost

In early January 1990, after things had begun to return to normal, Carl and Yolanda went to downtown Panama City to try to find out about the TV and typewriter they had left for repairs. The place where they had taken the TV was abandoned—completely demolished. There was nothing left. Apparently someone had opened fire on the American troops, because the place was leveled. Bits and pieces of electronic and amusement equipment was scattered everywhere. Television sets had been blown to bits. Fragments were all over the place. There was nothing of any value left. Carl and Yolanda talked to a fellow who was wandering around the area, picking up junk. He told them "Everybody who had a shop in here, all the young guys, are all dead. They died in the American invasion of Panama."

Yolanda just hung her head and said, "We tried to tell them, but they wouldn't listen to us. They gave their lives for what they thought was right for their country."

"I'm sure they thought they were right," Carl agreed.

"Hasta luego," Yolanda called to the fellow who had been talking to them.

"Hasta la vista," he called back.

So Carl lost his TV. Then he and Yolanda went to Central Street. People there said the American troops came through and the

Panamanian police vanished. The police and firemen were disbursed because of the invasion, leaving merchants with no protection. Parts of the city were looted, especially central Panama City where the major stores were located. We asked the shop owner, "Where is our typewriter?"

He replied, "They broke in here and stole everything I had."

Carl told him, "Well, then, you are responsible for our typewriter. Here is the repair ticket. You can pay for it."

"No, I don't have to pay for it. We all lose."

"Thank you, Jimmy Carter," Carl muttered as he and Yolanda walked away.

The 508 in Frankfurt and Panama City

One day soon after the invasion Carl was at the enlisted men's club at Fort Clayton, a large military installation just across the road from Miraflores Locks. While in Panama Carl liked to play the slot machines. The non-commissioned officers club had three floors, a beautiful kitchen, and an extremely large dining room with food served cafeteria style. On Saturdays and Sundays the food was served menu style. The food was just great. Down in the basement was a casino and a bar. Carl sometimes drank with some of the 508 soldiers from his old regiment. Carl ran into some members of the 508 who had participated in the invasion of Panama. They told him stories of what the Guardia in town tried to do to them. They dragged them out of their jeeps, shoved them around, called them names, and generally harassed them. When the war broke out, it was pay back time. Carl guessed they probably put a few extra shells in their rifles. They told him about how the concussion bombs had defeated the Panamanian soldiers. Then Carl told them this story, "I used to be in the 508-parachute infantry regiment in Germany during World War II. After the war was over while the regiment was still in Germany, some soldiers continued to harass the Germans. It didn't matter whether the Germans were men or women. The paratroopers would knock them down. One day an incident occurred which was the last straw. Some of the paratroopers went into Frankfurt, broke into a brewery and rolled kegs of beer down the street. They also cornered a string of trolley cars and created havoc all over Frankfurt. I thought the German beer was terrible. I don't even know what they wanted with it. We had plenty of American beer in the clubs, and it was dirt-cheap. The men confiscated two or three trolley cars and loaded the beer kegs inside. They broke the heads off the kegs. Then they began drinking beer and screaming and shouting all around the trolley car and driving the trolley all over Frankfurt. They finally crashed it. It took about forty MPs to round up the paratroopers and put them in the stockade. Several generals and the ambassador called us all out on the parade grounds. They told us what a fine war record we had, recalled how they had begged us to behave ourselves, but that we had continued to disgrace the regiment. Therefore we were deported from Germany and deactivated at Camp Kilmer. I still have pictures of this regiment. Although I didn't take part in this episode, I was deactivated in New Jersey along with all the others and sent to Fort Bragg, North Carolina. I had 31 days leave. When my leave was up, I was again at sea in the merchant Marine on a ship in Genoa, Italy. Good-bye, army."

The Cut Thumb

Carl used to go offshore in his 18' boat. He often caught big, beautiful fish. About two days after the invasion he was out in the back yard cleaning a big dolphin. It must have weighed 30 to 40 pounds. He had some sharp fish fillet knives. One of them slipped and he cut his thumb. It bled profusely. He wrapped it up, got in his car, and drove over to Gorgas hospital to the outpatient clinic. They looked at his identification card. They didn't have time for a lot of paperwork. A member of the medical staff put him in the line and he soon saw a doctor who cleaned and stitched up the cut and bandaged it.

Carl apologized to the nurse for coming in when there were so many injured people to be taken care of. Patients were in hallways and lined up in the reception room. The place was loaded with war casualties. Ninety-eight percent of them were Panamanians. It didn't matter who came in, Panamanians or Americans. All were treated. Among the wounded were American soldiers, Panamanian firemen, policemen, and civilians. At least they were dressed as civilians. By this time Panamanian soldiers had taken off their uniforms and thrown them away or destroyed them. Carl was really proud of the American medical group who took care of all comers regardless of race, color, creed, or national affiliation. They were doing a magnificent job. A nurse came right by him. She had a jar filled with a clear fluid. It looked like alcohol. Carl was always laughing and joking, so he said to her, "I wish my urine was that clear."

She laughed so hard she almost dropped the jar. Even though Carl was hurt, he always enjoyed his time in Panama, especially as a pilot, laughing and joking all the time. He had a wonderful time in Panama. He seldom had any trouble with any of the Panamanians. The only trouble he had was with some of the senior American pilots.

Just as Carl was getting ready to leave the hospital, he noticed Dirk Goodman, another pilot, in the hospital corridor. With him were another man who looked a lot like Dirk and a doctor. Carl asked the nurse if she knew why Dirk was in the hospital, explaining that Dirk was a friend of his and a fellow pilot. At first the nurse was reluctant to give Carl any information, but finally she relented and told him, "Yes, I'm familiar with his case. That's his brother with him. Dirk is a terminal cancer patient."

"TERMINAL!" Carl cried in surprise.

"Yes," she said, "He has cancer of the prostate."

"Did you know that he once rode his bicycle across the United States? He sure looks healthy."

"He most likely has a very healthy heart, but the malignancy has metastasized, spread throughout his body."

Carl just shook his head sadly and left the hospital. He wondered if Dirk had thought he was so healthy that he did not need regular check-ups. He determined that he would not make the same mistake.

Dirk died a few months later. Several years later, after Carl had retired and was living near the town of Boquéte, in Chíriqui Province, he heard from Scott Regan, a former pilot who was now retired and had become a coffee grower. Scott told Carl that Dirk had married his Jamaican maid shortly before he died. Scott said Dirk hated the Panama Canal Commission and President Jimmy Carter so much for giving away the Panama Canal Zone and the Panama Canal that he left the Jamaican maid his U.S. government annuity and hoped that she lived forever. Scott said, "Miss Jamaica" was in Boquéte selling all Dirk's coffee hold-ings as well as his beautiful house he had built for his retirement. She said she could not live off her annuity of $1500 a month. Can you imag-ine the size of these people's balls?"

Carl knew that she had worked for $90 a month when she was Dirk's maid. He thought that what she meant was that she didn't have enough money to build a house for everyone in her family and then feed them. In Panama the family and its welfare are all important. What the family did for a living before "Miss Jamaica" hit the jackpot is anyone's guess.

Scott also told Carl he had used Dirk's Guami Indian pickers to har-vest his coffee before the land was sold. After this admission of theft, Carl didn't see Scott any more.

9

1990 TO MARCH OF 1993

A deckhand on the pilot boat asked Carl, "Why did the Americans beat up so hard on the Panamanians?"

Carl answered, "Well, they asked for it."

"But why did they keep on firing and dropping firebombs after we were already beaten?" the deckhand pressed for an answer.

Carl replied, "It's like the sign at the entrance to military housing in Amador says, 'Thanks for a job well done.' This is the army's idea of a job well done."

After the invasion was over and Noreiga was in a Miami jail on charges of drug trafficking, there were no more riots or traffic tie-ups. Things calmed down and normal life returned.

The Wedding

Twenty months had gone by since Yolanda and Nelda had come to live in Carl's home. It was not very long after Yolanda's arrival that she and Carl became intimate. Yolanda wanted to get married. Carl protested for six months that the disparity in their ages was too great. Yolanda threatened to leave Carl. She had completed her college course. Finally Carl yielded and told Yolanda that he would marry her if she would not leave him. After Carl's affair with Carlotta had ended and his mother died, he began drinking heavily when he was not called for a transit. Then, too, this was a marriage he didn't really want, but he didn't want Yolanda to leave him. She had put joy and comfort back in his life. Yolanda and Nelda made all the arrangements. They obtained the license, arranged for the physicals, got the witnesses, arranged for the reception, and set the date—June 15, 1990—Yolanda's birthday.

On the appointed day Yolanda, Nelda, and Carl went to the courthouse. The girls came out of an office stating that more paperwork was needed from another office building in Panama City. "Okay," Carl said, "No wedding. Some other time."

Yolanda said it would just take a little while. Carl felt like a fish being reeled in. He tried to escape, but he had drunk too much to resist. They secured the needed document and went back to the courthouse. The witnesses were not there. "Oh," Carl said, "That's it," and headed for the door.

"Come back, Carl; they are just arriving."

"Oops, reeled in again. It looks like this fish will not get off the hook," thought Carl.

During the ceremony the judge realized that Carl was not fluent in Spanish and asked for an interpreter. Carl's friend, Jack, one of the witnesses, insisted he could speak Spanish and called Carl over to the corner and whispered to him, "I do not speak but a little Spanish. Just make out like you understand and say 'Si'."

In this way the ceremony was completed. The wedding party went back to Carl's home. The new bride and her sister had filled the house with guests. There was a large wedding cake and all kinds of goodies. A large meal was provided. Carl drank champagne and danced with all the girls. Before the reception was ended, Carl was very drunk. He left the party and went to bed.

The next morning Carl awoke, sat up in bed, held his head in his hands, and said aloud, "Lo! Behold the fool as he awakens from his folly."

Piloting and Canal Maintenance Skills Needed

Piloting is a stressful job. If a person cannot handle the stress, he will be in the hospital before middle age. To do a good job of piloting requires the ability to sense movement, and have a feeling for what the ship will do. As soon as the pilot comes aboard, he must have the feel of the ship. The best pilots are such people. Some "mechanical" pilots do everything by the book, learning the effect of a variety of actions. These pilots will get through, but the stress will shorten their lives. They may not live long after they retire. They are not usually as good as the more "instinctive" pilots. Pilots stay for the money, even the ones who bang ships around. There are frequent investigations when damage occurs, but it is a government civil service job, and pilots do not get fired.

Hiring of Blacks, Panamanians

By 1990 there were more Panamanians than Americans, particularly black people, working in the canal. Their ancestors were the hardest working canal builders. In spite of the fact that blacks were paid the lowest wages of any group of canal builders, eventually they found good jobs in the canal because they were bi-lingual, speaking both English and Spanish. They learned English from their parents and grandparents who had worked on the canal; they learned Spanish from Panamanians they associated with in the Zone.

The government was pushing the hiring of blacks. Many of them found jobs on tugboats. Their parents had taught them that promotions came from within Panama Commission personnel. Panamanians interested in becoming pilots transferred around to get a job on the tugboats in any capacity they could get; then they worked up the ladder. Some of them began as clean up boys, sweeping up shavings. Often they badmouthed American "gringos". When they became PITs, they had to belong to the MMP or face the derision of the pilots assigned to train them. Many of the pilots would not let them work unless they were specially assigned to do so by the Panama Canal Commission. If a PIT didn't take the con, under the direction of a pilot, he would never learn to be a pilot. Such PITs had to lick the pilot's boots to get to work. When they became pilots and advanced a few steps, they applied for port captain's jobs. The Commission pushed them into every possible position. This caused Americans to be somewhat indignant, since they did not like taking orders from Panamanians. Americans would retire; then Panamanians would step into their positions. Blacks became very able, well-trained workers. Where the money will come from to perform the costly repairs and maintenance of the canal locks after December 31, 1999 remains a question. Will tolls pay for this? They haven't in the past. Will the Panamanian Government pay?

Merchant Marine Pension Application Refused

One fine day in March of 1992 Carl arrived at the Cristobal boathouse. There were about a dozen other pilots waiting for the appropriate time to board their transits. Some ships were at anchor in Limón Bay; other ships were just arriving at the breakwater. The reason for such a large number of pilots so early in the morning, at 0400 hours was due to the large number of supers.

Captain Murray sat next to Carl and asked him, "Are you retiring soon?"

"Yes, I am planning to," Carl replied.

"Do you have your retirement credits with the Masters, Mates, and Pilots?"

The Masters, Mates, and Pilots (MMP) Union is affiliated with the American Federation of Labor. Carl had belonged to the MMP ever since he had advanced from seaman to third mate when he was in the U.S. Merchant Marine. Carl was hoping to get his pension for the years he had served in the Merchant Marine, as well as his Panama Canal civil service pension. Many of the pilots were counting on these two pensions. Carl explained to Murray, "I have at least 24 years of vested time, but I doubt that I'll get anything out of it, not much I am sure. I asked for an application for retirement in Houston before I came here to pilot ships for the government. They refused to give me one stating that the board would not approve it. I asked them to give me an application so I could submit it and see if it would be approved. I was told repeatedly, 'The board will not approve it.' Then when I insisted, they said there were no application forms in the office, and that I should try the next time I was in Houston.

When I turned 65, I called the union hall in Mobile, Alabama and asked the Gulf Vice-President for an application for retirement. I reminded the vice-president that I had been asking for this application for 15 years but had been denied. I got the same old story, 'The board will not approve it. Period.' Alice, the Houston representative, finally gave me the application, but she warned me, 'Don't you tell anyone where you got this application.' I answered her, 'My God, Alice, can't I ever collect this pension? For 15 years I have been denied an application for my pension. Every union in the maritime industry except the MMP has paid pilots their pensions while working for the U.S. Government, even the 20 or so US Navy pensioners from captain to third class enlisted men. Even pilots who have pensions from unlicensed unions collect their pensions!"

Murray tried to relate the facts, "Carl, it all happens this way. The union officials contribute their Political Action Committee (PAC) funds to New York State politicians. New York State laws control the MMP union pension fund. PAC money is given to New York State politicians at election time. Then they ask the MMP Board of Directors what they can do for them. Union officials want to change the pension rules to feather their own nests. They want to keep the pension fund solvent to insure their base captain's pay. For years the retirement pay was the same for everyone, but a lot of mismanagement was taking place. At least I heard that rumor. Then a wage-related pension was enacted. Union officials get masters wages, class A, B, and C. You know, Carl, classes A, B, and C have to do with different size ships. Union officials are on the payroll for 30 days each month. In addition, the president gets an additional

$25,000 on his base retirement as third vice president of the longshoreman's union. WOW! Carl, our pension for one year would probably equal one month's pension payment for a union official."

"I understand all this Murray," Carl added, "But they say that the ships' captains will also get this wage-related pension. I say that the American flag is disappearing from the high seas. Some ships go overseas and shuttle for a long time. The captain who is being relieved when he is in some foreign port is now finding himself losing pension time, since he is not available for a ship when one comes up at a U.S. port. Ships are being sold, scrapped, or laid up at dry-dock for long periods. It looks like no one thought of this, but the union officials and board members did. Thanks to crooked politicians and union officials, my pension has been reduced to next to nothing 'by law'."

Captain "Crash" Carson got up, looked at his watch, and remarked, "We have a launch. south four is coming through the breakwater. Let's go to work."

Later, aboard the transit, Captain Byrd, another pilot who had overheard the conversation at the boathouse, said to Carl, "If you go back to sea, you will be 70 years old. By the time you have served 10 years to get the best five years out of 10 years sea time for a wage related pension, you will be 80 years old. You will be lucky to be able to get up the gangway. Since you must have 10 years service to get a lump sum payment as well, you will never be able to get a lump sum. The union officials want to keep the money in the fund so they will be able to get the lion's share. In that way they can keep the fund solvent for themselves. They do not want to pay your pension now because you are piloting ships for the U.S. government. They will state that you are still engaged in the maritime industry. They won't process your pension application until you retire. The MMP union will state that port captains and other positions are not engaging in the maritime industry, but that's a lie. It's okay for port captains to work here and get credit toward their pensions with work as captain or crew on tuna boats and the like. Posh! I have had port captains relieve me of my transit for a number of reasons. Once I had an assignment to go to the Miraflores and take a ship to the ship-yard. The vessel had broken down. The transiting pilot had been taken off because he had worked longer than his 12 hours. When I started to board the pilot boat, I was called back and told the port captain was doing the job. I lost about $800 for my seventh transit. How about this not being maritime related?"

Captain Bittner spoke up, "You can expect your 24 years to be divided into quarters. Your 96 quarters will get you 96x6=$576 per month. An ordinary seaman's pension will most likely be more. I have less than 10 years. They will most likely just put my money in the general pot. I'll get nothing back for the money I've paid in. Don't dwell on it. We've all been had. Here is your radio. We are abeam of the arrow. Center one, coil in. Center one and two hold. Okay, fellas, you have the bow." This statement affirmed that the bow pilots had control of the bow machines, the locomotives, and they should keep the bow of the vessel in the center of the lock chamber.

A large lighted neon arrow is mounted at the end of the center wall of the lock. Its position indicates when a ship may enter the lock. When the arrow points to a three o'clock position, the lock is ready for a ship to enter. "We have the arrow," said by a pilot, means that the arrow points to the three o'clock position. When a pilot says, "Center one fast," it means that the line has been dropped on the bit between the locomotive on the center wall and the bow of the ship. The ship is then firmly attached to the locomotive.

After applying for his MMP pension to commence in March of 1993, Carl returned to the Isthmus of Panama and cancelled his membership in the Panama Pilots Association as instructed by the MMP. At this time the president of the Panama Pilots Association was "Trash Can Scalley," Hannibal C. Scalley. He was called "Trash can" because he fell asleep at his desk while teaching at the Massachusetts Maritime Academy. When he got up, his leg had been tied to the trash can. Trash went everywhere; "Trash Can" fell flat on his face.

After Carl cancelled his membership in the Panama Pilots Association, Scalley spread the word around the Commission and the other pilots that Carl was a labor "scab." He was mad because the association would be losing three months dues. Can you imagine calling a 70-year-old retiring man a scab over a few dollars? Pilots at this time earned in the neighborhood of $100,000 a year.

Steam Locomotive Relocation Riot

In 1914, when the canal was flooded and first opened to water traffic, the Panama Canal Company placed a steam locomotive on display beside the Ancon railroad station. It had been used on the Panama Canal Railroad during the construction of the Canal. In 1990 the canal administrator had the locomotive removed and shipped to the Smithsonian Institute in Washington D.C. There were riots all over Panama about taking the locomotive. The riots in Balboa lasted for a week. Finally the truth came out. The Panamanian government had been given an identical locomotive, along with one specimen of each type of equipment displayed at the Ancon Station, to be put on display in a Panamanian museum. All the riots died down and everything got very quiet. Someone in the Panamanian government had apparently sold the locomotive to another country, perhaps in South America, and pocketed the money.

Trent Transit

"Good morning, Carl."

"Good morning, Trent. It looks like we got a good easy job today. It looks like I'll get off in Gamboa. I have first control, so I guess you'll take it to Cristobal and drop anchor in Gatun Lake."

"Yeah, that's all right."

"I need another start, anyway. This will be seven for me. That's a thousand-dollar bonus. I'm already on overtime, so I'll have me a real whopping paycheck."

I don't have that kind of bonus money coming yet. This will be my sixth transit. Somehow or another I stayed on one ship all-night and lost out. What do you think about the loss of bow pilots, Carl?"

"Well, we kind of asked for it in a way. I remember getting drunk on the bow one time with another bow pilot. We didn't do any work. We didn't have any work to do. The control pilot could handle everything, so we just gave him crazy mixed-up signals and laughed all the time we were supposed to be working. He didn't like it a little bit, and I don't blame him. We were giving pilots a bad name. When the pilots enter into negotiations this time with the Commission, they are asking that their bonuses and overtime be included in their base pay. I'll bet the Commission will refuse; there'll be a lawsuit."

"Who do you think will win the lawsuit, Carl?"

"The pilot's association will. There is nobody who will be willing to risk losing pilots; they are the life's blood of the canal operation. I think we'll get a base pay of $140,000 with no overtime or bonus extras, maximum for retirement calculations, and bow pilots will be eliminated. I wouldn't be surprised if four pilots to a ship will be reduced to two pilots per ship. That's all that's needed, anyway. That will save the Commission the money they will have to put out to include overtime and bonuses in the base pay."

"Yeah, that sounds pretty reasonable. I guess we'll move on up here to the locks in a little while. Did you ride out in one of the new pilot boats out of the pilot station in Balboa?"

"Yeah, Trent. I rode on one. Those are real nice boats. They cost almost $500,000. Hell, man, I wouldn't give a $100,000 for one. Who in the hell do you suppose is paying all that money?"

"I don't know. It's government transit money and they're getting this canal all fixed up with new pilot boats and tugboats and doing a lot of work here for Panama with the treaty just a matter of a few years away. So that's the way it is."

"Hey, Trent, did you hear those Panamanian guys beefing about a whole lot of Americans who came down here and violated the treaty?"

"Yeah, I heard about that. I hear that Kincaid and his buddy, Vinson, have gone to the Commission with a pack of lawyers. They're raising hell up there."

"They were only supposed to hire Panamanians after October 30, 1979," Carl continued. "They're coming down here after 1980. They hired a whole bunch of them including some tow boat men from up around Alaska. A lot of military people came down with this load and they're getting all the privileges just like you and me who were here before the treaty was implemented. You know we get a good pension. We can leave at 65 with 15 years service. All the good stuff is included; you know, good pension, free housing and electricity. These new hires are supposed to get the same thing as the Panamanians if they come here after 1979. The Panamanians really got a complaint. But, anyway, I don't know who they are. I guess we'll have to work with them."

Trent answered Carl, "Somebody said one of these pilots told me how that happened. His wife is kin to one of the congressmen. When they got a bill through in Congress, they attached a rider to it to bring these pilots in because they were short of pilots. They gave them all the privileges as if they had been here for years. I think the Panamanians have a right to complain about it. They could have hired about a dozen Panamanian PITs and brought them in here. But I don't know. We're not running it. What do you think?"

"Yeah, you're right, Trent. I guess they'll be here and I doubt if there is very much that Panama will be able to do about it."

"Well. I don't know either. I guess they'll make it some way. I'll just call the 'Johnny come latelys'. We'll just see how they make out," Trent concluded.

"I understand that some of them who came down here were just second and third class petty officers in the navy," Carl continued, "That's just a sailor. My god, man, I wonder what these ships' captains will think who have been through maritime academies for four years, trained on sailing ships, and had to go to school to learn English. They had to be able to speak English to get their certificates. Then to come here and have some novice take over the navigation and movement of their ships with full control, and there's nothing they can do about it. That's the rule down here. That's the code of federal regulations. It's the only place in the world where a pilot can relieve a ship captain of control of his ship. U.S. Navy captains, four stripers, have to stand aside while former petty officers, now Panama Canal pilots, take over full control of their ship and everybody calls the pilot 'captain.'"

"You got me. I don't know what the hell it's all coming to down here. But I know one thing. I'm going to keep this job until I get my years in for retirement and I qualify for my pension; then I'm gone. Well, here we go. We're getting our tugs up here now. When we clear this lock, if you want to go down and take a rest you can. You'll have to take it to Gatun anchorage, and I'm getting off at Gamboa. This ship is only eighty-two feet beam, so I can take it through Pedro Miguel by myself, so go on down there and get some sleep."

"Yeah, Carl, thank you."

"I'll call you before we get to Gamboa with some hot coffee. The captain said he would have a nice lunch ready."

"Okay, thanks, buddy. Thanks a lot, Carl."

"Captain, let's put her on dead slow ahead. We'll enter the lock in a minute. We're gonna get a tug on the stern. Put him on the port side."

"Yes, sir, Mr. Pilot," replied the officer on duty, "Okay."

"Thank you."

Trent went below to a cabin prepared for him and slept for several hours. The transit proceeded without incident.

As it turned out, Carl was correct in some of his guesses. In January of 1999, he visited Panama and made a transit as a guest of a pilot friend of his, Julio Candanedo. There was only one control pilot at a time on the Panamax ship, Nordmax except for transiting the locks. No bow pilots are employed anymore. Base pay for a senior pilot is $99,000 a year. Bonuses and overtime are not included in the base pay, but a pilot can make $135,000 to $140,000 a year with overtime and bonuses included. Twenty American pilots had retired in December of 1998. Julio predicted that there would only be about five American pilots left in the canal after December 31, 1999. Julio is a very able Panamanian pilot. The second control pilot was also a very skilled, black, Panamanian pilot.

The Colombian Submarine

One morning in 1992 at 0600 MTC called Carl. "Good morning, Captain Turner," MTC began, "Your duty time this morning will be 0800 hours. You have S10, the Pijao, a Colombian submarine. Gatun time is 1200. You will be getting off at Gamboa. Captain Jack Summers will relieve you."

"Thank you, transit," Carl acknowledged his assignment. Upon his arrival at the Cristobal boat house, Carl called transit for the latest information. He was given the same information as earlier, except that he was asked if he needed a tug. Carl said that he did not need a tug. Looking at the transit card, he noticed that the submarine had never transited the canal before. It was a 120' German built variable engine speed diesel.

When Carl entered the sub, he was greeted by the captain, "Good morning, Mr. Pilot. We have a very nice day for transit. This is my first on this vessel. My name is Commander Ramirez."

"I am Carl Turner. Mucho gusto."

" Habla Espanol?"

" Si, pero no mucho, para mucho Espanol palabra," Carl replied, "So I think I will speak English."

Ramirez agreed to speak English, stating "English was taught at my naval academy. Here is coffee and some tasty cakes. Our baker is very proud of his pastry."

"Um-m-m-m-m," Carl exuded as he ate one of the cakes, "These are delicious, thanks. Captain, we can just about kill 30 minutes until south eight enters the channel. He is going on the west side, and we have the east side. We will have a pilot change at Gamboa at about 1600, so you will not have to anchor in the lake. I have been in ports in Colombia, so I know a little about your country. I always enjoyed visiting Colombia. Years ago loading coffee took some time. Now it seems everything is containerized. I am glad I'm here."

"Yes, you have a good job here, and the U.S. is very generous with dollars in the canal."

"Captain, let's go half ahead and starboard 10°. South eight is in the channel." Carl told the captain, "'Midships; port 15° rudder; 'midships and steady on 180°. Thank you, captain." Turning to the captain, Carl commented, "Captain, this sub is new, isn't it?"

"Yes, this is its first voyage since delivery. It was built in Germany for $97 million."

"Skipper, don't you think that is a lot of money, since a nuclear sub could annihilate you in a heartbeat?"

"Yes, but our Central and South American countries, as well as third world countries cannot compete with this sub. We do not intend to fight a world power such as your country. The money for this sub hurts our economy somewhat, but it is better than buying or being given obsolete vessels from the U.S.A. They are good only for scrap."

Submarines have a very large rudder forward of the propeller. Therefore, when the ship has no headway, it has no steering. When entering the locks Carl could not stop the sub and maintain his position. "Okay. Dead slow ahead, please," Carl told the captain.

"Dead slow, pilot. Mr. Pilot, I am in very slow, with just enough headway to steer," he added.

"Center wall, number one fast," Carl instructed a locomotive. The locomotive acknowledged with four bells.

"Okay, center wall, slack your wire."

The locomotive acknowledged the order with two bells.

"Side number one fast." The locomotive acknowledged. Carl looked astern and saw that the sub's stern was at an angle to the sea wall. "Hard to starboard."

When the sub was lined up to go into the lock chamber, Carl ordered, "'Midships." Then the sub straightened itself in the chamber so that it was parallel to the side wall and in the center of the chamber. By ordering "Port 10° rudder, Center number two fast and holding, Side number two fast, ahead slow" Carl was able to hold the stern off the center wall and steer the sub through the chamber. Then he told the locomotives, "Operators, slack your wires off about three feet and hold; do not tow at any time. Just stay along side and help to keep the vessel in the middle."

"Ding, ding," answered the locomotives.

"Stop all engines," Carl requested as the lock gates were closing. The sub glided into the chamber. The lock gates closed and the lock chamber filled. When the forward gates were opened, Carl ordered, "Slow ahead." Locomotives were alongside and holding only.

"All locomotives, cast off," Carl ordered while the sub was in the middle of the last lock chamber to prepare to depart the lock chamber and enter Gatun Lake. At 1305 the sub cleared the lock.

Piloting a submarine can be very dangerous. If the pilot steps back in the tower, it is a long way to the control platform. Carl was always mindful of this, while the captain and chief officer watched his every move. Carl appreciated their concern and thanked them for it.

"Pilot, now that we have a few leisure hours while we are crossing Gatun Lake, I would like to present you with one of my caps. As you can see, it is just like the one I wear. You can put your cap in your pilot bag."

Carl thanked the captain and put on his new cap.

"Let me tell you about the name of my ship," the captain continued, "The name is taken from a very famous tribe of Colombian Indians, the Pijao tribe. When the Spanish conquistadors were conquering Colombia, the Pijao knew exactly the methods of the conquistadors and knew they could not prevail. Rather than be captured and pressed into slavery, they took up defensive positions and sent warriors back to their village to slaughter old men, women, and all the children until not one Pijao was left alive.

When the conquistadors attacked, the entire warrior force was killed. Therefore, the Pijao Indians are now extinct. How about that, Mr. Pilot? Do you think this vessel is worthy of its name?"

"Captain, I do not know of a greater honor. I'm sure you and your crew will never forget it. I salute you and your crew," Carl gave the captain a snappy salute. Then he asked, "Captain, do you think that after all the American military has departed from Panama, your country will take back the former province of Panama?"

"The old people of Colombia have forgotten about Panama, France, and the United States. However, the young people have not! That is all I will say on the matter. By the way, do you have a pilot nicknamed "Greasy?" His name is really Gomez. I do not like this turkey."

"Yes, I know him. To the best of my knowledge he was born in Colombia and graduated from your Naval Academy."

"That's right. That man is a spy. He was born a Colombian. His father is American, so he has American citizenship. He taught in your Naval Academy in Maryland."

"Gomez lives in a house in Balboa in the U.S. Canal Zone. He has a very high fence around his house, paid for at his own expense; his yard is stacked with Doberman pincers."

"That's the traitor, Carl. If he ever comes back to Colombia, he better carry a stick. He is a known spy and traitor, just like the traitors who betrayed us in 1903."

"I'll remember that, Captain. Well, here we are at Gamboa. Your next control pilot will be Captain Jack Summers, USNR. That's right, a real retired U.S. Navy Captain. He is one of the retired naval officers working here. Don't let him pull his rank on you just because he has control of your bridge. Good-bye, Captain Ramirez. I wish you and your crew all the best, bon voyage."

"Good luck," the captain told Carl as the two men shook hands.

Carl wondered as he boarded the pilot boat what Ramirez meant by his statement that the young people in Colombia had not forgotten the French and American roles in the Panama Canal. He hoped it would not mean trouble after Panama assumed full control of the canal at noon on December 31, 1999.

Percy Functory

Late in 1990 Carl had a transit with Percy Functory, a pilot who was particularly disgruntled because he did not enjoy all the privileges of the pilots employed before 1979. He did not have free housing and electricity. He hated the Commission, too, because the legislation had not gone through congress to grandfather him in, and he didn't think he was going to get an eighteen year pension. He wouldn't have enough time on the job for the pension by the time the Panama Canal was turned over to Panama on December 31, 1999. He would have received only a Panamanian pension. Perhaps he could have applied the time he had on the Panama Canal job to a civil service pension in the United States, but no one knew at this time for sure.

This transit required two pilots. Carl took the pilot boat from the Naos Island Pilot Station to the ship. As was usual the pilot boat dispatcher gave Carl his computer print out. He was supposed to transit this day with a friend of his, but something happened in the rotation. Carl noticed on the print out that the second pilot was to be none other than Percy Functory. He winced when he saw this. John, the pilot boat captain, looked at Carl and asked, "What's the matter, Captain Turner? Something wrong with the printout?"

"You bet there is! I am riding with none other than nasty—nasty asshole Percy Functory."

"You're sure right about him. That man is mad at the whole world," John agreed.

"Functory thinks that giving everybody a bad time and disrupting transits will help him with the senators in the U.S. to grandfather him in with the pilots hired before the treaty."

"Captain Turner, I wish I had a $20 bill for every ship he has turned down, and I had to take him back to the boathouse."

"You are right, John. He never bends a little to help the ship's captain make his transit. You see, he knows the Code of Federal regulations by heart, and if he can find anything in the code that will help keep him at anchor, he will call for a pilot boat to take him ashore. This will give him a bonus start and early repeat the next day!"

"Yes, and he knows that the ship must wait for the Port Captain to come out and have the deficiency corrected. Usually the rejection will be for a very minor deficiency. What a jerk!" John added.

When they arrived at Balboa basin, a pilot boat already had Captain Percy Functory aboard. When he came to the bridge, being a normal person and having to work all day with this monkey, Carl said, "Good morning, Percy."

There was no answer.

The lockmaster was all flustered. Carl knew him. He was Carl's neighbor who had just won a court case to be promoted to lockmaster. He had claimed that he was not promoted because he was a third national from Poland and didn't speak English perfectly. Carl had gotten this information from a friend who worked at Miraflores Locks.

Carl felt sorry for the lockmaster. He told Carl he would get the loco-motives. "Okay, I'll hold the ship here until you find the locomotives. No problem."

Functory started his harassment. "Okay, Carl. Give that lockmaster hell. Make him move the arrow to 45°. Get on his ass. How the hell are these monkeys going to run this canal when the competent Americans are gone? By the way, the tug didn't give you a full astern. I noticed the water about his stern. He couldn't have been doing much over 'slow astern.'"

Then Percy got on the radio on the lockmaster's frequency giving everyone hell. Carl admonished him, "Now, Percy, don't be shitty. Remember that I am senior pilot here. Not only that, but I am control pilot. Now just shut down your radio and get your ass off the bridge. I really do not need you here with your attitude."

Percy looked startled.

"All right, Carl, but you give that lockmaster hell. Look at him. He ain't doin' his job right."

Carl told Functory, "Look, Percy, why don't you keep your damn mouth shut? I know what I'm doin'. If you're going to harass me and try to get me to harass everybody in the locks, why don't you go down below? I'll do this job up here without you."

"You know how these people are, Carl. They're so damn stupid. Every time I come through here I have a hard time."

Carl interrupted with "Percy, it's because you're giving them a hard time. You gotta bend a little bit; bend a little bit."

"Look at that, Carl. The guy has left his workboat real close to the bow. These are the dumbest people—"

Carl again interrupted, "Look, Percy, GET YOUR ASS DOWN BELOW! GET OFF THE BRIDGE! I DON'T NEED YOU UP HERE! YOU'RE A PAIN IN THE ASS!"

"I don't have to go down below. I can stay up here. The Comission assigned me this—"

"Well, okay. I'll get on my radio and tell them that you are harassing me and I want to put this ship on the lock wall. I'll ask them to come down here and take your ass off. I'm control pilot on this ship, not you."

Without another word Percy took his radio and went below. "Can you imagine somebody who has that much hatred built up in him with a good job like this?" Carl thought.

When the ship got to the other side of the Canal, Carl mistakenly picked up Percy's radio. Percy sneered, "Now I'm in control. Get your greasy hands off of my radio."

Carl just gave it a toss over to him and said, "I hope it doesn't even work now."

Thank God that transit was over. Carl got home late that night. As soon as he got inside the door, the telephone rang. The caller identified herself as Percy Functory's wife. "Did you get sick on that ship with Percy?" she asked.

"No, I didn't get sick." Carl replied.

"Percy is sick. That food on that ship must have been poisonous. I'm taking him to the hospital now."

"Well, lady, it didn't bother me a bit, and I didn't see anybody else on the ship who was sick, so get him over there and pump his stomach out and give him a damn enema too. Tell them to stick the tube in his ear and blow it out the other end, because he needs it."

SLAM went the telephone. What a character! When the legislation to grandfather him in went through, Carl worked with Functory again. Then he was the *nicest* guy to work with that you would have ever seen. Settling his beef sure changed his personality! He's still down there, getting in his eighteen-year pension.

First Injury

Early in 1991 Carl sustained his first job-related injury. He was boarding a German container vessel as it was coming through the breakwater doing at least six knots. Gatun Locks were available, so the ship did not anchor in Limón Bay. When a ship is underway, it is customary for the pilot boat to match the ship's speed so that a pilot can climb the pilot ladder as easily as though both vessels were stopped. When Carl started up the pilot ladder, the pilot boat stopped his engines. The ladder was hung up on the pilot boat fendering. Carl was pulled under the gangway platform. His right thumb was twisted and pulled out of joint. The control pilot, Polack, reported the injury to MTC. Carl told MTC that he could make it to the Pacific side all right, but to have someone take him to Paitilla Hospital. The canal bo's'n met Carl at the boathouse on the Pacific side and took him to Paitilla Hospital. An orthopedic physician looked at Carl's thumb and asked, "Have you had this thumb operated on before?"

Carl answered, "No, a doctor at Gorgas Hospital treated it and told me that his treatment worked sometimes; I don't consider that an operation."

The orthopedic physician, Dr. Punjab at Paitilla Hospital, put Carl's thumb and hand in a cast and told him that this should work. It did not; four weeks later when the cast was removed Carl's thumb was still out of joint and became even more painful. Carl showed his hand to the chief pilot, Poncho Menendez. A staff member told Carl that the injury was more than two months old, and he would have to pay for his own medical care. Carl was instructed to see Patty Arquesta at the sick and injury department. When Carl saw Patty Arquesta, she asked him to get a letter from Dr. Punjab. Carl did this. Dr. Punjab's letter stated "Right thumb *re-injured*". Carl took the letter to Patty Arquesta who said to Carl, "No, this will not do. Take the letter back and have him give you another letter that states 'Right thumb injury re-occurred'. This letter you have will never do."

Actually the letter Carl had would do very well, as it was accurate. Carl would have received the appropriate medical attention, which included an operation, and full pay while he was off work, as well as bonuses that his replacement pilot would have earned. Patty Arquesta did not want the letter to say, "Right thumb *re-injured*". Such a letter would have entailed a lot of paperwork for her and would not have been a feather in her hat. With the new letter she could claim she was saving the Commission money. She knew her report would look better to the Panama Canal Commission if she could show that no injuries had occurred. Carl had never read the portion of the Federal Code of Regulations that dealt with accidents or injuries, but he felt sure that Patty Arquesta had and that she knew very well what she was doing.

Carl returned to work. His right hand was swollen. The pain became excruciating. He finally stopped working and asked Patty Arquesta to find him a doctor who could operate on his hand and take him out of his misery. She told him, "I know of a doctor who is a hand specialist. We use him sometimes."

"Please make an appointment for me as soon as possible," Carl pleaded.

Later that morning Patty Arquesta called Carl to tell him she had made the appointment for 1300 hours that same day with Dr. Gonzales. Carl kept the appointment. Dr. Gonzales examined Carl's hand and said, "I will operate. It will cost you $600 cash."

Dr. Gonzales set up the operation for 1000 hours the next morning. Although he felt that the Canal Commission should have paid for this work-related injury, Carl went to the Treasury Bank and got the cash demanded. The operation took about 40 minutes. Carl returned to work in two weeks. The operation corrected the problem; Carl's thumb has never given him any trouble since.

Military Base Maintenance

One day in 1992 Carl was in the pilothouse carrying on a conversation with some Panamanian pilots. Panamanians did all the jobs on the military bases. That was a lot of money flowing in to Panama. Now that they know the American military is going to leave in seven and a half years, Panamanians are asking the U. S. to pay several billions of dollars to lease bases in Panama. Carl told them, "The only reason the U. S. hasn't done it and won't do it is that all this was paid for with the $10 million the U. S. government gave Panama in 1903. Not only that, but the U. S. bought up private land to make the Canal Zone and paid out five million dollars for it. Some of that is land you are standing on. They are not going to pay for land they already own, Buster. The U.S. is not going to lease anything in Panama in the future. They are going to *give* it all to Panama."

One Panamanian pilot asked, "The U.S. leases bases all over the world. Why not Panama?"

"Son, we own these. The others we don't!"

Second Injury

In the early spring of 1992 Carl was assigned to harbor pilot duty from 1600 hours to 2400 hours. His name had come up on the rotation, so he had harbor duty for eight hours. It may be that he would have two successive harbor pilot duty days, or he may not have another one for a long time. He had several dockings and undockings that lasted until approximately 2200 hours. Then he was asked to go to the Pacific anchorage and board one of the many small tankers used to load bunker fuel in ships at anchor. All went well until he had docked a vessel at Pier 18E. Carl did not debark to the dock, but rather to a pilot boat, since he had another job moving a ship from one side of the harbor to the other. His pilot boat came alongside. When a pilot leaves a vessel at night, there is supposed to be a seaman who lights the way to the pilot ladder. Just as Carl reached the pilot ladder, he looked around for the seaman with the light. The crewman was nowhere to be seen. All the lights were turned off, leaving Carl in total darkness. He carefully began to climb down the ladder. Carefully he reached for first one rung, then the next and the next until he reached the last rung. As he stepped on the last rung with one foot on the pilot boat, the rung broke. Carl went down. The right side of the pilot ladder had oil on it. His right hand slipped; he caught his entire weight with his left arm. He felt a sharp pain like a bee or wasp sting in his shoulder. The crew of the pilot boat caught him as he dropped the four feet to the deck. In spite of the pain, Carl finished his harbor pilot duty. He was thankful that his last task was moving a ship from one dock to another. He did not have to climb any ladder.

The next morning Carl called the pilot office and told the story of his injury. The chief pilot sent him to Gorgas Hospital where he had his arm x-rayed. His injury was diagnosed as a torn tendon in his left arm. He reported for physical therapy for two months; then he was put on light duty for another month. He would normally have been assigned work in the office, but the chief pilot had no office work for him to do at this time. At the end of this period, Carl reported for pilot duty and piloted for about two months when his arm began to hurt again. The pain became intense, and he remembered his former injury. He had gotten effective treatment at Paitilla Hospital but not at Gorgas Hospital. Therefore, he requested treatment at Paitilla Hospital this time. The doctor at Paitilla gave Carl cortisone shots in his shoulder and arm. The pain stopped immediately. Since he had no more pain, he told the doctor that he could now go back to work. The doctor said that he was not yet ready and gave him an "Unfit for Duty" slip.

Carl reported to the chief pilot's office, but was unable to see him right away. He was told to take his slip to Patty Arquesta. He did so. While she was reading the report, the chief pilot appeared and shoved Carl hard against his left arm and asked gruffly, "What arm is injured? Where are you hurt this time?"

Carl felt a sharp pain in his left arm and shoulder.

The chief pilot backed away, turned to Patty Arquesta and told her angrily, "Put this man to work!"

Patty Arquesta answered, "We can't do that."

"Why not?" the chief pilot shouted.

"He has an 'Unfit for Duty' slip," she defended.

"For how long?" the chief pilot bellowed.

"The 'Unfit for Duty' slip has no expiration date," she responded.

"Get this man out of here! Now!!" thundered the chief pilot.

Carl went home. He reported to Paitilla Hospital for more physical therapy, hot soaks, lifting small weights. Finally he felt as though he could again climb pilot ladders. Since his arm was still weak and very tender, he climbed the ladders by reaching for the rung above him with his right hand, then stepped up while holding himself in place with his right hand. He repeated this procedure with each rung. He never reached up with his left arm. He never lifted any weight with his left arm and shoulder.

All during this period Patty Arquesta wanted Carl to take an office job, but none was available. One day she called him on the phone and said, "I have filled out this report on your status after talking to the doctor. Do not let anyone else fill one out for you. With this report you can get a medical disability pension."

Carl thanked her but never applied for the medical disability pension. He wondered if Patty had a twinge of conscience about his thumb injury. A few months later a friend of Carl's, Captain Mendenhall, was debarking the same vessel that caused Carl's injury. The crew turned out the lights as he debarked. He just walked off one deck and crashed onto the deck below. The resulting injuries ended his piloting career. Carl guessed there was no railing on the ship to protect him or to hold onto.

A few weeks after returning to work after his shoulder injury, Carl reported to the U.S. Occupational Health Office for a physical to certify that he was now fully recovered. The examination was very thorough. Carl was told that he was losing his hearing due to an ear infection. He was sent to Paitilla Hospital, where a doctor gave him antibiotic ear drops. After two more weeks of off duty, he reported back to the otolaryngologist who gave him a "Fit For Duty" slip.

Back Carl went to the U.S. Occupational Health Office. A female doctor again put Carl through his paces. Finally she told him to stand flatfooted and chin a bar. He gathered up all his will power and strength. His shoulder, while healed for normal activity, would be in a great deal of pain with this kind of strain. With great difficulty Carl struggled to the top of the bar. Then the female doctor said, "Once more."

This time Carl didn't think he would make it; but, with sheer determination, he did. He received another "Fit For Duty" slip and reported to the chief pilot. Carl gave him his "Fit For Duty" slip; Carl reported for pilot duty. He was determined to make his 15 years on the job to qualify for his pension and retire. If Carl served for 15 years and reached 65 years of age while on the job, he would also qualify for his pension and a $60,000 lump sum.

Worms

In early February of 1993, about a month before Carl's retirement date, he woke up one morning and thought there was a string caught in his anus. He pulled it out. He was shocked to see a worm about a foot long, alive and wiggling. He put the repulsive squirmer in a jar of water and hustled it to Gorgas Hospital in about five minutes. It was early in the morning, so the doctor Carl saw was an emergency room physician. He took one look at Carl and asked, "What's the matter? You look pale as a ghost."

Carl displayed his jar with the worm in it and told the doctor his story. The doctor gave Carl pills to take. He downed them immediately. Then the doctor inquired, "How did you get these worms? Don't you have indoor plumbing?"

"Yes. As a matter of fact, I do," Carl asserted.

The doctor explained, "Well, do you see the Panamanian people wash off every vegetable and fruit in your house? There must be some way you ate unwashed vegetable or fruit."

"Oh, yes, I know. I often ride my bike on the causeway. Sometimes I jog to keep my cholesterol down. Just in front of the general's house is a tree full of the sweetest mangoes in Panama. I just pick up the fruit from the ground, peal the skin off with my teeth and eat the fruit."

"That will do it! The worm's eggs live on the skin of the fruit. When you touch the skin with your teeth, you ingest some of the eggs. They hatch and grow inside of your digestive tract. You were lucky enough to expel one of the worms."

The doctor gave Carl additional medication to take five days later. He was then to come back in a week with a stool sample.

The doctor queried, "Why don't you take your mangoes to your maid? She would know what to do with them."

"Doctor, that tree is always full of mangoes. Panamanian boys swim across the inlet from Panama Bay and rob the other trees along the road. However, my tree is in front of the general's house, and a U.S. soldier guards the area around his house very closely, so they don't bother it. I am going to take a sack next time. I guarantee you the mangoes will be thoroughly soaked and washed! By the way, doctor, what made that worm come out?"

"You didn't eat for a while and they were hungry," the doctor answered.

"I know I have been drinking and didn't eat very much. Most of the time I just drank beer at the Army Club on my four weeks off."

The doctor elaborated, "Pilot, did you know that some people, mostly children, like the boys who swam the inlet for mangoes, get these worms. In extreme cases they will crawl out of their mouths, enter their lungs and live there. The children become anemic. By the time they get to a doctor for an exploratory operation, they just sew them up and they die shortly."

Carl again spoke to the doctor, "These worms come from animals. That makes us like animals."

"That's right," affirmed the doctor.

"Whew! I'm going home and take a few valiums for my nerves!"

Chinsky and Carl at the Albrook Garden Shop

Late in 1992 Carl's sister-in-law, Nelda, and Carl and Yolanda's maid, Lidia, liked to go to Rodman Naval Base on weekends and dance with the sailors at the enlisted men's club. Lidia met a chief petty officer nick-named Chinsky, a naturalized American citizen from Kurdistan. The girls brought their sailor friends to Carl and Yolanda's home on Empire Street in Balboa. Chinsky asked Carl if he could purchase anything for him in one of the military stores, the commissary or PX. Carl told him, "Yes. I would like to get into the garden shop at Albrook Air Force Base. My home is being built in the province of Chíriquí, near the city of David. I sure would like to get some patio furniture and some other things."

"No problem," accommodated Chinsky.

"Let's hook up my 18' fishing boat to the back of my Montero. We can haul our purchases home in that. I'll go by the bank and draw out some cash," Carl suggested.

Chinsky agreed to the plan. Carl knew he no longer had purchasing privileges since they had been taken away in 1985 as a part of the gradual withdrawal of the American presence in Panama after the Carter-Torrijos Treaty. Nevertheless, Chinsky did, since he was in the U.S. Navy. The two men hooked up the boat; Carl drew $1,500 in cash from his U.S. treasury account. They drove over to the parking lot behind the store and parked the truck and boat. Carl told Chinsky he would drive to the loading platform behind the store to pick up his purchases when they were placed on it. Carl knew what he wanted before they entered the store. He had been in this exchange when he had purchasing privileges and knew their inventory. Carl selected a refrigerator for Yolanda's father, a gas stove, large gas barbecue pit, rotary tiller, freezer, patio table, chairs and umbrella, lawnmower, yard rakes, garden hoses, electric hedge clippers, gloves, rose fertilizer, and extension cords for his new home.

When Carl and Chinsky went to the cashier to pay, the Panamanian store manager told Chinsky, "Your squadron is only on temporary duty here. I can't sell you all these goods as a temporary resident. You do not occupy housing."

Carl wondered how the store manager knew this. Chinsky grabbed the manager by the shirt, lifted him off the floor and told him, "Listen, you! My I.D. card gives me purchasing privileges all over the world. This place is included!"

He sat the manager down and continued, "If you want me to get my commander here, I will."

"Okay," the manager assented, "How are you going to pay for all this merchandise? We do not accept credit cards."

"Cash," Chinsky said, "Put it on the platform aft."

He peeled off the money needed from a fat roll of bills.

"You will have to wait until tomorrow for a truck to deliver it," cautioned the manager.

"We have our own truck," strutted Chinsky.

Carl went to the parking lot and drove the Montero and the boat to the loading platform. When he saw this rig, the manager's mouth flew open; his chin fell to his chest; his eyeballs stood out on their stems. "I have worked for the government all my life in this business and never have I seen such a sight," he exclaimed in astonishment.

"Load the goods, boys and let us go," Chinsky instructed, delighted with himself and Carl's ingenious "truck".

The boat was loaded high, but everything was included in one load. As they passed out the main gate, the guards just stared at Carl and

Chinsky open-mouthed. Chinsky stuck his torso out the window and shouted, "Navy over Army and Air Force" all the way to Empire Street.

People stared and laughed. Carl enjoyed the whole event. "Have a good day," Chinsky shouted all the way home.

10

1993 TO 1999

Carl Retires

A month later, in March of 1993, Carl retired from piloting in the Panama Canal. By this time the construction of his home between Davíd and Boquéte was well under way. Yolanda had found house plans she liked in a home design book. As Carl reflected on his years working in the canal, observing the changes that had taken place and would continue to take place in the near future, he wondered about the effects of these changes on Panama's people. Just how much would they benefit from the canal? Would the tolls find their way into politicians' pockets? Carl knew the people in Chíriqui cared nothing about the canal. They could not see how it has ever benefited them.

Exodus of American Pilots

Panamanians replaced American pilots and other canal workers at the rate of at least five percent a year, beginning in 1979. As soon as they could, American pilots retired. By January of 1999, less than 50 American pilots remained in active service in the canal. One of the pilots with whom Carl spoke predicted that many of these would retire on December 31, 1999. Only a few if any would remain to have their salaries, pensions, and privileges regulated by the government of Panama. By this time Panama had raised the upper limit of social security payments from $1,000 per month to $3,000.

Third National Certificates

Once in the boathouse one of the real senior pilots getting ready to retire told one pilot, "I know family members of the oligarchy send their sons to nautical schools in other countries. Their colorful diplomas look good on their resumes and help them get pilots' jobs. I believe you are one of them. I sure wish you'd give me a photocopy of your graduation degree from Argentina or Mexico or whatever country you got it from. It may not be worth the paper it is written on, but I'll bet it is really beautiful. I'm planning to open a candy factory when I get home. I'd like to use some of these diplomas to wrap candy boxes with. They're so colorful! They would help sell my candy. They're out of this world."

Earthquakes, Repair, Use of Panama Canal

If they ever did have a major earthquake in Panama and cave in the locks, Carl wondered where a couple of hundred square miles of water would go. They've never had a major earthquake there, but they have had tremors. He had felt them in his own house. They woke him up, and he saw chandeliers swaying. There have been major earthquakes just south of the Darien Peninsula in Colombia. Panama's mountain range is the same range that runs through Colombia. What would the people do? They do not pick up their own garbage. They have sidewalks, even in town, with holes that would swallow you up if you fell in them. The stoplights all turned green in every direction right after Panama took over the Zone, causing cars to all slam into one another from all directions. How are these people ever going to put the canal back together? It would take a mountain of money to build another canal. The only other country that could possibly undertake the task might be Japan if they would be willing to turn loose billions, perhaps trillions of dollars. A sea level canal is out of the question to build in Panama because of the mountainous terrain and the difference between the tides in the Pacific Ocean and the Caribbean Sea. The Pacific Ocean shelf, before you get to the Panama Canal, would require dredging out miles into the ocean on each side to get the depth needed for ships larger than the present panamax ships to go through the isthmus. If they ever did have a major disaster, there would be a lot of Panamanians, who had profited both from American generosity and Panamanian graft and corruption, who would have their sources for economic prosperity come to a screeching halt.

Some say that the canal was handed over to Panama on a silver platter. That's not true. The Panamanian government knows that the one thing more valuable than silver is gold. The U.S. government turned the canal over to Panama on a gold platter, not a silver one. Everything to be turned over to Panama is in the treaty—housing, buildings—the whole lot. Everything has to be brought up to new condition, requiring complete renovation. Panama has to approve of each item before it is accepted.

Panamanian Mail Service

The Panamanians would mail a letter in the Canal Zone for two cents rather than mailing it in Panama for three cents. There was a big squabble about it, with Panama saying that this practice causes a hardship on the Panamanian postal service. The truth about the postal system is that a person cannot send anything of value safely through Panamanian Postal Service. Just an ordinary letter is fine, but money will be gone immediately. Even a personal check or anything of any value whatsoever is either x-rayed or opened at the post office and immediately pocketed. Carl knew this to be true, since he sent Yolanda $400 before they were married, when she was living with her father in Nuevo San Pablo. The money never left Panama City.

In order to send anything of value one must go to the bus station and show the proper identification. Information from the identification papers is written down. The valuables to be sent are inventoried, placed in a container, and sealed. The bus company is paid for transporting the package. When the package arrives at its destination, the recipient must produce all the information that has been taken down at the other end, including the cedula number, picture and other identification. Only then can the recipient pick up the package. No one should send anything other than a letter through the rotten Panamanian mail system.

When Carl was at his home in Boquéte in January of 1999, a guest of his decided to write a letter to her son in Florida. Yolanda had business at the post office, so she checked on the progress of outgoing mail. She learned that no mail had left Boquéte for the past week and was not likely to do so for several days to come. It seems that the courier who takes the mail from Boquéte to Davíd had a death in the family and was taking time off from work. No one had bothered to secure a replacement for him, so the mail stayed in Boquéte. Carl's guest later learned that the letter to Florida took six weeks to arrive at her son's home.

Auto Inspection, Fruit Trees

In Panama an annual auto inspection is required. If there is any mechanical problem, it must be repaired, re-inspected, and passed before a license tag is issued. Carl thought this regulation was really a joke, because he saw cars driving all around Panama that were just a junk heap held together with bailing wire. They were ready to fall apart. People just paid off the inspectors and got their stickers. Before the Zone was turned over to Panama in 1979, an auto tag in Panama cost $1.50. Inspections were free. Americans inspected the cars; Panama issued the stamps; Americans paid the fee. After the treaty was implemented, the Americans turned the total auto inspection operation over to Panamanians in the Zone. So all the thousands of military and civilian civil service people had to get Panamanian license tags. Canal Zone license tags disappeared. Cars were still inspected in the same place, but now the inspection fee was six dollars. Tags went from $1.50 to $30.

Panamanian inspectors and clerks appeared in the inspection stations. Suddenly the money began disappearing. Panamanian personnel were stealing the money as fast as it came in, so Americans were put back in charge of all the inspections. The United States collected all the money from inspection fees and license tabs and turned it over to the Panamanian treasury. It will be interesting to see how things will be handled after all the Americans leave at noon on December 31, 1999.

Carl observed an instance of Panamanian "patriotism" which was based on a total lie. A Panamanian colonel climbed up on a dias in a public square and made a lengthy speech about how the people of Panama would never be subjected to the rules and regulations of the United States. He exhorted, "Now our children can go into the Canal Zone and pick the fruit from the trees!"

The truth is that Panama never planted any fruit trees in the Zone. Americans planted them all. The American government spent a great deal of money planting palm, papaya, and other fruit trees. The trees did well and bore prolifically. Panamanian children did go into the Zone climb the trees, and pick the fruit. They damaged the trees in the process.

The day after the colonel made his big speech, he flew out of Panama with $20 to $30 million of Panamanian money. Even if his whereabouts is known, the unofficial policy is that no one will tell, since many of the government officials are related to one another. They are all members of a small group of wealthy families, the oligarchy. A great deal of nepotism is practiced in awarding jobs. It is commonly said that, to get a good job in Panama, one has to have "palanca."

Communist Links

Yolanda told Carl that when Ramón was president of Panama, Fidel Castro came to Panama on a visit. Carl guessed that Panama pressured the United States to turn over the Canal Zone to Panama, playing a human rights theme. The U.S. was embarrassed because of the Mei Li massacre and failure in Vietnam. It was rumored that Cuba, The USSR, and Nicaragua, in cooperation with Panama threatened to attack the U.S. and engage in jungle warfare similar to that in Vietnam if the canal were not turned over to Panama. Castro asked Ramón when he was going to kick all the gringos out of Panama. Ramon replied that this would happen as soon as Castro kicked the Americans out of Guantanamo. Of course, there is no way of knowing if this conversation ever took place, but the story was widely circulated in the Canal Zone.

It is well known that Omar Torrijos and Manuel Noreiga were dictators with communist or at least socialist leanings. In May of 1999 elections were held for a new president. The leading candidates were Martin Torrijos, son of Omar Torrijos and Mireya Moscoso, widow of Arnulfo Arias. Arias had been elected three times as president of Panama and deposed by military coups. Moscoso won the election, promising to end government corruption and privatization policies. The outgoing president, Pedro Balladares, was making strides toward a capitalist economy by turning over utilities and other companies to private parties. It is feared by some that the new president will revert to government control of industry.

Yolanda's brother-in-law has a government job working on highways. He has been told that he will soon lose his job now that there is a new president. It seems that palanca is still very much alive and well. So far, Juan still has his job. Perhaps the new president, who owns a coffee plantation near Boquéte, wants to keep the good will of her neighbors.

Future of Pilots

Late one Saturday afternoon Carl was sipping beer on his patio with his old friend and fellow pilot, Geoff Jones. As usual they were talking shop. "Well, I think the fun is going to start in December with so many pilots retiring. There will be a mad rush to rehire as many as are willing to stay," Carl began.

"Working for Panamanian wages will be a come down. Beginning on January 1, 2000 pilots will only get the Panamanian social security for their retirement regardless of the high American wages they were paid before," Geoff added.

"There'll be more fun when the last American goes. Who will get the spoils? Whose pocket will the fees go in? I mean not just canal transiting fees, but also car inspection fees, airport fees, and all the others. Who will be allowed to use all the facilities the Americans leave behind?" Carl wondered.

"Yeah, I can't see the Indians using the golf courses, clubs, pools, living in the military housing and getting the jobs. Those poor wretches live in shacks and work from dawn to dusk on the coffee plantations for poor wages. They are so far out in the country they get little or no education."

"That's right, Geoff. In Boquéte, where I'm building my house, I see the Guamis on Friday and Saturday nights. The men are drinking the cheap booze the coffee plantation owners supply them in the taverns they own. They drink up everything they earn during the week while their wives and children sit on the curb for hours waiting for them to come out so they can go home. They get in a lot of fights, too, when they get drunk. This goes on from generation to generation. I don't see much hope of improvement." Carl had watched these events from the safety of his locked car. He had parked half a block away so he would be out of the fray.

Geoff probed for more information, "How far do you think the Panamanians will lower the wages? Do you think Panama will keep similar wages to the American wages?"

"Hell, no! A Panamanian pilot has told me that Panama has promised to keep the same wage scale. When can you remember Panama keeping its promises to its labor force? Panama is a poor country. It's like some of the Panamanian pilots I ride to work with say, ' The democratic business men build up the country and the military government tears it down'. Panama is in debt because of the military dictators, Omar Torrijos and Manuel Noreiga. There will be more debt in the future. Just wait and see. Colombian guerillas will cause or give Panama an excuse to build up another army and down the economy will go again," Carl concluded.

"We'll just have to wait and see what happens. It will be interesting to watch what unfolds. We both have early transits tomorrow, so I'd better go so we can both get some sleep. Good night, Carl."

"That's right, Geoff. I'll be seeing you." Carl said as he walked Geoff to the door.

Balboa High School

In June 1999 Balboa High School graduated its last senior class of 525 students. Most of them are bi-lingual, "Zonians", children of U.S. military personnel, civilian base workers, or employees of the U.S. government's Panama Canal Commission. Now they will be moving to new homes or college—many to the United States. According to the newspaper article, "They say they will miss the mix of American, Caribbean and Latin American cultures they found in Panama. A group of "Zonian" seniors hanging out in the gym wonders how they'll adapt to being Americans living in the United States for the first time." [iv] Carl wonders how well to do Panamanians who paid to send their offspring to U.S. Defense Department schools like Balboa High School will give a first class education to their children.

The Boa-Constrictor

He recalled the story of an incident in the city of Boca Del Toro, the capital of Boca Del Toro province on the Island of Colón in an Elementary School. Choloe, a six-year-old first grader had been misbehaving in class. Panamanian teachers are notorious for their severity with Indian children. Choloe had the misfortune to be a Guami Indian.

The Panamanian teacher had corrected him several times when she decided to put him out of class. Behind the school was a tool shed where lawnmowers, garden tools, and fertilizer were kept. The teacher put the little boy in this dark, windowless shed and locked it. A few hours later when she came back to get him, he was nowhere to be seen. She called for help. Two other teachers came to help in the search. They discovered a huge boa constrictor with an enormous lump in its stomach. No one knew how the snake had gotten in, but it was surmised that it had crawled in under some loose floorboards. One of the teachers took a machete down from its hooks on the wall and cut the lethargic snake's head off. Then he carefully slit the snake open. By this time the child's teacher was hysterical. The dead child was like a rag doll inside the snake. Every bone was crushed. The teacher was arrested and is still in prison.

POSTSCRIPT

Carl enjoyed his time as a pilot in the Panama Canal for the most part. He had his mother with him until she died in 1987 at the age of 88. He lived in comfortable, even elegant homes with beautiful, tropical surroundings. He made an excellent salary.

Carl especially enjoyed the work. Having served in the U.S. Merchant Marine in positions from ordinary seaman to captain of huge vessels, it was a pleasure to associate with captains and other officers and seamen on the ships that transited the canal. He was never more in his element than when he was at the con of a Panamax with only two feet to spare on either side of the lock wall. Safely and successfully transiting the canal gave him a great deal of satisfaction.

He is proud to know that he never had any ship damage causing an investigation by the Board of Local Inspectors.

He enjoyed the conversations he had with military personnel, especially paratroopers from the 508. Playing slot machines in the various clubs was a pleasurable pastime. Carl often gave his winnings away; he was very generous, especially to those less fortunate than he. Fishing was very rewarding, since there was an abundance of fish. Fishing was his favorite sport.

Carl was fortunate to meet his beautiful Panamanian wife, Yolanda, while he was piloting the Panama Canal. Now that he is retired, they live in a lovely home built on a hectare of land between Boquéte and Davíd, in northwestern Panama. He has a good life there tending his fruit trees and vegetable garden. Yolanda enjoys caring for the house and the gorgeous tropical orchids and other flowers in their yard.

As Carl looks back with fondness on all the good times he had, he tries to let the difficult times fade into oblivion, as he remembers his fifteen years of piloting the Panama Canal.

THE END

Endnotes

[i] *The Seattle Times.* Article from *Newshouse News Service.* Elizabeth Sullivan. October 7, 1999, page A17.

[ii] *The Seattle Post-Intelligencer.* From *The Associated Press.* A School—and a way of life—come to a close on Panama base". By Michelle Ray Ortiz. May 15, 1999. Page A12.

[iii] McCullough, David. *The Path Between the Seas, The Creation of the Panama Canal 1870-1914.* Simon and Schuster, 1977. Page 472.

[iv] *Seattle Post-Intelligencer.* From *The Associated Press.* By Michelle Ray Ortiz. "A School—and a way of life—come to a close on Panama base". May 15, 1999. Page A12.

Printed in the United Kingdom
by Lightning Source UK Ltd.
102691UKS00002B/81

9 780595 181070

CW01091070

Gallery Books
Editor: Peter Fallon

A BOOK OF STRAYS

Michael Hartnett

A BOOK
OF STRAYS

Edited by Peter Fallon

Gallery Books

A Book of Strays
is first published
simultaneously in paperback
and in a clothbound edition
on 14 September 2002.

The Gallery Press
Loughcrew
Oldcastle
County Meath
Ireland

*All rights reserved. For permission
to reprint or broadcast these poems,
write to The Gallery Press.*

© The Estate of Michael Hartnett 2002

ISBN 1 85235 321 X (*paperback*)
    1 85235 322 8 (*clothbound*)

A CIP catalogue record for this book
is available from the British Library.

The Gallery Press acknowledges the financial assistance
of An Chomhairle Ealaíon / The Arts Council, Ireland,
and the Arts Council of Northern Ireland.

Contents

Christ, come to Templeglantine
where a thousand Christmas candles
welcome You, White Star, new from the womb.
You will get a linen bed here,
a goose-down pillow for Your head here:
for every house is an inn here
and every inn has room.

I have tried to write for the people . . .

I have tried to write for the people,
made ballads for the Irish farmers,
dubious couplets for the workers,
songs for the sleek suburban housewives,
verses for the civil servants.

I have written for certain poets
poems as they like them written,
stolen an occasional rhythm
simply to give my friends some pleasure:
all these lines I am now regretting.

I have hopefully watched the critics
for a patronizing mention,
hoping to see in what direction
they thought my latest work was heading.

I have written down this evening
poems of no social value,
of a purely private meaning,
poems of my own dishonour,
poems of personal confession;
I have desecrated metre,
seldom used the peg of rhyming;
I have written private love-songs,
my own songs without a message:
I am an enemy of the people.

I stand in the streets . . .

I stand in the streets.
I admire the geological accidents,
and the man-made hills.
I admire the violated spectra,
eroded wood, eroded stone:
I admire erosion.
I admire what the poets have to say
though none of them knows the truth.
They do not know
man is a being who posits unattainables,
love being posited.
For our granite girdered
tree-lined problem
love is a desirable answer,
but do not misinterpret me as a saint:
when I say love
I am talking about women.

The Poet as Saint

I thought upon this friend.
He, the rich effusive man
preaching love for love's ends,
words and metres huge as
his Christ-love for his hundredth Judas.
He is father to many poets
and he is lover of their songs.
Largesse is his forte, as well as love:
and the great energy denoting love
and the lax compassion denoting love.
We have sat in Malaga
arguing over servants' ways
mistaking love of the master
for love of what the master pays.
We have argued over style
in the grey sheltered limestone bays
of Clare and not agreed: but we
shall be poets in coming days.

Enamoured of the miniscule . . .

Enamoured of the miniscule,
of the careful and compact,
I fail to introduce the fact
of current misery into
the line and, careful of the rule,
therefore cannot ask my proper dues,
become, not a poet of the heart,
but a *leipreachán* at his last,
making unwearable golden shoes.

The Critic as Carnivore

What would all the critics do
if all the poets died?
Alexandria could not hold
all the volumes they'd write.

What would all the critics do
if poets were not born?
Kindergarten could not hold
its hundred, thousandth moron.

The critic is a sporting man,
he dabbles some in verse:
'If they can do it, so can I!'
— except he does it worse.

Critic wanted: please apply
with hate as your credential;
competence is not required
but hindsight is essential.

If I were King of England . . .

If I were King of England
and you were Prince of Wales
we'd have a lark on the Royal Ark
with females and with males.

Oh happy days in England!
Oh gorgeous nights in Wales!
I could wear the ball-gowns,
and you could wear the tails!

You could bring Myfanwy round
and I some Swansea friends
and we'd all strive together
to pursue each others' ends.

We'd quieten Northern Ireland,
allow none to hunt or shoot;
we'd put the 'gay' in Gaelic
and blow the Orange flute.

We'd pacify the churches,
get rid of all sects at once,
by ordering all the clergy
to dress up as nuns.

We'd drink the malt of Scotland
and make sure no drop was spilt,
and you could flaunt your sporran
and I could twirl my kilt.

With dishy footmen at the Palace
at night to see us bed-ward —
you, my sweet Prince Alice,
and I, your sweet Queen Edward!

A New Ballad on the State of the Nation

Come hear my sad narration
about this Christian nation
where the cynic reigns supreme;
our national sports are Emigration,
Homelessness and Degradation,
and Abortion is a constant theme.

Embezzlement and Murder
stretch our patience further
and the farmers play Pollution on the green;
and the Irish language
is squashed into a sandwich,
caught between Illiteracy and Greed.

No lady now may enter
The Well Woman Centre
(a real lady wouldn't, anyhow),
and the latest Papal bill
was passed against the Pill
supported by some past-it Papal cow.

Our bishops moan and mumble
as their edifices crumble
and all the boys and girls abroad do roam.
In this land of milk and honey
let the church pay the mickey-money —
that'll keep the Catholics at home!

Glass melts with caustic soda
as the MultiNats unload a
million tons of shit off Aughinish.
I'll wear shabby quaint apparel
and rent a one-roomed barrel
and if I become a Cynic — that's my wish!

Who Killed Bobby Sands?

Who killed Bobby Sands?
'I,' said Margaret Thatcher,
'with my snow-white hands,
I killed Bobby Sands.'

Who saw him die?
'I,' said Humphrey Atkins,
'with my diplomatic eye,
I saw him die.'

Who caught his blood?
'I,' said a Provo,
'with my little black hood,
I caught his blood.'

Who'll dig his grave?
'I,' said Edward Kennedy,
'I'm safe across the wave,
I'll dig his grave.'

Who'll carry his coffin?
'We,' said some terrorists
shaking hands and scoffing,
'we'll carry his coffin.'

Who'll be the chief mourner?
'I,' said Charlie Haughey,
'in my neutral corner.
I'll be the chief mourner.'

All the children of Ireland
wrung their little hands
when they heard of the death
of poor Bobby Sands.

Reconstructionists

The GAA decided
the time had come to explain
to very puzzled tourists
the rules of the Hurling Game.
So, as things are quiet in winter,
their decision was to ask
the lads from the Office of Public Works
to help them with their task —
to build an Interpretive Centre;
to unbaffle Icelanders,
Dutchmen, Danes and Turks,
to educate our visitors
and not leave them in the dark,
and to site this latest venture —
where else, but in Croke Park!

The day came for unveiling
and there in snow-white ranks
stood shining sheds of limestone,
with Celtic septic tanks
to service all the toilets
with their sparkling tiles and taps;
and there was a lecture room
hung with very detailed maps
to point the way to Thurles
for Libyans, Letts and Lapps;
and a foyer aglow like the Book of Kells
with an undecipherable graph
that's explained the whole year 'round
by the full-time staff
of two. And for all the lovely money
a Foreign Currency Exchange
clad in gleaming quartz-stone
left over from Newgrange.

And a genuine Irish *siopa té*
with genuine soda bread
made brown with genuine turf dust
to sink in your belly like lead
(one slice of that and, d'you know what,
you'll swear that you've been fed!).

The Fathers of the Nation
rejoiced and they were glad
(the Mother of the Nation
was somewhere west of Chad);
but none of these wise leaders
had foreseen the tiny hitch —
the lads from the Office of Public Works
had built their Temple of Plumbing
in the middle of the pitch!

Hallo Ducky

(a Muscovy duck)

A tale I'll tell and now reveal —
it happened once near Abbeyfeale.
Mickey Joe was a bit of a card,
he stole a duck out of a yard;
then he saw before him, in his way,
the farmer's wife and her daughter May.
In his trouser the duck he hid
afraid they'd see what he just did.
'Fine mornin', Mickey,' said young May
and the mother barely said 'Good Day'.
And May talked on as gay as a lark
and the duck got anxious in the dark.
Young May was full of last night's dance
and feathers came down the leg of Mick's pants,
and he stood and stuttered, nearly dumb,
with two webbed feet stuck up his bum.
All of a sudden fly-buttons went pop
and out came a neck with a big red top.
The ladies gave a quick jump back
and nearly died when the duck went 'Quack!'
'Oh Mother, Mother,' cried the daughter,
'is *that* what all the girls are after?
I'd sooner go barefoot a ten-mile walk
than trust a man whose lad can talk!'

Con Murphy's Pal

1

We watched him grow from *banbh* up,
as small and friendly as a pup;
his two brown eyes would melt a stone
as he sat there in the shed alone,
his small heart heavy with distress
until Con brought in his mess.

2

He grew in beauty day by day,
happy in his straw and hay,
with his back as smooth as silk
from barley-meal and sweet new milk:
his noble head and handsome snout
over the half-door looking out.

3

He thought Con Murphy was his friend
but he was much mistaken;
for this friendship had to end
when Con, he longed for bacon.
And Ritchie Trant no mercy would grant
and Willie Woulfe, he dropped no tear;
in spite of his cries, to his great surprise,
they cut his throat from ear to ear.

4

And myself with razor and shaving-brush
made his skin as smooth as a baby's bum.
I sang him a song as the blade sped along
and thought of fine dinners to come.
And Paddy Kelly slit his belly
and butchered him into pieces;
we had liver and lard and guts by the yard,
enough blood to fill the half-tierces.
And Mary Con with her apron on
did something a bad wife couldn't —
with onions and spice and oatmeal nice
turned the guts and blood to black puddens.

5

Pray heed me now, both pig and sow,
all hungry men are fickle:
they'll feed you well and when you swell
they'll drop you in the pickle.
They'll mind you from harm and keep you warm
when the weather is cold and bad;
and then one day when you're happy and gay
they'll come and they'll cut your gad!

Three Squibs

1

Abbeyfeale, Abbeyfeale
where the people eat meal,
nettles, thistles and mangolds,
and the people back there
have lice in their hair
and snots from their noses like candles.

2

Abbeyfeale is a fair old place,
Kilmorna wouldn't grow a haw;
Lyreacrompane is the worst place of all —
but f*** me, Duagh!

3

Do you recall Seán Archer
who plagued us poets for ages,
who wore the critic's cap a while
and ponced about *Hibernia*'s pages?

Do you recall the book of verse
he wrote, all by himself?
You can't recall the title?
Neither can anyone else!

The Ballad of Salad Sunday

for Sheila and Ned Dwyer

You've heard of Newcastle and its famous Dog Fair,
and of Sandwich Sunday — no one was there;
you'd not think we'd be caught out three times in a row —
but once again, people, we're made a pure show!

Come all ye young travellers who live in this town,
all crime that's committed to ye is put down;
be now found 'Not Guilty' by the householder breed
who were ate up last Sunday by profit and greed.

The fifth day of June, nineteen eighty-three,
they expected to profit by you and by me;
yet in spite of their salads and watery tay
more went to watch donkeys in honest Athea.

I heard that the shopkeepers up in the square
were sending back bread and tearing their hair;
they turned over so little, it made their hearts scald
(I will mention no names — but there's two of 'em bald!).

I heard of a publican who rented a space
not far from his own house, John Bourke's is the place,
put girls behind counters all dressed in white coats
and had enough greens to feed twelve hundred goats.

One cleared the locals out of his place,
no cards or no darts were allowed — just in case —
but two pick-axe handles were ready to wave
at the thousands expected who mightn't behave.

Let no local farmer buy meal or buy hay
for there's free bales of lettuce to be had, I hear say;
and regardless of breed or regardless of number
their cows can now feed on free wynds of cucumber.

There's ducks in the river now bigger than swans
and the waterhens there wouldn't fit into ponds,
and the rats eating salads, mouths back to their ears,
for the flutes of Newcastle they send up 'Three Cheers!'

Maiden Street Ballad

1

Come all you young poets and listen to me,
and I hope that my words put a flea in your ears;
a poet's not a poet until the day he
    can write a few songs for his people.
You can write about roses in ivory towers
and dazzle the critics with your mental powers,
but unless from your high horse you cannot come down
    you're guilty of poetic treason.

2

You can write about writers in verse that is free
and rob all the stories from our history;
you can rhyme about China and philosophy —
    but who gives a shite for your blather?
Your friends are your friends, for better or worse,
to speak to them straight put rhyme in your verse;
if the critics don't like it they can all kiss my arse —
    as long as it's read by my father!

3

So relax and I'll tell you what I'm going to do,
take a sup from your drink, start unlacing your shoes;
you'll be in a bad way when I'm finished with you,
    and ringing up doctors and nurses.
My song's not so long — it's about my own life,
and the things that I saw as a man and a child —
but it won't keep you up too late in the night
    for it only has fifty-three verses!

4

My father was born in a house in North Quay,
Ned Harnett, his father, was a tailor by trade;
he came to this town on the boat from Athea
    to make suits for the rich and the needy.
My mother, the daughter of farmers so bold,
in the townland of Camas she made her abode,
'til my father he promised her silver and gold
    and stole her away from Raheenagh!

5

Nineteen forty-one was a terrible year,
the bread it was black and the butter was dear;
you couldn't get fags and you couldn't get tea —
    we smoked turf-dust and had to drink porter.
To work in the bog brave men volunteered
when Hitler was bombing the land and the sea,
and to cap it all off I appeared on the scene
    and threw everything into disorder.

6

In Newcastle West I spent most of my years,
so you'll be amazed at what you will hear —
the old stock will be shocked by what I reveal
    'twas in Croom that I spent my first fortnight!
Well, in a turf-lorry I came home from Croom
and we took an apartment in Massey's back room
and my Ma fed me goody and milk from a spoon
    supplied by the late JJ Dalton.

7

We left Connolly Terrace and moved to Church Street,
a few doors from Tom Luddy who made harness so neat —
but we wanted to live among the élite,
    so we moved to a new situation.
We rented a mansion down in Lower Maiden Street,
Legsa Murphy our landlord, three shillings a week,
the walls were of mud and the roof it did leak
    and our mice nearly died of starvation.

8

Now before you get settled, take a warning from me
for I'll tell you some things that you won't like to hear —
we were hungry and poor down in Lower Maiden Street,
    a fact I will swear on the Bible.
There were shopkeepers then, quite safe and secure —
seven Masses a week and then shit on the poor;
ye know who I mean, of that I am sure,
    and if they like they can sue me for libel.

9

They say you should never speak ill of the dead
but a poet must say what is inside his head;
let drapers and bottlers now tremble in dread:
    they no longer can pay men slave wages.
Let hucksters and grocers and traders join in
for they all bear the guilt of a terrible sin:
they thought themselves better than their fellow-men —
    now the nettles grow thick on their gravestones.

10

So come all you employers, beware how you act
for a poet is never afraid of a fact:
your grasping and greed I will always attack
    like Aherne and Barry before me.
My targets are only the mean and the proud
and the vandals who try to make dirt of this town,
if their fathers were policemen they'd still feel the clout
    of a public exposure in poetry.

11

But now to get back to the story at hand
about the street of my youth where my bum was once tanned;
when you hear what I'll tell you, then you'll understand
    why I smile now whenever I go there.
'Tis said that in Church Street no church ever stood,
and to walk up through Bishop Street no bishop would,
and 'tis said about Maiden Street that maidenhood
    was as rare as an ass's pullover.

12

We had no television and no radio,
no Donncha Ó Dúlaing, and no *Late Late Show*;
when the nights they got dark to bed we did go
    and provided our own entertainment.
The poor, as you know, always breeding like rats,
ended up with a house full of wall-to-wall brats,
and when they grew up they had all to make tracks
    to England on board of the boat-train.

13

Off went Smuggy and Eye-Tie and Goose-Eye and Dol,
off went Ratty and Muddy and Squealer and Gull;
then the Bullock and Dando and Gallon were gone,
    all looking for work among strangers.
The old men who stayed, Time soon thinned their ranks —
like Gogga and Ganzie and Dildo and Sank,
and the Major and Bowler felt Death's icy hand;
    old Maiden Street went to the graveyard.

14

Behind Nash's Garage we played pitch-and-toss
or sat on the footpath the tinkers to watch
as they walloped each other because of a horse
    outside Bill Flynn's pub of an evening.
Oh gone are the days of our simple past-times
when rawking an orchard was the worst of our crimes;
we fought with our fists and we never used knives
    and ran like the hare when the priest came.

15

We played marbles and skellit and, blue with the cold,
we started up bone-fires right out in the road;
we had negotiable comics and our chainies were gold
    and marble-sweets were twelve a penny.
We cracked nuts in the autumn, caught collies in crocks
and hunted for craw-fish at the back of the Docks;
we ducked into Latchfords, myself and Mike Fox,
    and ate Peggy's Leg for our dinner.

16

The old street it finally gave up to the ghost
and most of the homes there they got the death-blow
when most of the people were tempted to go
    and move to the Hill's brand-new houses.
The moving it started quite soon after dark
and the handcars and wheelbar's pushed off to the Park
and some of the ass-cars were like Noah's Ark
    with livestock and children and spouses.

17

For we all took our furniture there when we moved,
our flourbags and tea-chests and threelegged stools
and stowaway mice ahide in old boots —
    and jamcrocks in good working order.
And our fleas followed after, our own local strain —
they said, 'We'll stand by ye whatever the pain,
for our fathers drew life from yere fathers' veins
    and blood it is thicker than water!'

18

'Tis said their descendants still live in the Park
with the strength and the cuteness and teeth of the shark;
they can jump seven feet and see in the dark —
    but they only attack passing strangers.
They're respectable now for they live with the toffs
and every flea there has his own private dog
and every summer to Bally they're off
    though hundreds get drowned in the waves there.

19

In nineteen fifty-one people weren't too smart:
in spite of the toilets they pissed out the back,
washed feet in the lavat'ry, put coal in the bath
    and kept the odd pig in the garden.
They burnt the banisters for to make fires
and pumped up the Primus for the kettle to boil,
turned on all the taps, left the lights on all night —
    but these antics I'm sure you will pardon.

20

For in a few years we all settled down
and quickly became the pride of the town —
we swapped our old army coats for eiderdowns
    and stopped being so wild and so airy.
We have motorcars now and we sometimes play squash
and, dirty or clean, quite often we wash;
we have more than one shirt and more than two socks
    and we holiday in the Canaries.

21

But now what can I say of a small country town
that is not like Killarney, known all the world round?
That has not for beauty won fame or reknown
    but still all the same is quite charming?
I have seen some fine cities in my traveller's quest,
put Boston and London and Rome to the test,
but I wouldn't give one foot of Newcastle West
    for all of their beauty and glamour.

22

Go out some fine evening, walk up to the Park
when the sun shines on Rooska and the Galtees are dark
and all the nice gardens are tidy and smart
    and the dogs lie asleep in the roadway,
and the blue of the hills with their plumes of white smoke
in a hazy half-circle do shelter our homes
and the crows to the treetops fly home in black rows
    and the women wheel out their new go-cars.

23

When the children in dozens are playing at ball
and Dick Fitz and Mike Harte stand and chat by the wall
and a hundred black mongrels do bark and do brawl
    and scratch their backsides in the street there;
when the smell of black pudding it sweetens the air
and the scent of back rashers it spreads everywhere
and the smoke from the chimneys goes fragrant and straight
    to the sky in the Park in the evening.

24

When the chestnut's in flower each spring by the Bridge
and the boys stand around and whisper and wink
and the trout rings the water to nuzzle the midge
    and the bell from the chapel is calling;
where the blackheaded bullfinch shows off the haw
and the wagtail with her bill full finds her nest in the wall
and the river from brown turns to white in its fall
    and the swallow, she kisses the water.

25

If you've nothing to do, stroll up the Demesne,
it's there you'll discover all kinds of game:
there's pheasants, there's rabbits, there's pigeons, there's hares
    and girls ahide in the bushes.
There's football and handball and hurling and squash,
there's coursing of hare, there's gallop of horse,
while the noise of the traffic in trees it gets lost
    in the music of blackbirds and thrushes.

26

I have drank in New York and missed Barrett's pub,
I have eaten in Paris and missed home-cooked grub,
I have longed for my own when I shoulders did rub
    with very hospitable gentry.
I have slept in Newfoundland and dreamt of the Coole,
in Trinity College missed the old Courtney School,
but if you think you can go back then you are a fool
    for the Past is signposted 'No Entry'.

27

Sometimes I have reason and cause to lament
the number of pubs that I like to frequent
but I always leave when my money is spent
    unless I am forced to remain there.
Dinny Pa's and the Dollar I have been inside
when from wife or from weather I am forced to hide;
to Mike Flynn's I have walked up just for exercise
    and if thirsty have been known to stay there.

28

McCarthy's, Pat Whelan's, they've both heard my shout
and I have been known to peep in to Peep-Out's
and before I leave Church Street I turn about
    and walk Mister Barrett's old Greyhound.
'Tis there you will find a rest from all strife —
John Barrett, he knows me as well as my wife —
for didn't I give him the best years of my life
    for he has the cure for what ails me!

29

In Tom Meaney's on Sundays there is a fine quiz,
at which Desmond Healy thinks he is a whiz:
and Joe White he keeps shouting 'Bzz, bzz, bzz, bzz!'
    though he seldom knows his own answers!
And down in Mike Kelly's there's free nuts and cheese
and a fine pint of porter that's certain to please:
where some better class clients, pretending to spree,
    dine free there on Sundays, the chancers!

30

With jokes and with crack the Tally-Ho rings
and I'd go there more often but Mike Cremin sings,
and when Horan joins in, to the doorway I spring
    and go straight across to John Whelan's.
'Tis there you will find the Barber enshrined —
he'd gallop for porter out to the Bruff Line;
I'm ashamed to confess he is a cousin of mine
    but what can you do with relations?

31

There's Dinny the Postman out with Tony Roche
pouring brandy and ginger down poor Tony's throat;
you can hear Dinny laugh miles up the Cork Road
    as he adds up his Christmas donations!
And then there's young John whose moustache will soon grow
and Ger who drinks nothing for one month in four —
a shit and a shower and he's ready for more:
    oh, I'm blest with some lovely relations!

32

If you want to read papers you don't buy at home,
if you want to drink porter with a rich creamy foam,
if you want a hot whiskey with more than one clove,
    you must pay a call to John Barry.
Go there in the evening if you want a good laugh,
'41' on a Tuesday, great fun and great crack;
but when Peg's in bad humour you'd take it all back
    and wish she had stayed down in Kerry!

33

Go back to the Shamrock, the home of the ducks,
where the counter it groans to keep Doyle standing up;
with Dick on the phone on some blowen tryin' his luck
    it's Tony and Peg do the work here.
You'll see Jimmy Deere and he making soft farts,
you'll see Terry Hunt, he's a martyr for darts —
he spends every week-night nearly bursting his arse
    to bring home a ham or a turkey.

34

I've been seen in Ned Lynch's and in Gerry Flynn's,
in Walshe's and Cremin's, forgive me my sins;
and in Donal Scanlon's when the new spuds come in
    sometimes I have a small jar there.
More than once in the Heather with Dan, Gerry and Jack
I've lingered too long and missed the bus back —
dropped into Moss Dooley and stayed for the crack
    and had to walk home over Barna!

35

In Cronin's and Cullen's to pints I've said yes
('twas in Dolly Musgrave's I drank my first glass)
and above in the Sunset I often play chess
    with Bill Buckley in darkest December.
Once under the weather, I slipped and I fell
and I woke in a bar that I didn't know well —
then I saw to my horror I was in the Motel
    with a couple of Fianna Fáil members!

36

In the Central Hotel you will find Arthur Ward
and Vera, his missus, who lets no one get jarred —
the occasional priest, the occasional Guard
    who are there just to keep things in order.
And at Seamus Connolly's behind in the Quay
you'll hear Irish spoken to this very day:
Bail ó Dhia ort, a Shéamais, 's orainn go léir,
    's go bhfóire Dia ar ár náisiún-sa.

37

Now if you get the notion I'm mad for the drink
you won't be far out, but it's not like you think:
for a pub is a sociable place to be in
    provided you can hold your liquor.
So now to get back once more to my tale
to some sights and some scenes I saw in my day;
of things that will never again come our way
    I will paint you a few verbal pictures.

38

I awoke one fine morning down in Maiden Street
to John Kelly's forge-music ringing so sweet,
saw the sparks flying out like thick golden sleet
    from the force of his hammer and anvil;
and the red horse-shoes spat in their bucket of steam
and the big horses bucked and their white eyes did gleam —
nineteen forty-nine, I remember the year —
    the first time I got my new sandals!

39

I remember that one time the town had four bells,
Protestant, Catholic, and Library as well,
and John Lenihan's hand-bell above them did swell
    as he called out 'Take Notice! Take Notice!'
And the hearse pulled by horses went slow through the streets
and the men took their hats off in rain or in sleet
and the shops closed their doors respecting the grief
    of the crying and black-coated mourners.

40

The day of the pension my Nan came to town
in a flurry of hairpins with her shawl wrapped around,
with a dozen of eggs and maybe a half-crown
    and a bag of new spuds in her ass-car.
I remember the women ahide in the snugs
as we carried the milk home in gallons, not jugs,
and we drank cabbage-water from pannies, not mugs,
    and we were physicked with spoons of Cascara.

41

We had cod liver oil and Parrishes food
and castor oil to put us in the mood
and if Epsom Salts didn't do any good
    we had senna-pod tea for our breakfast!
We had turnips for dinner, we had turnips for tea,
and half stones of pandy piled up on our plates;
we feasted on cabbage, we fattened on kale
    and a feed of boiled meat if we smelled it!

42

In the old Courtney School we were a hard bunch:
the boys from the town ate the country boys' lunch,
and the rats ate the legs off every bench
    and the swallows shat into the inkwells.
Where the smoke from the fire brought tears to our eyes
and the boodies and woodlice crawled up our thighs,
and Finucane and Coughlan knocked sparks off the boys
    and the priest ate the head off the tinkers!

43

I remember quite well the Confraternity Band —
in the Procession they sounded so grand;
the front, they played one tune while in the back rank
    they struggled with 'Faith of our Fathers'!
In the old Market Yard I looked up at the lights
where Paudie Power danced as he swung Peggy Hynes;
now the lights have gone out and the music has died
    and Time, it has slowed down the dancers.

44

I remember the days of the cows at the fairs,
the standings, the Corkies, and *banbh*s in rails,
and men from the mountains with scollops for sale
    when everyone slipped in the cowdung.
There was spitting on hands, there was drinking in pubs,
and milking of milk from big cows' fat dugs
and the jobbers in gaiters and the cute country mugs
    saved sixpence and drank a few pounds' worth!

45

And then I left home and I started to roam,
making my living by the writing of poems:
until I got wed ('twas the wife who proposed)
    and I had to stop gallivantin'.
We've a son and a daughter, a cat and a hen,
a dog and an acre of weeds to fence in,
and we dwell in the shade of Tom White's green hill
    in exile out foreign in 'Glantine.

46

I have told ye no big lies, and most of the truth —
not hidden the hardships of the days of our youth
when we wore lumber jackets and had voucher boots
    and were raggy and snot-nosed and needy.
So now — there you have it, the long and the short —
and there may be some people that I have forgot;
if you're not in this ballad, be thankful you're not,
    but anyway, buy it and read it.

47

So now to conclude and to finish my song:
it wasn't composed to do decent men wrong;
if I had known it would go on so long
    I'd have finished before I got started.
And in times to come if you want to dip
back into the past, through these pages flip
and, if you enjoy it, raise a glass to your lips
    and drink to the soul of Mike Hartnett!

On Those who Stole Our Cat, a Curse

On those who stole our cat, a curse:
may they always have an empty purse
and need a doctor and a nurse
    prematurely;
may their next car be a big black hearse —
    oh may it, surely!

May all their kids come down with mange,
their eldest daughter start acting strange,
and the wife start riding the range
    (and I don't mean the Aga);
when she begins to go through the change
    may she go gaga.

And may the husband lose his job
and have great trouble with his knob
and the son turn out a yob
    and smash the place up;
may he give his da a belt in the gob
    and mess his face up!

And may the granny end up in jail
for opening her neighbours' mail,
may all that clan moan, weep and wail,
    turn grey and wizened
on the day she doesn't get bail
    but Mountjoy Prison!

Oh may their daughter get up the pole,
and their drunken uncle lose his dole,
for our poor cat one day they stole —
    may they rue it!
And if there is a black hell-hole
    may they go through it!

Unfriendly loan-sharks to their door
as they beg for one week more;
may the seven curses of Inchicore
      rot and blight 'em!
May all their enemies settle the score
      and kick the shite of 'em!

I wish rabies on all their pets,
I wish them a flock of bastard gets,
I wish 'em a load of unpayable debts,
      TV Inspectors —
to show 'em a poet never forgets
      his malefactors.

May rats and mice them ever hound,
may half of them be of mind unsound,
may their house burn down to the ground
      and no insurance;
may drugs and thugs their lives surround
      beyond endurance!

May God forgive the heartless thief
who caused our household so much grief;
if you think I'm harsh, sigh with relief —
      I haven't even started.
I can do worse. I am, in brief,
      yours truly, Michael Hartnett.

The Ghost of Billy Mulvihill

As I looked out my window
    in the heart of Dublin 4
the ghost of Billy Mulvihill
    went walking past my door.
He wore a heavy top-coat,
    his face was pale and thin;
he waved up at my window
    but I would not let him in.

What was he doing walking
    on Upper Leeson Street,
a cardboard suitcase in his hand
    and hobnails on his feet?
He flashed up at my window
    his old big-toothed grin,
but I moved back in the shadow
    and I would not let him in.

As I moved behind the curtain
    and beat a coward's retreat
the ghost of Billy Mulvihill
    walked up Leeson Street.
He vanished in the traffic
    with his suitcase full of sin:
I knew he wanted comfort
    but I would not let him in.

That night as I sat writing —
    the clock said nearly four —
the ghost of Billy Mulvihill
    stood on my kitchen floor.
'The fight you're fighting, Mikie,
    is a fight you'll never win.'
I locked the doors inside my head
    and I did not let him in.

Aere Perennius

And there you are, Paddy,
watching your canal
and — to use your own rhyme — banal
in bronze, you suffer the embrace
of winos at all hours
who clasp your neck and sing,
'If all the world was sweet sweet wine
an' all the sea was gin,
if all the flowers were Baby Powers
whor a pickle we'd be in . . . '

So, too, new claimants tamper
with the facts,
dull strangers with degrees
who prune, to fit conceptions
you would never back,
your statements and your acts;
who, to give you ancestors and heirs,
to bring you into line
with academic aims,
number all your bones
and stake false claims.

They forget I knew you, Paddy,
if only for a while;
fresh from Newcastle West
at twenty, with a sheaf of verse
tucked in my belt,
I understood the smokescreen of your talk
about fillies, about stallions:
I sometimes placed your bets.

It is easy to forgive
a world that forgets
but not a world that changes

with subtle sentences
a life that was and is.

Let me escape a similar fate.
I'd rather be forgotten out of hand
than wronged in bronze:
let the sad facts stand.

House Devil

In a certain public house
as I charmed some man's spouse
(an art that only poets can really master),
every Culchie, every Dub
in the hubbub of that pub
was totally determined to get plastered.

All the male and female flirts
(three-piece suits and mini-skirts)
began to split into the hunted and the hunters,
and two wino friends of mine
sat there drinking German wine
disguised as ordinary punters.

Up to the counter, said 'Hallo!'
and the barman said 'No, No!
All ye do is come in here to borrow money!'
I said 'Well, you, you have some neck —
today I got a cheque,
so cash it for me pronto, sonny!'

And then a man, about my size,
darker hair and darker eyes,
came up and made this salutation:
'My dear Michael, have a drink!'
but I had to stop and think —
there was something damp and cold in his persuasion.

With the vodka, 80 proof,
I thought I saw a hoof,
black and hairy underneath the table;
perhaps I was in the rats
but said 'I must go feed my cats,'
and staggered out of there while I was able.

And as I left the pub
the incredible hubbub
changed it to a manic Tower of Babel;
as I beat my dazed retreat
at the top of Leeson Street
the moon shone like a Guinness-bottle label.

Aubade

When you wake in the dawn
with your eyes full of sand
(more than the grains on Ballyheigue Strand)
and you think that Paul Durcan
is holding your hand —
is it time to send for the doctor?

When you think you have suffered
a mild heart-attack
and you lie there talking to Pasternak
and into the room walk Heine and Schumann;
and at the foot of the bed a man and a woman
are most harmoniously singing —
could it possibly be Garcia Lorca
and Hildegard von Bingen?
Is it time I rang up the doctor?

When getting up is decidedly risky
and your hotwater-bottle
is drained of hot whiskey;
when your butts are all smoked
and your pipe has no dottle,
when you look for your ivory Venus to pawn
and you find you've already hocked her —
then it is time,
(it is certainly time)
to ring up your doctor!

Morning Ireland

Suicidal prisoners moved to Ballymun.
Politicians form a Gang of One.
British troops defuse their daily bomb.
Senator stands trial with aplomb.
Georgian building rebuilt overnight.
Abandoned baby lost on derelict site.
Farmers and badgers reach an accord.
Poet gets the Brown-nose Verse Award.

I switch off Hanly, play the *Shepherd's Hymn*,
coughing up my morning clot of phlegm.

Parables for Clane

for the staff of Clane General Hospital

1

The field behind the hospital slyly
changes its November coat
(as many creatures do)
so that winter, passing by
with ice upon its tongue,
will not know it's there;
while, up the road, the odd pampered rose
and bright green lawns — much less wily —
die and shrivel in the blackfrost air.

2

As perfect as one of my discarded fingernails
the moon in its last crescent
in pure stillness lies upon the water.
A trout, the same shape,
same curve, same colour in the late light
as that moon, leaps with great grace
smashing it as if it were a china plate
and falls back with a flat splash.
Soon, the fragments and the ripples all re-gather
and, again, the moon in its last crescent
in pure stillness lies upon the water.

3

Butterstream takes a hint
from the Red Valerian
near a bored clump of mint,

and across the shrinking channel
the brooklime offers its green hand
to the reluctant watercress.
And none of them seems to guess
that after some time
there shall be no more water left,
no brooklime, mint or cress;
except growing, growing as fast as it can,
the Red Valerian.

4

Indoors the seasons change no coat or fashion.
Ladies, white and blue, appear and disappear,
dispensing comfort, care, compassion.
When I confuse despair with ordinary fear
and the fabric of my soul starts to unravel
I head for Clane. I stare at the Butterstream.
I plod (and exchange 'Good mornings'
with other mended souls) the gravel.

Identity Crisis in the Outpatients, St Vincent's Hospital, Elm Park

Do I really exist? Will I wake with a scream
and find I was dreaming another man's dream?
Are all my thoughts theological lumber?
Why has God got an unlisted number?
Or was Nietzsche correct? Is God really dead?
Earthly existence — is it all in the head?
Where am I going? Where *do* I come from?
Has Saddam Hussein got a nuclear bomb?
Life after death — is it all a great lie?
What is humanity and — what am I?
'Ah yes,' said the nurse, scanning her list,
'you're the infected sebaceous cyst.'

For Bishop Newman and Jim Kemmy

We had plans and charts and maps
and now we meet the 'great perhaps'.
> *And, in the silence that descends,*
> *I think of all my now-lost friends.*
Religion and strife were all —
life to us was just a hobby.
Now to whom can we appeal,
who can we fooster, who can we lobby?
> *And, in the silence that descends,*
> *I think of all my now-lost friends.*
Two of the most unlikely pals,
Socialist and bishop —
a set in Limerick's piercing eyes
'very risky';
discussing life and love and death
over a bottle of whiskey.
> *Now, in the silence that descends,*
> *I think of all my friends.*

Harvest Song

for S H

Now is the time for sawing the logs,
    now is the time for wintering in;
now we must cloister our cats and our dogs
    and remember our sins, sin by sin.

Now is the time we have to remember
    all we have gained, all we have lost;
now is the time we must store up our timber:
    now is the time to read Robert Frost.

Angela Liston

The rules you make,
the strictures you insist on,
have made me a beggar before you,
    Angela Liston.

I have been kicked around the place,
been mocked and have been pissed on;
but I find my way home to you,
    Angela Liston.

And my wrinkled, anxious forehead
amazingly has been kissed on;
and I am blessed by you,
    Angela Liston.

For All the Children

Oh my darlings, oh my dears,
I have lived for fifty years;
and my hair is a river of tears —
oh my darlings, oh my dears.

Notes on 'Maiden Street Ballad'

'Maiden Street Ballad' (to the air of 'The Limerick Rake') was 'composed by Michael Hartnett in Glendarragh, Templeglantine, County Limerick, in the month of December 1980 as a Christmas present for his father, Denis Harnett [sic]'.

The author's preface to the first edition of the poem, published by The Observer Press (no date) 'with the help of members of Newcastle West Historical Society', read: Everyone has a Maiden Street. It is the street of strange characters, wits, odd old women and eccentrics, also a street of hot summers, of hop-scotch and marbles: in short, the street of youth. But Maiden Street was no Tír na nÓg. It was one of the remnants of those depressed areas to be found in every city and garrison town, such as the many 'Liberties' and 'Irishtowns'. Human warmth and poverty often go hand in hand: well-to-do suburbanites do not intermingle at home as much as the poor do. In country places, this intimacy, (manifested in the 'rambling house') still exists, but is dying out. Maiden Street, of course, is a memory distorted by time in the minds of all who lived there. The period 1948-51 is dealt with in this ballad. Though the scheme of new houses, 'The Park', figures here as a kind of enemy, it is, of course, not really so. Like the battle of Aughrim it dealt the death-blow to a society which was dying, an inbred, poor and weak society. But it also introduced the people of the street to electric light and flush toilets. The ballad, of course, is not about *all* the people of Maiden Street — some were well-to-do, but not *us*. And it is the *us* I talk about. The street, its stories, its heroes and villians, would need an entire novel to describe it: I barely touch the surface.

I must now digress (as I do in the ballad itself: setting out to describe the street I mix in a long piece about the pubs in Newcastle West, but it's almost the duty of a long ballad to digress and to capture some of the flavour of the town because I believe the cement that binds the Irish people together is not religion or patriotism, but porter) and talk about the ballad itself. What is the difference between a ballad and a poem? Well, a ballad can often contain poetry — all the best ones do — but a poem must depend on an inner emotion and not on narrative, geography or history — it must not have a programme, as this ballad does. For a good many years people have asked me to write about Maiden Street, to produce a kind of *Cannery Row*: this is the closest I could get to it. I used the metre of 'The Limerick Rake', the best Hiberno-English ballad ever written in this county. I have not hesitated to use all the conventions of such a song. In this way I have been able to purge from my system the folk-images and rhythms that all my reading in modern literature could not eradicate (not that they could *not* be used to create a 'modern' work: but I simply don't wish to use them).

The object of this ballad is to invoke and preserve 'times past' and to do so without being too sentimental. Too many songs gloss over the hardships of the 'good old days' and omit the facts of hunger, bad sanitation and child-neglect. But this ballad is not all grimness. I hope it is humorous in spots. It was not written with mockery but with affection — part funny song, part social history. Ballads about places, however bad they may be, unite a community and give it a sense of identity.

I have no doubt that some people will find some parts of this work a little offensive and in bad taste: well, it's meant to be a *little* offensive and in bad taste! Also, it's romantic and slightly sentimental. The notes provided are by no means full or even trustworthy! 'Maiden Street Ballad' is meant for local consumption and most of the references will be readily understood in that context.

[The following notes, on the first twenty stanzas only, appeared when the poem was published first.]
stanza 3, The ballad has in fact only forty-seven verses but
   line 8 'fifty-three' gives a better rhythm!
   4, 1 My father was born in 1914 in the house in North Quay now occupied by Nash's Garage Showroom. It is also the site of the original Courtney School (hence Schoolhouse Lane, behind North Quay).
   4, 2 My grandfather was born in Athea, County Limerick, c.1850 and died in 1929.
   4, 5 My mother, Bridget Halpin, was born on a small farm in the townland of Camas, six miles southeast of Newcastle West. In the 1930s, attracted by the

bright lights, she came to Newcastle West and regretted it ever since!

6, 3　To qualify as 'old stock' a family has to be established in the town for at least three generations. If you meet someone in the street whose name you can't recall, it's a very handy phrase to know.

6, 5　The hospital in Croom had a maternity unit until recently. All my family were born there. I think it was my brother Billy who came home in a turf-lorry. The handlebars of my father's bike were too breezy and my mother wouldn't fit in the saddle!

6, 6　In 6 Connolly Terrace, the home of the late Harry Massey.

6, 7　If made from good bread, white sugar and creamy milk, it was not to be despised. It was much used as a baby food before the coming of the tinned and packeted variety. White bread was crumbled into hot (not boiled) milk and sweetened with sugar. Such foods go back to the dawn of Celtic society — the sweetener then being honey. It is not true that a common Christmas dinner was a bowl of goody with a sprig of holly in it!

11, 5　I have put into rhyme here the old Newcastle West saying: 'Church Street without a church, Bishop Street without a bishop, and Maiden Street without a maiden'. The poor 'Dock Road' always had a bad reputation. Some scut suggested to me that the street was originally called Midden Street!

11, 8　I have heard on good authority that an enterprising tailor, at the turn of the century, during a very bad winter, did make asses' pullovers — but he didn't prosper. The local harness-makers were against him and, worse still, he was ran out of his native place when twelve of the pullovers he sold shrank in the wet weather and a dozen donkeys were choked to death. This story has absolutely nothing to do with the fact that my grandfather left Athea about the same time!

12, 8　An air of hope and sadness always hung over the local railway-station. I myself, complete with cardboard suitcase, took 'a single ticket to Euston' in 1960.

13 It used to be said that if a stranger walked from Forde's Corner he'd have a nickname before he got to Leslie's Ating House. The list given here is only a small sample. The nick-name 'Smuggy' is interesting — it's from the Irish *smugach*, meaning 'snotty'.

14, 1 The game of 'pitch-and-toss' seems to have vanished from the town. It was a pleasant sight to see men and boys on a summer evening cursing and swearing over a few pence in the dirt, or running like hell from the Guards.

14, 4 That pub, now The Silver Dollar, is run by Billy Flynn's daughter, Margaret, and her husband, John Kelly.

14, 6 The word 'rawking' is from the Irish *ragairne*, 'mischiefmaking in the late hours'. I may have over-romanticized in this stanza: I do remember some vicious fights.

15, 1 We called this game 'Skellit' in the '40s and '50s. The correct anglicization should be 'skellig' from *Sceilg*. *Sceilg Mhichíl* is the famous rock off the Kerry coast. It was a place of pilgrimage and in later times men went there to select their wives. Any marriageable woman who was not engaged or married before Shrove Tuesday was sent there to be 'selected'. By our time it had degenerated into a street-game played like this: the boys went about with ropes 'capturing' the single girls, saying they were taking them to 'Skellit', giving them a good squeeze (with the ropes, of course) and tying them to trees and lampposts until they said they'd get married. I remember it last being played in 1949. Did this remnant of a 'pagan' custom die out in the Holy Year of 1950? The fairies of Knockfierna did. [See 'Maiden Street' in *Collected Poems*.]

15, 2 The ritual lighting of bone-fires (bones were originally used) on St John's Eve still went on in the '40s and '50s but we did not know why. Like 'Skellit', it was a custom without a heart, without a reason.

15, 3 The swapping of comics is not dead. But there is a difference nowadays — the newer the comic today, the better. Denis Deere, now in London, once gave me two *Captain Marvel* comics, a *Knockout* and a *Film Fun* for a very old *Beano*. This was the pre-Biffo *Beano*: Big Eggo was on the cover before him. 'Chainies' were pieces of china, the patterned type being the most valuable.

15, 4 As their name suggests, marble-shaped and marble-sized sweets with an aniseed flavour, sometimes indelicately called 'aniseed balls'. I once bought sixpence worth — 72 sweets! I rattled for a week.

15, 5 The word we used for minnows.

15, 6 The freshwater crayfish. The rivers around Newcastle West abound in them. They are edible and delicious but are not eaten in the area.

15, 7 'Laffcherd's' was also known as 'ablow'. Nash's Cinema was called 'above'.

15, 8 A stick of candy about six inches long flavoured with peppermint or vanilla. The name could have come from 'peg-leg' or perhaps there was a real Peggy. Pity she wasn't alive today: she'd make a fortune with legs that flavour!

17, 2 Flourbags were in great demand for bed-sheets and nightshirts. Tea-chests served as cradles and play-pens. Jamjars were the poor man's china. To drink hot tea from a jamjar demanded great skill, as did the filling of it. First the milk and sugar were put in — to avoid splitting the glass. Then the tea, to the very top. It had to be stirred very gently. It was not held in the hands, at first, but laid on the table in front of the diner, who sucked at the top. By the time the tea had gone down too far to be sucked, the jar was usually cool enough to be handled. This, of course, was a slow process, but in those days meals were leisurely affairs.

19, 6 The Primus lamp was the Aga of the poor. It was cheap to run — on paraffin oil and methylated spirits. It filled the house with poisonous fumes. It was faster than lighting a turf or coal fire. A pint of paraffin oil was a common 'message' to be sent for in those days. Small was beautiful then: a shopping list could consist of a half-stone of cao [sic], a half-ounce of tea, a quarter-pound of butter, a quarter-pound of sugar and two Woodbines!

20, 3   Old army and LDF coats were used as bed covers. I knew a man in the '50s who still slept under the coat he was demobbed in in 1918!

Afterword

Michael Hartnett presented the idea for this book in a letter of 26 March 1996. 'The clouds are moving away,' he wrote. 'Here is *A Book of Strays*.' We were working together at that time to finish his translations of Aodhagán Ó Rathaille (*c.* 1670-1729). We had an Agreement in place that Gallery would publish his *Collected Poems* and we'd started discussing the shape, scope, and make-up of that book. Was 'Collected' the same as 'Complete'? Would it contain poems in English *and* Irish? What about the translations?

The original table of contents for *A Book of Strays* included a number of recent poems which I let Michael know I hoped would form the core of a new collection. They appear with other 'New Poems' at the end of the *Collected*. Those contents also embraced a handful of translations. Since I'd long had in mind a Gallery book to round up various Hartnett translations, Michael agreed to reconsider the range of the book he had proposed, to dismantle its contents, and to return to the idea of it in due course, when *Collected Poems* was out and on its way. But he died in October 1999. Gallery published *Collected Poems* on the date we'd agreed — 18 September 2001 — on what would have been his sixtieth birthday.

With the support, in particular, of Michael's children, Niall and Lara, I returned to the *Strays* and to the book of translations to complete the Hartnett oeuvre.

I've placed first in this book, as a kind of epigraph, Michael's own translation of an Irish verse he sent out as a Christmas card from Glendarragh, Templeglantine, following his return, in 1975, to County Limerick with his wife Rosemary and their young children. The poem is a prayer, and the verses which follow it — satires, burlesques, ballads published anonymously ('A New Ballad on the State of the Nation') or pseudonymously ('by the Wasp'), squibs, and stanzas to traditional airs — derive from equally ancient impulses and sources.

Michael Hartnett's *first* poem, however, was written and published when he was thirteen. The manuscript is headed '18 June 1955', and he transcribed these lines in the (Limerick) *Echo* offices on 9 August 1983:

A bridge, a stream, a long low hedge,
A cottage thatched with golden straw,
A robin at the water's edge
Picks the luscious red ripe haw.
A donkey plods along the way
Weary from his heavy load,
Thinking of the soft lush hay
That grows in fields round Camas Road.

A timid hare sits in the ditch,
A copper fox with bark so shrill
Stirs the kine in grass so rich
O'er which there wafts a thrush's trill.
Dark shadows fall o'er a land so still.
The dusk is here as I write this ode;
A silver flash from a dancing rill:
The sun goes down on Camas Road.

These sixteen lines, and the date, fix a moment, or occasion, and a mood, and announce an eye for particular detail. But it's no surprise, despite the familiarity of the location, that they're expressed in a language and register which are not Michael's own. The poems I've assembled are ones which, by and large, serve *and survive* their occasions and bear their author's inimitable signature.

In many of these poems, Michael Hartnett lived out his sense of the poet as a chronicler of his race. 'I have tried to write for the people . . . ' he wrote, anticipating his now famous declaration at the end of 'A Farewell to English': 'I have come with meagre voice / to court the language of my people.'

The central theme, for instance, of his popular 'Maiden Street Ballad' is the impact of the move made in 1954 by the inhabitants of that street to a new housing scheme in Newcastle West. He relished the response to his lampoon, 'The Ballad of Salad Sunday', which earned bold headlines in the same *Limerick Echo and Shannon News* whose front page reported on 6 August 1993: POET CAUSES MAYHEM WITH SALAD SAGA!

Other poems own to a more literary provenance. 'Hallo Ducky' is 'based on Pope's imitation of Chaucer'. Others address politics in sudden outbursts ('Who Killed Bobby

Sands?'), while others again are more personal — recording aspects of his alcoholism and experiences, real or imagined, in hospitals and with doctors. More intimate appreciations are sounded in 'Angela Liston'. Others are simply entertaining, or marked by candour ('The Ghost of Billy Mulvihill'), or are comradely addresses to the spirits of Patrick Kavanagh and Jim Kemmy or younger friends like Paul Durcan and Seamus Heaney. They include characteristically lovely poetry: 'The moon shone like a Guinness-bottle label.'

While the final four lines here are possessed of a haunting music, the most poignant of Michael Hartnett's occasional poems, or strays, might be one which appears in Irish in the margins of a manuscript notebook and which might be rendered in English as:

> *Michael's my name.*
> *I've lived longer than Seán Ó Riada,*
> *longer than Behan.*
> *Great is my shame.*

Peter Fallon
August 2002

For the record: to the original dedication 'for Bill Ambrose, John Cussen' Michael Hartnett appended 'Donal Flanagan, John Hathaway, Des Healy'.